CONSTITUTIONAL LAW: THE COMMERCE CLAUSE

by

DAN T. COENEN
J. Alton Hosch Professor of Law
University of Georgia

TURNING POINT SERIES®

FOUNDATION PRESS
New York, New York
2004

Turning Point Series is a registered trademark used herein under license.

© 2004 By FOUNDATION PRESS

      395 Hudson Street

      New York, NY 10014

      Phone Toll Free 1–877–888–1330

      Fax (212) 367–6799

      fdpress.com

Printed in the United States of America

ISBN 1–58778–507–2

TEXT IS PRINTED ON 10% POST CONSUMER RECYCLED PAPER

TURNING POINT SERIES

CIVIL PROCEDURE

Civil Procedure: Class Actions by Linda S. Mullenix, University of Texas (Available 2004)

Civil Procedure: Economics of Civil Procedure by Robert G. Bone, Boston University (2003)

Civil Procedure: Preclusion in Civil Actions by David L. Shapiro, Harvard University (2001)

Civil Procedure: Jury Process by Nancy S. Marder, Illinois Institute of Technology (Available 2004)

Civil Procedure: Territorial Jurisdiction and Venue by Kevin M. Clermont, Cornell (1999)

CONSTITUTIONAL LAW

Constitutional Law: The Commerce Clause by Dan T. Coenen, University of Georgia (2004)

Constitutional Law: Equal Protection by Louis M. Seidman, Georgetown University (2002)

Constitutional Law: The Religion Clauses by Daniel O. Conkle, Indiana University, Bloomington (2003)

CRIMINAL LAW

Criminal Law: Model Penal Code by Markus D. Dubber, State University of New York, Buffalo (2002)

INTERNATIONAL LAW

International Law: United States Foreign Relations Law by Phillip R. Trimble, UCLA (2002)

LEGISLATION

Legislation: Statutory Interpretation: Twenty Questions by Kent R. Greenawalt, Columbia University (1999)

PROPERTY

Property: Takings by David Dana, Northwestern University and Thomas Merrill, Northwestern University (2002)

CORPORATE/SECURITIES

Securities Law: Insider Trading by Stephen Bainbridge, UCLA (1999)

TORTS

Torts: Proximate Cause by Joseph A. Page, Georgetown University (2002)

*For my beloved parents,
Clayton J. and LaVerne A. Coenen*

*

Acknowledgments

I greatly appreciate the help provided by Professors J. Randy Beck, Brannon Denning, Walter Hellerstein, John C. Inscoe, Paul M. Kurtz and James C. Smith, and Dr. Randy Reid, in reviewing drafts of large portions of this book. I am also thankful to Kay Bramlett for her fine work in typing the manuscript and to my able student assistants, Michael A. Caplan, Cara Runsick Mitchell and David M. Stewart.

*

About the Author

Dan T. Coenen is the J. Alton Hosch Professor of Law at the University of Georgia, where he has taught constitutional law for 16 years. His many published works include extensive treatments of constitutional federalism and the Commerce Clause. Professor Coenen attended the Cornell Law School, where he served as Editor in Chief of the Cornell Law Review. He went on to work as a law clerk for Supreme Court Justice Harry A. Blackmun and as a practicing lawyer at a major North Carolina law firm, of which he became a partner in 1985. During his career in academics, Coenen has been selected by students for numerous awards and honors. In 1998, he received the Josiah Meigs Award for Excellence in Teaching, the University of Georgia's highest recognition for achievement as a teacher.

*

TABLE OF CONTENTS

TABLE OF CONTENTS

TABLE OF CONTENTS

TABLE OF CONTENTS

*

CONSTITUTIONAL LAW:
THE COMMERCE CLAUSE

*

CHAPTER I

THE COMMERCE CLAUSE—WHO CARES?

At the heart of the American identity lies the idea that "We the People" have organized ourselves under a distinctively inspired and effective form of government established by the Constitution of the United States. The Constitution and its Amendments reflect themes at the heart of our nation's history: the centrality of human dignity and equality, the values of individual and collective self-determination, and the need to counter governmental excesses with a system of "checks and balances" built around a "separation of powers." From the beginning, however, American constitutional thought has focused on, perhaps more than any other subject, the proper division of powers between the federal government and the states.[1]

Struggles over this subject pre-dated ratification. Indeed the Philadelphia Convention of 1787 was called to address one overarching problem—the shared sense that the federal government was too weak, and the states were too strong, with respect to the power to regulate interstate and foreign

1. *See* ROBERT G. MCCLOSKEY, THE AMERICAN SUPREME COURT 17 (2d ed. 1994) (revised by Sanford Levinson) (describing "the nation-state relationship" as the "greatest of all the questions left unresolved by the founders").

1

commerce. At the Constitutional Convention itself, and in the state ratification conventions that followed it, conflicting views about how to deal with this state of affairs spurred deliberation and compromise. The end result was the adoption of a new charter of government that, in one of its most prominent provisions, gave Congress the authority "[t]o regulate Commerce with foreign Nations, and among the several States, and with the Indian Tribes."[2] From that day to this one, these 16 words have played a defining role in the allocation of lawmaking authority between the central government and the states.[3]

Once the Constitution was ratified, debates about the proper scope of federal power quickly came to the fore. These controversies pitted more nationally-minded "Hamiltonians" against less nationally-minded "Jeffersonians" on issues such as whether Congress had constitutional authority to charter a national bank, including under the Commerce Clause.[4] As the eighteenth century gave way to the nineteenth, concern over congressional power to

2. U.S. CONST. art. I, § 8, cl. 3.

3. There are a number of treatments of the Commerce Clause. The most recent is BORIS I. BITTKER, BITTKER ON THE REGULATION OF INTERSTATE AND FOREIGN COMMERCE (1999). More dated treatments include FREDERICK H. COOKE, THE COMMERCE CLAUSE OF THE FEDERAL CONSTITUTION (1908) and E. PARMALEE PRENTICE & JOHN G. EGAN, THE COMMERCE CLAUSE OF THE FEDERAL CONSTITUTION (1898). The subject is also dealt with extensively in LAURENCE H. TRIBE, AMERICAN CONSTITUTIONAL LAW (3d ed., vol. one, 2000).

4. *See, e.g.*, JOHN M. BLUM ET AL., THE NATIONAL EXPERIENCE 141–43 (1963).

enact the Sedition Act helped bring about the promulgation of the Virginia and Kentucky Resolutions and Thomas Jefferson's defeat of John Adams in the presidential election of 1800. In ensuing decades, as the abolitionist movement grew, so did claims of state immunity from federal control. The most far-reaching of those claims met a bloody end on the battlefields of the Civil War.

The post-bellum expansion of federal power gave rise to new debates about the reach of congressional authority, especially with regard to protecting the nation's African–American citizenry. State/federal conflicts multiplied, particularly under the Commerce Clause, as the industrial revolution produced a more integrated economy and Congress responded to this new reality by enacting unprecedented worker-protection, financial-regulation and human-welfare laws. The resurgence of the civil rights movement in the 1960s brought with it new battles over the scope of the commerce power, particularly as Congress took up an agenda of fashioning protections for racial minorities, women, the aged and persons with disabilities. In later years, the pendulum swung again, as officials in all branches of the federal government looked hard at whether sweeping post-New Deal invocations of the Commerce Clause had overshot constitutional boundaries. In short, the history of American constitutionalism—and indeed the history of America itself—is in large part the history of dividing up power between federal and state authorities. And the history of dividing up these powers is, to a substantial extent, the history of the Commerce Clause.

All American leaders have played a role in this history, and some leaders—George Washington, Thomas Jefferson, Franklin Roosevelt, Lyndon Johnson and Ronald Reagan among them—have made particularly significant contributions. From the earliest days of the nation, however, the Supreme Court has placed itself at the center of the storm by applying the Commerce Clause in hundreds of cases pursuant to its self-declared role as the "ultimate interpreter of the Constitution."[5] This book focuses on the Supreme Court's work in the cases that have come before it—that is, on the *law* of constitutional federalism. In doing so, it addresses each of the two great legal issues concerning the allocation of legislative power. First, it examines the extent to which principles rooted in the value of state autonomy limit the power of the national Congress, particularly under the Commerce Clause. Second, it considers the extent to which principles rooted in the need to protect the interests of the nation—particularly under the "dormant Commerce Clause" principle—preclude otherwise permissible exercises of state lawmaking authority. In working through these matters, this book canvasses key historical developments. It concentrates, however, on the current state of Supreme Court doctrine.

5. United States v. Nixon, 418 U.S. 683, 704 (1974) (quoting Baker v. Carr, 369 U.S. 186, 211 (1962)).

The tale of constitutional federalism is a rich and continuing story. As a result, any treatment of this body of law must strive to do more than merely set forth "hornbook" rules. At a minimum, such a treatment must explore the aims, structures, interstices and possibilities of existing doctrine. It must address how judicially crafted rules relate to and shape one another, as well as how those rules have practical relevance in the real-world work of lawyers and judges. It must consider how the law in this area has always been—and will continue to be—open-textured, dynamic and evolving.

This book takes on all these subjects, but it also attempts to do something else. Too often too many students find too little excitement in studying the law of state-federal relations, at least to the extent that that law concerns the Commerce Clause. But why should that be? The struggle between centralized and decentralized power, after all, lies at the root of the American experience. For this reason, this book seeks to move beyond simply exploring the law of constitutional federalism. At least between the lines, it seeks to show why the study of the Constitution's division of lawmaking powers is essential to understanding, and fascinating to undertake, for anyone who seriously seeks to probe the meaning of the "United States of America."

CHAPTER II

COMMERCE CLAUSE BASICS

In a critical move, the Framers of the Constitution vested in the federal government only a limited number of lawmaking powers. Most of these powers—such as the authority to "coin Money," to "provide and maintain a Navy," or to "grant Letters of Marque and Reprisal"[1]—have stirred little debate. The power "[t]o regulate Commerce ... among the several States," in contrast, has proven enormously controversial. The source of controversy lies in the opportunity that the Commerce Clause gives Congress to regulate highly localized matters, historically overseen by state governments, on the theory that they bear some relationship to interstate commercial activity. May Congress impose minimum-wage and anti-discrimination requirements on the operators of a local "mom and pop" café? May Congress criminalize the possession of heroin, marijuana or handguns, or the disruption of access to local abortion clinics? May Congress control hunting or fishing within a state, or the filling of small ponds, or the destruction of a rare localized plant species? We return in due course to these questions about congressional power under the

1. U.S. CONST. art. I, § 8.

Commerce Clause. Properly thinking about them, however, requires a sense of why the Constitution limits congressional power and of how the Supreme Court shaped debate about such matters in early, seminal decisions.

A. Why and How the Constitution Divides up Lawmaking Power

As the delegates to the Constitutional Convention gathered in 1787, questions about how to allocate state and federal lawmaking power crowded their thoughts and conversations. One option was to leave in place the existing Articles of Confederation. Under the Articles, however, things had gone badly for nearly a decade. The Articles created a federal Congress, but that body lacked the power to impose taxes or to regulate interstate commerce. Although in theory the national legislature could deal with war-related matters and foreign affairs, even in these areas it lacked a practical effectiveness both because it lacked funds and because no federal executive or judiciary was in place to carry out congressional mandates. The result was that individual states operated much like independent countries, bound together by a loose-knit alliance that depended on the continuing goodwill of its members. "Congress, in short, had responsibility without power. It could recommend endlessly but no one either inside or outside the United States paid much attention to what it recommended."[2]

To make matters worse, the spirit of collaboration that marked the days of the American Revolution had eroded—at least in commercial relations—during the pre-Constitution period. Individual states erected tariffs and imposed duties on goods that moved across their territory at the expense of "outsider" exporters and importers in other states.[3] These strategies, in turn, "engendered rival, conflicting and angry regulations."[4] As Joseph Story observed, "thus a state of affairs disorderly and unnatural grew up, the tendency of which was to destroy the Union itself."[5] Leaders who had endured the snows of Valley Forge viewed with horror the prospect that internecine commercial conflict might abort the American experiment. As a result, in 1786, the leadership of Virginia proposed a gathering of representatives from all the states "to take into consideration the trade of the United States; to examine the relative situations and trade of the said States; to consider how far a uniform system in

2. JOHN M. BLUM ET AL., THE NATIONAL EXPERIENCE 122 (1963).

3. *See generally* H.P. Hood & Sons v. Du Mond, 336 U.S. 525, 531–34 (1949) (detailing this history).

4. *Id.* at 534 (quoting James Madison *in* III RECORDS OF THE FEDERAL CONVENTION OF 1787, 547 (Max Farrand, ed. 1937)).

5. JOSEPH STORY, COMMENTARIES ON THE CONSTITUTION OF THE UNITED STATES, § 515 (Carolina Academic Press 1987) (1833). As Professors Rotunda and Nowak have noted, "Joseph Story lived at an ideal time and under ideal circumstances to reflect upon the nature of our constitutional system," including because of his service as an Associate Justice of the Supreme Court from 1811 to 1845. RONALD D. ROTUNDA & JOHN E. NOWAK, *Introduction* to STORY, *id.,* at v.

their commercial regulations may be necessary to their common interest and their permanent harmony...."[6] It was this call that led to the Convention of 1787, which ultimately put to paper the Constitution of the United States.[7]

The Framers of the Constitution might have terminated the trade wars that marked the post-revolutionary period by creating a single nation, ruled by a unitary government, unencumbered by any state boundaries at all. But the delegates gathered in Philadelphia knew that this path was not open to them. As John Marshall would later write: "No political dreamer was ever wild enough to think of breaking down the lines which separate the states, and of compounding the American people into one common mass."[8] The Framers understood the political reality that both powerful leaders and ordinary citizens thought of themselves, first and foremost, as Virginians, New Yorkers, Georgians or New Hampshirites. Delegates to the Convention thus would have to find a way to strengthen the national government's hand without diminishing the prerogatives of state governments too much.

In the end, the Framers steered a middle course between leaving matters as they stood and obliterating state boundaries altogether. They dealt with the worst flaws of the Articles of Confederation by

6. *Hood*, 336 U.S. at 533.

7. *See id.* (noting that "sole purpose" for calling the Convention was to address the debilitating proliferation of state-imposed obstacles to a free flowing commerce).

8. McCulloch v. Maryland, 17 U.S. 316, 403 (1819).

fashioning a much-energized federal government that could exert its will directly on its citizens, that contained strong executive and judicial branches, and that possessed new powers to lay taxes and to "regulate Commerce ... among the several States."[9] Using three main strategies, however, the Framers also took steps to ensure that the new federal authority would not overwhelm the state governments.

First, the Framers devised a system that, simply put, made it difficult for the central government to legislate at all. Enactment of any law required the concurrent action of two very different chambers of the legislative branch: the Senate (made up of two representatives from each state, with members chosen for staggered six-year terms)[10] and the House of Representatives (made up of differing numbers of representatives from each state based on state population, with all members elected to brief and identical two-year terms).[11] In addition, all enacted bills were subject to presidential veto, which in turn could be overridden only by the concurrent action of two-thirds of the Senate and two-thirds of the House.[12]

Second, the Framers built into the processes for selecting federal officers vital roles for the states. Under the original Constitution, state legislatures

9. U.S. CONST. art. I, § 8, cl. 3.

10. U.S. CONST. art. I, § 3, cl. 1.

11. U.S. CONST. art. I, § 2, cl. 1.

12. U.S. CONST. art. I, § 7, cl. 2.

chose senators.[13] Even under the modern Constitution, Senators and Representatives come from particular states, and each state is equally represented in the Senate regardless of its population. Under Article II of the Constitution, presidential electors are selected from within each state in a manner established by the state legislature, rather than by federal authorities.[14] In short, the Framers protected the repositories of local authority from being swallowed up by the federal government in part by crafting the structure of the central government in a way that took account of state boundaries, state interests and state institutions.

Third, the Framers—even while declaring that federal law took priority over incompatible state law[15]—insisted that the federal government could legislate only in specified fields. Most important, the Framers refused to give the federal government a general police power to regulate the health, safety or morals of the national community. They also rejected proposals made early in the Convention to vest in Congress an ill-defined power "to legislate in all Cases for the general Interests of the Union, and also in those Cases in which the States are separate-

13. In 1913, the provision for state legislators' election of Senators was displaced by the Seventeenth Amendment, which provided that Senators must be "elected by the people" of the states. U.S. CONST. amend. XVII.

14. U.S. CONST. art. I, § 1, cl. 2.

15. *See* U.S. CONST. art. VI, cl. 2 (setting forth the so-called Supremacy Clause).

ly incompetent."[16] Instead the Framers took a
"laundry list" approach, setting forth in Article I,
§ 8, seventeen separate purposes that Congress
could pursue with legislative enactments.[17] Among
those grants of authority lay the power to regulate
interstate and foreign commerce. Also granted were
powers "[t]o lay and collect Taxes"; to enact "uniform laws on the subject of bankruptcies"; to pass
laws concerning patents, copyrights, and counter-
feiting; "[t]o establish Post Offices," as well as
"Armies" and "a Navy"; to create lower federal
courts, and "[t]o declare War." To the seventeen
enumerated grants of power the Framers added
another source of authority of vital consequence:
the power "[t]o make all Laws which shall be necessary and proper for carrying into Execution ... all
... Powers vested by this Constitution in the Government of the United States."[18] The critical
point—that Congress could not do anything it
wished, even though it could do much—was reaffirmed in the Tenth Amendment, which provides:
"The powers not delegated to the United States by
the Constitution, nor prohibited by it to the States,
are reserved to the States respectively, or to the
people."[19]

These constitutional provisions, while laying
down the essential architecture of American federalism, gave rise to large questions that recur in this
book: How far does Congress's opaque commerce

16. II THE RECORDS OF THE FEDERAL CONVENTION OF 1787, 131
(Max Farrand ed. 1966) (original work published 1937).

17. U.S. CONST. art. I, § 8, cl. 1–17.

18. U.S. CONST. art. I, § 8, cl. 18.

19. U.S. CONST. amend. X.

power, particularly when coupled with its even more opaque necessary-and-proper power, extend? What limits, if any, do the Tenth Amendment and non-textual postulates of state autonomy place on federal authority? What limits based on the need for federal cohesiveness does the Constitution place on the power of state officials? In particular, to what extent do the grant of the commerce power and the vision of a national common market that it reflects inhibit state action that interferes with free-flowing interstate trade? In wrestling with these questions over the course of two centuries, the Supreme Court has both defined the essential features of our constitutional system and resolved some of the most contentious political battles of the American past.

B. *McCulloch v. Maryland*

In the spring of 1789, the first Congress assembled, and George Washington took his constitutional oath as the first President of the United States. No sooner had the nation's new government been born than questions began to arise about how far its powers reached. Taking the lead in this debate were President Washington's nationally minded Secretary of the Treasury, Alexander Hamilton, and his more states-rights-oriented Secretary of State, Thomas Jefferson. Early disagreements concerned such questions as whether Congress could or should assume state war debts, aid domestic manufacturers and initiate a federal program to build canals, bridges and roads. The most contentious debate of the Washington presidency, however, focused on whether Congress had the power to charter a national bank.

Hamilton argued that the Necessary and Proper Clause authorized a National Bank Act because a proper construction of the clause permitted enactment of any law "incidental, useful or conducive to" the exercise of Congress's previously enumerated powers. More particularly, this principle supported creation of a national bank because it "has a relation, more or less direct, to the power of collecting taxes, to that of borrowing money, to that of regulating trade between the States, and to those of raising and maintaining fleets and armies." Jefferson responded that Congress could not create a bank because the Constitution's laundry list of powers did not authorize the chartering of corporations and the Necessary and Proper Clause was properly read to permit only the enactment of laws "without which the [specific grants] of power would be nugatory." He insisted, in particular, that recognizing a federal power to charter a bank would require such an energetic interpretation of the Necessary and Proper Clause that it "would swallow up all the delegated powers" and authorize congressional interference with even "the most ancient and fundamental laws of the several States; such as ... rules of descent."[20] In the end, President Washington acceded to the pleas of his Secretary of the Trea-

20. The preceding quotations are taken from KATHLEEN M. SULLIVAN & GERALD GUNTHER, CONSTITUTIONAL LAW 97–98 (14th ed. 2001) (setting forth selected writings of Hamilton and Jefferson to President Washington).

sury, and dismissed those of his Secretary of State, signing into law the original National Bank Act in 1791.

The Bank Act by its terms lapsed in 1811, before any challenge to its constitutionality had found its way to the Supreme Court. In 1816, however, Congress passed the Second National Bank Act, and President Madison (although a career-long ally of Jefferson and ardent opponent of the first Bank Act as a member of the first House of Representatives) signed the bill into law during the "period of nationalistic optimism that followed the end of the War of 1812."[21] The constitutionality of this act came before the Supreme Court in *McCulloch v. Maryland,*[22] a case of such singular importance to the development of the commerce power that it warrants extensive examination.

In essence, the Act of 1816 created a federally regulated bank that competed directly with existing banks chartered by individual states. For the most part, local authorities had opposed adoption of this law. When Congress passed it anyway, the states struck back. Among the most aggressive was Maryland, which enacted legislation that imposed a charge of $15,000 per year on any bank not chartered by it unless that bank bought stamps from the state for each note it issued. One feature of the Maryland law exposed officers of the National Bank to penalties for failing to pay these charges, and the *McCulloch* case was initiated as a suit to collect

21. *Id.* at 99.

22. 17 U.S. 316 (1819).

such a penalty from the cashier of the Baltimore branch of the Bank of the United States. After the state courts ruled against the defendant, the case came before the Supreme Court, which invalidated the Maryland statute.

In his opinion for a unanimous Court, Chief Justice Marshall identified the first issue in the case as whether Congress had the constitutional power to create a national bank. Endorsing the Hamiltonian position, he concluded that it did. The Chief Justice began his analysis by contrasting the language of the Constitution with the language of the Articles of Confederation, under which the federal Congress possessed only those powers "*expressly* delegated" to it.[23] The Chief Justice observed that the Framers "had experienced the embarrassments resulting from the insertion of this word in the articles"[24] and he added that, if a Constitution were "to contain an accurate detail of ... all the means by which [the government's enumerated powers] may be carried into execution," it "would partake of the prolixity of a legal code."[25] As a result, only the Constitution's "great outlines should be marked, its important objects designated, and the minor ingredients which compose those objects be deduced from the nature of the objects themselves."[26] "[W]e must never forget," Chief Justice Marshall declared,

23. *Id.* at 378 (emphasis added).

24. *Id.* at 406.

25. *Id.* at 407.

26. *Id.*

"that it is a *constitution* we are expounding."[27]

The Chief Justice, however, did not stop there. He also argued that (1) the Constitution vested the war-making and other "great powers" in the federal Congress; (2) "a government, intrusted with such ample powers, on the due execution of which the happiness and prosperity of the nation so vitally depends, must also be intrusted with ample means for their execution";[28] and (3) this conclusion was all the more compelled in construing a document "intended to endure for ages to come"[29] and to provide for a "vast republic."[30] In short, Chief Justice Marshall relied on "general reasoning" from the history, structure and purposes of the Constitution, as well as on common sense, to conclude that broad "incidental" powers followed from the assign-

27. *Id.* (emphasis in original). Marshall added that a liberal view of "deduced" powers found support in other features of the constitutional text as well. For example, no enumerated power even obliquely indicates that Congress has the power to grant titles of nobility; thus the express prohibition on the grant of such titles in Article I, § 9, suggested that the Framers' understanding of the authority to grant these titles was deducible as means "necessary and proper" to carry Congress's enumerated powers into effect. After all, if such a power were not deducible in this way, it would not exist at all; thus there would be no need to prohibit its exercise in Article 1, § 9. And such a power was plainly not, as Jefferson had suggested, needed to avoid rendering any enumerated power nugatory.

28. *Id.* at 408.

29. *Id.* at 415.

30. *Id.* at 408. Particularly in this context, the Chief Justice observed, Congress had to have broad flexibility to fashion practical approaches to the "various" and often-unforeseeable "*crises of human affairs.*" *Id.* at 415 (emphasis in original).

ment of critically important enumerated powers to the federal Congress.[31]

There was, however, a fly in the ointment. The problem, according to the Jeffersonians, was that the text of the Constitution rendered Chief Justice's appeal to the "dictates of reason" beside the point.[32] The Constitution, after all, specifically treated the subject of incidental powers, and it stipulated that Congress had only those powers "necessary and proper" for carrying into effect its otherwise enumerated grants of authority. On any fair interpretation, the Jeffersonians argued, establishment of a national bank was not "necessary" for spending federal money, collecting federal taxes, raising armies or regulating interstate commerce. Instead the federal government could use the existing state banks for those purposes.

Chief Justice Marshall, however, found this textual argument unimpressive. In his view, two interpretations of the word "necessary" were available: the Jeffersonian interpretation under which the term meant "indispensable" and the Hamiltonian interpretation under which the term meant "convenient, or useful, or essential."[33] In endorsing the second and far more expansive of these two definitions, Chief Justice Marshall began by relying on "common usage," asserting that "in the ordinary affairs of the world" a means necessary to an end "is generally understood" to denote "any means

31. *See, e.g., id.* at 386.

32. *Id.* at 409.

33. *Id.* at 413, 418.

calculated to produce the end," rather than being confined to "those single means, without which the end would be entirely unattainable."[34] This common-meaning argument found support in the linguistic reality that the critical term admitted "of all degrees of comparison" because "a thing may be necessary, very necessary, absolutely or indispensably necessary."[35]

The Chief Justice added to this linguistic exegesis two additional, and no less significant, points. First, he argued that endorsement of the Jeffersonian interpretation would wreak havoc with the operation of the federal government. Existing federal law, for example, prohibited robbing the mail, yet such a prohibition was not "indispensably necessary" to

34. *Id*. at 413—14.

35. *Id*. Any doubt in this regard, Chief Justice Marshall added, was negated by the Constitution itself, which in Article I, § 10 authorizes state imposition of duties on imports and exports only to the extent they are "*absolutely* necessary for executing its inspection laws." *Id*. (emphasis in original). In other words, according to Chief Justice Marshall, the Framers knew how to use the term "absolutely necessary" when they meant "absolutely necessary," and they had not included the term "absolutely necessary" in the Necessary and Proper Clause of Article I. In addition, the Framers' use of the word "proper" in that clause carried significance for the Court because, "[i]f the word 'necessary' was used in the strict and rigorous sense for which counsel for the State of Maryland contend," the full clause would require either the "extraordinary" conclusion that some indispensable means for carrying out the enumerated powers were improper or the alternative conclusion that the word "proper" had no effect whatsoever. *Id*. at 418–19. For this reason, the very "necessary and proper" language on which Maryland based its argument cut, in Chief Justice Marshall's view, against and not for Maryland's constitutional position.

carrying out Congress's enumerated power to "establish post offices and post roads."[36] Likewise, outlawing perjury was "conducive" to pursuing the due administration of justice in federal courts, but it was not indispensable to "constitut[ing] tribunals inferior to the supreme court."[37] By way of these examples, Chief Justice Marshall constructed the sort of "parade-of-horribles" argument that would recur in constitutional discourse from his day to this one, particularly in debates about the scope of congressional power under the Commerce Clause.

Second, Chief Justice Marshall defended his interpretive stance against the Jeffersonians' argument that the convenience-based Hamiltonian view of the Necessary and Proper Clause would produce a federal lawmaking power subject to no meaningful limits. In keeping with his broad view of federal power, the Chief Justice decreed that "where the law ... is really calculated to effect any of the objects entrusted to the government, to undertake here to inquire into the degree of necessity, would be to pass the line which circumscribes the judicial department, and to tread on legislative ground."[38] Yet, in a passage that would surface often in later opinions, he emphasized that the Constitution places *some* limits on congressional authority: "Should congress, in the execution of its powers, adopt measures which are prohibited by the constitution; or should congress, under the pretext of

36. *Id.* at 417.

37. *Id.* at 381.

38. *Id.* at 423.

executing its powers, pass laws for the accomplishment of objects not intrusted to the government; it would become the painful duty of this tribunal ... to say, that such an act was not the law of the land."[39] Chief Justice Marshall did not explain when or how the Court would determine that congressional action constituted an impermissible "pretext." With this passage, however, he left the door open for later judicial examination of whether congressional enactments reached beyond the federal commerce power.

The Court's decision that Congress had the authority to charter a national bank did not resolve the *McCulloch* case. Rather, the Court still had another question to answer: Even assuming that Congress could create a national bank, did it follow that the Constitution required invalidation of the tax that Maryland had imposed? The Chief Justice began his analysis of this second issue by conceding there was "no express provision" in the Constitution that rendered the Maryland statute invalid. He went on, however, to speak of "a principle which so entirely pervades the Constitution" and is "so interwoven with its web, so blended with its texture, as to be incapable of being separated from it."[40] This principle, which emanated from the Constitution's express recognition of the primacy of federal law, mandated that states lacked the power to "defeat the legitimate operations of a supreme govern-

39. *Id.*

40. *Id.* at 426.

ment."[41] Because "the power to tax involves the power to destroy,"[42] a "fair construction" of this principle required an invalidation of Maryland's effort to impose its tax on the national bank.[43]

The Court found further support for this ruling in a "just theory" of governmental taxation.[44] According to the Chief Justice, the "only security against ... abuse" of the taxing power lay in the fact that "the legislature acts upon its own constituents"—a fact that ordinarily provided "a sufficient security against erroneous and oppressive" imposition of governmental burdens.[45] "But when a state taxes the operations of the government of the United States, it acts upon institutions created, not by their own constituents, but by people over whom they claim no control."[46] The intolerable nature of this sort of "action of a part on the whole"[47] was so patent that the Chief Justice detected "a total fail-

41. *Id.* at 427.

42. *Id.* at 431.

43. *Id.* at 427. The Court added that settled principles of governmental autonomy in the field of interstate relations helped to support this conclusion. It reasoned that just as surely as it would be intolerable for one state to suffer controls placed on its operations by other states, it was intolerable for a state to handicap the operations of a duly enacted federal program. The Court did not, in making this observation, advert to the fact that the Bank of the United States was (unlike state-chartered banks operating in other jurisdictions) conducting business operations within the territorial limits of Maryland.

44. *Id.* at 430.

45. *Id.* at 428.

46. *Id.* at 435.

47. *Id.* at 436.

ure" of the claimed right of the state "to tax the means employed by the government of the Union."[48]

Chief Justice Marshall's opinion in *McCulloch* is not immune to criticism. For example, it might be said that, in endorsing Congress's use of the Necessary and Proper Clause, the Chief Justice expended most of his energy attacking a straw man. In particular, he gave almost no attention to the possibility that the word "necessary" might have some meaning short of "indispensable"—such as "substantially related" or "highly important"—that would have departed from the most extreme version of the Jeffersonian position but still cast doubt on the Bank Act. Likewise, in railing against the Maryland tax, Chief Justice Marshall never acknowledged that Congress could have protected the national interests at stake in the case by simply enacting legislation that explicitly preempted programs such as the one adopted by Maryland.

Even so, *McCulloch* remains "perhaps the greatest of our constitutional cases."[49] The decision embodied styles of analysis—centered on text, history, structure and a democracy-correcting judicial role—that would pervade constitutional decision making throughout American history. Of no less importance, *McCulloch* launched the two great themes that have echoed through the Court's efforts to mark the proper balance of state and federal power

48. *Id*. at 430.

49. CHARLES L. BLACK, JR., STRUCTURE AND RELATIONSHIP IN CONSTITUTIONAL LAW 5 (1969).

under the Commerce Clause. First, the ruling left no doubt that federal lawmaking authority, though limited in some nebulous way, was expansive and largely beyond the power of the judiciary to constrain. Second, *McCulloch* recognized the possibility of implying from the "web" and "texture" of the Constitution judicially enforceable constraints on both state and federal power.

C. *Gibbons v. Ogden*

Article I, § 8, cl. 3 grants Congress the power to regulate certain matters with respect to "[c]ommerce." From the beginning there has been consensus that this term embraces "buying and selling, or the interchange of commodities."[50] It follows, as a textual matter, that the congressional power with respect to interstate commerce permits it to regulate purchase and sale transactions that cross state lines—perhaps, for example, by requiring non-deceptive packaging of items sold by a seller in one state to a buyer in another or by preempting state laws that impose tax-related or other burdens on cross-border exchanges.[51] Are there other subjects that Congress may regulate under its Article I commerce power? Five years after *McCulloch*, while

50. Gibbons v. Ogden, 22 U.S. (9 Wheat.) 1, 189 (1824).

51. Others have suggested that the clause was meant to vest Congress only with a power to preempt state laws and not with a power to regulate private parties themselves. The Court, however, has long rejected this restrictive interpretive stance. *See* BORIS I. BITTKER, BITTKER ON THE REGULATION OF INTERSTATE AND FOREIGN COMMERCE § 2.02, at 2–4 to 2–7 (1999).

John Marshall still sat as Chief Justice, that question came before the Court in the case of *Gibbons v. Ogden*.[52]

In the early 1800s, Aaron Ogden began to run a steamboat ferry between New York City and Elizabethtown, New Jersey, pursuant to a monopoly granted by New York State. Thereafter, Thomas Gibbons obtained a license under a federal statute to engage in "the coasting trade" and, pursuant to this authorization, began to operate a competing ferry service. When Ogden brought suit for an injunction, Gibbons responded that the federal statute under which he held his license preempted the New York monopoly grant. Ogden countered by arguing that the federal statute, to the extent it authorized Gibbons's competing activities, exceeded Congress's commerce power because it did not regulate the buying and selling of commodities at all. Chief Justice Marshall, however, made short shrift of Ogden's contention, reasoning that "all America understands, and has uniformly understood, the word 'commerce,' to comprehend navigation." More important, the Chief Justice took the occasion to define the commerce power broadly. "Commerce," he wrote, "is traffic, but it is something more: it is intercourse," and regulating commerce entails "prescribing rules for carrying on that intercourse." The Chief Justice noted that Congress could not reach trade that "is carried on between man and man in a State, or between different parts of the same State and [that] does not extend to or affect other

52. 22 U.S. (9 Wheat.) 1 (1824).

States."[53] But even this assertion held out the tantalizing possibility that Congress could regulate wholly intrastate activities on the theory that they "affect other States," whether or not they directly concerned the sort of border-crossing movements involved in the *Gibbons* case itself.

Finally, Chief Justice Marshall laid out two ideas that have played a role ever since in supporting a broad conception of the commerce power. First, he described that power as "plenary," adding that it "may be exercised to its utmost extent, and acknowledges no limitations, other than are prescribed in the constitution."[54] Second, he observed that, as long as Congress acted pursuant to this power, protection of the people from the risk of its abuse must come not from the judiciary but from "[t]he wisdom and the discretion of Congress, their identity with the people, and the influence which their constituents possess at elections."[55] In sum, the Court in *Gibbons*, like the Court in *McCulloch*, recognized the existence of limits on federal power but offered up a rhetoric available for later use to support a sweeping conception of how far that power reached.

D. Values of Centralization and Decentralization and Judicial Efforts at Accommodation

---

McCulloch and *Gibbons* introduced key themes that continue to dominate constitutional discourse

53. *Id*. at 189–90, 194.

54. *Id*. at 196—97.

55. *Id*. at 197.

concerning the proper scope of congressional authority under the Commerce Clause. Drawing on the open-textured language of the Constitution, they endorsed the view that a broad conception of federal power would wisely facilitate congressional flexibility and an ability to adapt to new conditions over time. At an even deeper level, the Marshall Court's commitment to expansive congressional authority squared with the transformative political theory that underlay James Madison's conception and defense of the American Constitution. In Madison's view, the greatest danger presented by democratic self-rule lay in the risk that a "powerful faction" would capture the processes of government and use them to oppress "the weaker party."[56] This problem, as Madison saw it, grew as the size of the self-governing group diminished, because

[t]he smaller the society, the fewer probably will be the distinct parties and interests composing it; the fewer the distinct parties and interests, the more frequently will a majority be found of the same party; and the smaller the number of individuals composing a majority, and the smaller the compass within which they are placed, the more easily will they concert and execute their plans of oppression.[57]

Madison thus argued for a broad empowerment of the federal government, and a reciprocal disempow-

56. THE FEDERALIST No. 10 (James Madison).

57. *Id.*

erment of the states, on the theory that a great "advantage ... in controlling the effects of faction ... is enjoyed ... by the Union over the States composing it."[58]

Neither Madison nor Marshall, however, envisioned such an enlargement of federal power that it would do away with a constitutional system built around the existence of "two distinct governments,"[59] including state governments that retained "numerous and indefinite" powers.[60] It was for this reason that the Court in *McCulloch* recognized that both "the letter and spirit of the constitution" put limits on congressional authority.[61] These limits, in turn, reflected the benefits that political theorists have long understood to flow from vesting geographically defined subunits of government with control over significant public policy matters. A strong system of state and local lawmaking, for example, encourages citizen participation and fosters a sense of connection with government by keeping it near at hand. The dispersion of power within a federal system facilitates the development of distinctive programs that respond to distinctive local wants, while also permitting each state to "serve as a laboratory ... and try novel social and

58. *Id.* It is worth noting in this regard that the federal law challenged in *Gibbons* had the effect of breaking a state-granted monopoly, a form of governmental favoritism that often has subverted, rather than supported, the public interest for the advantage of the few.

59. THE FEDERALIST No. 51 (James Madison).

60. THE FEDERALIST No. 45 (James Madison).

61. *McCulloch*, 17 U.S. at 421.

economic experiments without risk to the rest of the country."[62] Perhaps most important, a "vertical" division of government authority protects "our fundamental liberties" by helping to ensure that tyrannical power may not be too readily seized by any single group of public officials.[63]

The Court in *McCulloch* and *Gibbons* recognized that sorting through competing claims of federal and state power would require a fair accommodation of competing constitutional values in the context of expounding a vague constitutional text. Those decisions also at least hinted at three forces that would play a prominent role in later judicial decisionmaking concerning the scope of the congressional commerce power: (1) that, on the one hand, a variety of considerations—including the existence of process-centered protections for the states built into the Constitution's structuring of federal lawmaking institutions—counseled against a strong judicial role in protecting state autonomy interests; (2) that, on the other hand, the view that Congress may freely regulate any local activity as long as it somehow affects interstate commerce would threaten to

62. Reeves, Inc. v. Stake, 447 U.S. 429, 441 (1980) (quoting New State Ice Co. v. Liebmann, 285 U.S. 262, 311 (1932) (Brandeis, J., dissenting)). *Accord, e.g.,* Gregory v. Ashcroft, 501 U.S. 452, 458 (1991).

63. *Id.* (quoting Atascadero State Hosp. v. Scanlon, 473 U.S. 234, 242 (1985)). *See id.* (adding that "[j]ust as the separation and independence of the coordinate branches of the Federal Government serve to prevent the accumulation of excessive power in any one branch, a healthy balance of power between the States and the Federal Government will reduce the risk of tyranny and abuse from either front").

remove all limits on federal authority in violation of the Framers' basic plan; and (3) that, in any event, the Court must accord the Commerce and Necessary and Proper Clauses a practical and adaptive reading, so as to give Congress the ability to deal effectively with "exigencies ... best provided for as they occur" as not only years, but "ages," pass.[64] Against this complex backdrop, the Supreme Court has wrestled with the meaning of the commerce power in hundreds of published opinions. It is impossible to capture the ebb and flow of this work, in any way that fairly depicts its richness, in a summary account. It may aid understanding, however, to divide the Court's work into three main historical periods: (1) the period that extended through

64. *McCulloch*, 17 U.S. at 415. One other force that inevitably comes to bear in commerce-power adjudication emanates from the reality that disputes over state and federal power never arise in a vacuum. Rather, each such *structural* dispute invariably involves an underlying controversy about *substantive* rights and interests. Aaron Ogden, for example, did not sue Thomas Gibbons (or at least he did not do so primarily) because of an abstract commitment to state rights. Rather, Ogden sued because he wanted to protect his monopoly and the economic advantages it afforded him. In more modern times, hotel and restaurant operators did not challenge the Civil Rights Act of 1964 (or at least they did not do so primarily) because they harbored philosophical objections to a nationally oriented conception of the commerce power. Rather, they sought to resist specific regulatory controls that forced them to behave in a way they did not wish to act—in this instance, by desegregating their business operations. The interaction of the law of federalism and underlying substantive values is extremely complex. Thoughtful observers of constitutional law, however, must be prepared to consider how that interaction has played itself out in both their own views of the law of federalism and the Supreme Court's work.

1936, during which the Court identified various "prongs" of the commerce power and ultimately invalidated important federal New Deal programs; (2) the period from 1937 to roughly 1986, during which the Court moved sharply away from the position of judicial vigilance that marked the early years of the New Deal era and assumed a posture of great deference in evaluating issues of congressional power; and (3) the post–1986 period, during which the Court has continued to adhere to the Court's pre–1986 precedents but also has embraced doctrines that have led to the invalidation of significant exercises of the commerce power.

CHAPTER III

THE COMMERCE POWER THROUGH 1936: THE QUEST FOR LIMITING PRINCIPLES

In the period prior to 1937, the Court forged the basic structure of commerce-power doctrine. In particular, it suggested that Congress could deal with commerce-related matters on any one of three separate theories.[1] First, it could regulate the channels and instrumentalities of interstate commerce (the channels/instrumentalities theory), including by prohibiting the cross-border movement of specified goods or persons—that is, through use of the so-called "commerce-prohibiting" technique.[2] Second,

---

1. The Court also carried forward the spirit of *Gibbons* by continuing to define "commerce" broadly. *See, e.g.,* United States v. Simpson, 252 U.S. 465, 468 (1920) (Clarke, J., dissenting) (describing and criticizing view taken by eight-Justice majority to the effect that interstate commerce includes "isolated movements of small amounts of private property, by private persons for their personal use" across state lines); Thornton v. United States, 271 U.S. 414, 425 (1926) (characterizing the ranging of cattle across state lines as interstate commerce even if those cattle are not driven or transported).

2. It is worth noting that the Court has not been entirely clear in identifying the distinction (if any) between "channels" and "instrumentalities" of commerce. On one understanding, the former term focuses on corridors of movement and trade (sea routes, air routes, highways, rail and communications lines,

Congress could regulate even wholly intrastate activities on the theory that they were in the stream of interstate commerce (the in-commerce theory). Third, Congress could regulate local activities if they "affected" interstate commerce in a substantial way (the affecting-commerce theory). Although this three-part conception of the commerce power has been much refined since 1936, it continues to provide the core framework for analyzing commerce-power questions to the present day.

A. The Channels/Instrumentalities Theory and the Commerce–Prohibiting Technique Through 1936

Gibbons in effect held that Congress could remove obstructions to commerce—there, in the form of transporting people—across state borders by way of ship. In *The Daniel Ball*,[3] the Court expanded on *Gibbons* by upholding federal licensing and inspection requirements for a steamboat that operated entirely within a single state on a river that emptied into Lake Michigan. According to the Court,

electrical wires, pipelines, etc.), whereas the latter term focuses on vehicles and other tools used in exploiting those corridors (planes, trains, ships, etc.). The key point is that the Court's cases suggest a specialized and broad power to regulate such channels and instrumentalities (however each term might be defined) that stands apart from its power to regulate the persons or things that move in commerce by way of such channels and instrumentalities and local activities that affect interstate commerce.

3. 77 U.S. 557 (1870).

the congressional power extended to the case because the river was part of "a continued highway
for commerce, both with other States and with
foreign countries," and the boat "was employed as
an instrument of that commerce."[4] Later decisions
clarified that the Commerce Clause reached the
instrumentalities and channels of shipment by land
as well as by water.[5] These cases laid the basis for
recognizing a comprehensive federal power over the
infrastructure of interstate movement, including—
in due time—an expansive authority over railways,
aircraft, and the facilities of telephone and telegraph communications.[6]

4. *Id.* at 564–65. Another early ship-related commerce-power
case is *United States v. Coombs*, 37 U.S. (12 Pet.) 72 (1838), in
which the Court upheld on commerce grounds a federal
criminal provision against theft of shipwrecked cargo from land
above the high water mark. According to Justice Story, this
statute was "perfectly within the constitutional authority of
Congress" because "[a]ny offense which ... interferes with,
obstructs, or prevents [foreign or interstate] commerce and navigation ... may be punished by congress, under its general
authority to make all laws necessary and proper to execute their
delegated constitutional powers." *Id.* at 78. The opinion does not
clearly indicate whether the goods in the case were destined for
interstate (as opposed to intrastate) delivery and whether that
fact mattered to the Court in assessing the combined effect of the
Commerce Clause and the Necessary and Proper Clause with
respect to the challenged statute.

5. *E.g., In re* State Freight Tax, 82 U.S. 232, 275 (1873).

6. *E.g.,* Fischer's Blend Station, Inc. v. State Tax Comm'n,
297 U.S. 650, 654–55 (1936) (concluding that "the transmission
of information interstate is a form of 'intercourse,' which is
commerce"). *See generally* Pensacola Tel. Co. v. W. Union Tel.
Co., 96 U.S. (6 Otto) 1, 9 (1878) (observing that powers under
the Commerce Clause "are not confined to the instrumentalities
of commerce ... known or in use when the Constitution was

Cases such as *Gibbons* and *The Daniel Ball* ensured that Congress had ample power to facilitate the conducting of commerce across state lines. Those cases, however, did not address another question: Could Congress invoke its authority over the channels of commerce to block interstate movements of goods or people to achieve "police power" objectives of protecting the general well-being of the citizenry? This issue first came before the Supreme Court in the *Lottery Case* (*Champion v. Ames*),[7] which involved an attack on a federal law that prohibited interstate shipments of lottery tickets. The challengers of the law argued that it violated the Constitution for both textual and historical reasons. As to the text, they asserted that the law did not "regulate" interstate commerce in lottery tickets; rather it *prohibited* such commerce. As to history, they argued that the law lacked any connection with the Framers' underlying concerns about removing impediments to free interstate trade.

A five-Justice majority of the Supreme Court saw things differently. As to the challengers' textual argument, Justice Harlan reasoned that prohibition is a form of government regulation (as an earlier decision sustaining congressional power to block interstate movements of diseased cows indicated).[8] As to the challengers' historical argument, Justice

adopted, but they keep pace with the progress of the country, and adapt themselves to the new developments of time and circumstances").

7. 188 U.S. 321 (1903).

8. *Id.* at 358–359. The quarantined-cow case was *Reid v. Colorado*, 187 U.S. 137 (1902).

Harlan emphasized the Court's insistence in *Gibbons* that the congressional power to regulate commerce among the states "may be exercised to its utmost extent."[9] In other words, because a prohibition on moving lottery tickets across state lines was in its very nature a regulation of interstate commerce, further inquiry into constitutional history or congressional motives was beside the point.

The dissenters, led by Chief Justice Fuller, first attacked the majority's attempt to characterize the lottery-ticket prohibition as a "regulation" of interstate commerce. They noted that the exclusion of diseased animals from trains and steamboats—unlike the exclusion of lottery tickets—made commerce-regulating sense because diseased animals were "in themselves injurious to the transaction of interstate commerce."[10] More fundamentally, Chief Justice Fuller worried that the Court had recognized a *de facto* federal police power, thus taking a "long step in the direction of wiping out all traces of state lines, and the creation of a centralized government."[11] According to Chief Justice Fuller, the Lottery Act embodied just the sort of "pretext" anticipated and condemned in *McCulloch* because it involved an invocation of the commerce power to regulate matters of morality reserved for state control by the Tenth Amendment.

The Court in the *Lottery Case* took care to limit

9. *Lottery Case*, 188 U.S. at 347.

10. *Id.* at 374 (Fuller, C.J., dissenting).

11. *Id.* at 371 (Fuller, C.J., dissenting).

its holding to the facts presented.[12] Before a decade passed, however, the Court had signaled that Congress could use the commerce-prohibiting technique to block the cross-border transportation of most anything it chose to target. A significant move in this direction came in *Hoke v. United States*,[13] which involved the constitutionality of a federal prohibition on transporting women across state lines for immoral purposes. Writing for a unanimous Court, Justice McKenna reasoned that "if the facility of interstate transportation can be taken away from the demoralization of lotteries, the debasement of obscene literature, the contagion of diseased cattle or persons, the impurity of food and drugs, the like facility can be taken away from the systematic enticement to and the enslavement in prostitution and debauchery of women...."[14] Four years later, in *Caminetti v. United States*,[15] the Court relied on *Hoke* to sustain the conviction of a man for taking a woman across state lines to make her "his mistress and concubine," even in the absence of any plan of "commercialized vice."[16]

12. *See id.* at 357 (emphasizing particular importance of "guarding the people of the United States against the 'widespread pestilence of lotteries' ").

13. 227 U.S. 308 (1913).

14. *Id.* at 322.

15. 242 U.S. 470 (1917).

16. *Id.* at 483–84. Justice Day, writing for the majority, assumed *arguendo* "that Congress has no power to punish one who travels in interstate commerce merely because he has the intention of committing an illegal or immoral act at the conclusion of the journey." *Id.* at 491. This case was different, however, because it involved the "transportation of passengers in inter-

In *Hipolite Egg Co. v. United States,*[17] the Court turned its attention to the interaction of the commerce-prohibiting technique and Congress's authority under the Necessary and Proper Clause. At issue in the case was the legality of the confiscation of "preserved eggs" that had been unlawfully shipped across state lines because their labels did not conform with federally established standards.[18] The defendant argued that the seizure violated the Constitution because the eggs "had passed out of interstate commerce" when they were commingled with other items at the place they were received.[19] The Court, however, declined to engage in a metaphysical inquiry about whether the eggs were "in" or "out" of interstate commerce at the time of the seizure.[20] Instead, with a tip of the hat to *McCulloch*, the Court reasoned that the power to confiscate mislabeled eggs, whether or not they remained in interstate commerce, was "an appropriate means to [the] end"[21] of preventing "trade in them between the states."[22]

The Court's reasoning in *Hipolite Egg* raised large questions about Congress's ability to "boot-state commerce." *Id.* Notwithstanding this qualification, Justice McKenna and two other Justices dissented. *Id.* at 496.

17.   220 U.S. 45 (1911).

18.   *Id.* at 49.

19.   *Id.* at 50.

20.   *See generally infra* notes 33–44 and accompanying text (discussing separate in-commerce theory of the commerce power).

21.   *Id.*

22.   *Id.* at 58.

strap" its commerce-prohibiting power to justify regulation of intrastate activities. Could Congress prohibit all manufacture of lottery tickets, all intrastate sales of preserved eggs, or all sexual relations between unmarried persons on the theory that laws of this kind would help to head off at the pass violations of the bans on cross-border transit involved in the *Lottery Case*, *Hipolite Egg* and *Hoke*? On this score, the Court's rhetoric seemed far-reaching. "The principle," the Court declared in *Caminetti*, "is the simple one ... that Congress has power over transportation 'among the several states' ... and that Congress, as an incident to it, may adopt not only means necessary but convenient to its exercise, and the means may have the quality of police regulations."[23]

Within 18 months of making this pronouncement, however, the Court moved to cabin the commerce-prohibiting power in *Hammer v. Dagenhart*,[24] a case that grew out of complex societal changes that marked the opening decades of the twentieth century. The late 1800s had seen sharp increases in immigration, urbanization and the growth of heavy industry within the United States. As these movements accelerated in the early 1900s, so did the social problems they bred—the emergence of urban ghettos, the blight of widespread poverty and the exposure of countless laborers to unsafe, if not barbaric, working conditions. In response came

23. *Caminetti*, 242 U.S. at 492 (quoting *Hoke*, 227 U.S. at 323).

24. 247 U.S. 251 (1918).

cries for reform. As novelists, sociologists and muckraking journalists decried the human costs of corporate profit making, political movements that favored ameliorative legislation (loosely collected under the label of "progressivism" and most famously personified in Theodore Roosevelt) began to take hold at both the state and federal levels. Reformers made important inroads when some state legislatures enacted protective measures such as minimum wage and maximum hour laws. Many local officials, however, feared that adoption of such measures would cause employers to flee to states that touted more "pro-industry" legal regimes. The result was a heightened demand for federal action, particularly through use of the commerce-prohibiting technique.

A major breakthrough came with Congress's adoption of the Child Labor Act of 1916. Built squarely on the commerce-prohibiting technique, the Act barred the interstate transportation of goods produced in factories that employed children under the age of 14 or that employed children between the ages of 14 and 16 at night, more than eight hours per day, or more than six days per week.[25] When the law was challenged, however, a five-Justice majority found a constitutional violation.[26] Writing for the Court, Justice Day reasoned that its commerce-prohibiting precedents had all involved items that were intrinsically "harmful."[27]

25. *See Hammer,* 247 U.S. at 268 n.1.

26. *Id.* at 276.

27. *Id.* at 271.

Here, in contrast, "the goods shipped are of themselves harmless,"[28] and upholding the law would improperly bring "all manufacture intended for interstate shipment ... under federal control to the practical exclusion of the authority of the states."[29]

The Court's opinion in *Hammer* spurred one of the most famous opinions of the "great dissenter," Oliver Wendell Holmes, Jr. Invoking the *Lottery Case* and its progeny, Justice Holmes insisted that the power of "prohibiting the carriage of certain goods in interstate or foreign commerce" was given to Congress "in unqualified terms."[30] He continued: "The notion that prohibition is any less prohibition when applied to things now thought evil I do not understand. But if there is any matter upon which civilized countries have agreed [it is that there is evil in] premature and excessive child labor." For Justice Holmes it was singularly wrong-headed to say that prohibition "is permissible as against strong drink but not as against the product of ruined lives."[31] In 1918, however, even Justice Holmes's eloquence could not save the Child Labor Act from fears that an unchecked congressional

28. *Id.* at 272.

29. *Id.* Notably, Justice Day advanced this distinction after resurrecting the prohibition-is-not-regulation argument that had not been a winner in the *Lottery Case*. The commerce power, he explained, "is one to control the means by which commerce is carried on, which is directly the contrary of the assumed right to forbid commerce from moving." *Id.* at 269–70.

30. *Id.* at 277 (Holmes, J., dissenting).

31. *Id.* at 280.

ability to employ the commerce-prohibiting technique would swallow up the states' police powers.[32]

B. The In–Commerce Theory Through 1936

After *Hammer* the commerce-prohibiting technique held little promise for justifying most federal laws that dealt with working conditions. It followed that, if such laws were going to take hold, lawyers would have to devise another strategy for defending them against federalism-based attack. The seeds of such a strategy lay in Justice Holmes's 1905 opinion for the Court in *Swift & Co. v. United States,*[33] which concerned an injunction under the Sherman Antitrust Act against meat-packing firms that conspired to hold down cattle prices in midwestern stockyards. In sustaining the federal action, Justice Holmes explained: "When cattle are sent for sale from a place in one state, with the expectation that they will end their transit, after purchase, in another, and when in effect they do so, with only the interruption necessary to find a purchaser at the stock yards, and when this is a typical, constantly recurring course, the current thus existing is a

32. Even so, in keeping with the rationale of *Hammer* the Court continued to uphold exercises of the commerce-prohibiting technique as to goods that were seen as threatening "the spread of any evil or harm. . . ." Brooks v. United States, 267 U.S. 432, 436 (1925) (stolen cars). *See, e.g.,* United States v. Simpson, 252 U.S. 465, 467 (1920) (holding that commerce power permits prohibition of transporting liquor across state lines, even for purpose of purely personal consumption).

33. 196 U.S. 375 (1905).

current of commerce among the states, and the purchase of the cattle is a part and incident of such commerce."[34] In *Stafford v. Wallace,*[35] decided four years after *Hammer,* the Court again invoked the current-of-commerce theory in upholding the unfair trade practice prohibition of the Packers and Stockyards Act of 1921. As stated by Chief Justice Taft: "The stockyards are but a throat through which the current flows, and the transactions which occur therein are only incident to this current from the West to the East, and from one state to another."[36]

Swift and *Stafford,* however, left many questions open. Could Congress, for example, invoke the in-commerce theory to regulate activity—including child labor, wages, and working hours—that did not concern, at least directly, prices or product-marketing practices? Could Congress use this theory to regulate activities at the beginning or the end, rather than in the middle, of a product-distribution process? In short, just how long, wide and deep was this "stream of commerce" that the Court had empowered Congress to regulate?[37]

34. *Id.* at 398–399. It was in this context that Justice Holmes coined the oft-quoted passage that "commerce among the states is not a technical legal conception, but a practical one, drawn from the course of business." *Id.* at 398.

35. 258 U.S. 495 (1922).

36. *Id.* at 516.

37. Addressing one aspect of this question, the Court agreed in *Chicago Board of Trade v. Olsen,* 262 U.S. 1 (1923), that the principle of *Swift* and *Stafford* was not limited to cases involving cattle. Relying squarely on those cases, the Court upheld price-related regulations applicable to grain "stored on its way from

Telling answers to these questions came in the Supreme Court's then-seminal decisions in *A.L.A. Schechter Poultry Corp. v. United States*[38] and *Carter v. Carter Coal Co.*[39] Each of these cases grew out of events stirred by the stock market collapse of 1929. As the Great Depression gripped the nation— with joblessness, mortgage foreclosures and business failures reaching unprecedented proportions— the Republican-controlled government under the leadership of President Herbert Hoover took a cautious attitude toward large-scale federal intervention. One consequence of this choice was a sweeping Democratic victory in the election of 1932, and as a result President Franklin Roosevelt took office in 1933 with a mandate for reform. The new President's initiatives plunged the federal government into broad regulation of securities markets, welfare programs and labor conditions. At the heart of this "New Deal" lay the National Industrial Recovery Act of 1933 (NIRA), which delegated authority to the President to promulgate "codes of fair competition" that regulated, among other things, minimum pay and maximum hours in marketplaces throughout much of the nation.

Schechter Poultry involved the prosecution of two operators of a small wholesale poultry market in Brooklyn for violating wage and hour rules (as well

the West to the East as it is being sold on the exchange." *Id.* at 36.

38.   295 U.S. 495 (1935).

39.   298 U.S. 238 (1936).

as inspection, licensing and disclosure rules) imposed by a code of fair competition, promulgated under the NIRA, for the poultry industry in metropolitan New York City. The operators predictably argued that application of the NIRA to their localized business exceeded the reach of the commerce power. Lawyers for the government predictably responded that the market was part of the "stream" of interstate commerce, because 96% of poultry purchased for resale in New York (and thus passed along by wholesalers like the defendants) came from other states. Writing for the Court, Chief Justice Hughes concluded that the current of commerce recognized and relied on in *Swift* and *Stafford* did not flow this far. Rather, as he explained, "[w]hen defendants had made their purchases, whether at the West Washington Market in New York City or at the railroad terminals serving the City ... for local disposition ... [t]he interstate transactions in relation to that poultry then ended."[40] Thus, "decisions which deal with a stream of interstate commerce—where goods come to rest within a state temporarily and are later to go forward in interstate commerce—and with the regulations of transactions involved in that practical continuity of movement, are not applicable here."[41]

What *Schechter Poultry* did to the mouth of the stream of commerce, *Carter Coal* did to its source. At issue in that case was the constitutionality of the

40. *Schechter Poultry*, 295 U.S. at 542–43.
41. *Id*. at 543.

wage and hour provisions of the Bituminous Coal Conservation Act of 1935. Could Congress regulate the basic causes of labor discord within the coal industry on the theory that the industry provided the well-spring of a great stream of commerce that carried essential fuel to every metropolis and hamlet of the nation? The answer was "no." In *Swift* and *Stafford*, Justice Sutherland explained, "[i]t was nowhere suggested . . . that the interstate commerce power extended to the growth or production of the things which, after production, entered the flow."[42] Any lingering doubt about whether "*Swift* and kindred cases" reached beyond a "restricted field" had been removed by *Schechter Poultry*.[43] "In the *Schechter* case the flow had ceased. Here it had not begun. The difference is not one of substance. The applicable principle is the same."[44]

In short, the in-commerce theory was not destined to sustain the boldest expressions of New Deal regulatory energies so long as the Supreme Court remained unshaped by the guiding hand of Franklin Roosevelt. Advocates of federal power, however, had one last arrow in their quiver. Harkening back to *Gibbons*, they argued that Congress could pass laws, including the laws at issue in *Schechter Poultry* and *Carter Coal,* on the theory that they concerned matters that "affect" interstate commerce.

42. *Carter Coal*, 298 U.S. at 305.

43. *Id*. at 306.

44. *Id*.

C. The Affecting–Commerce Theory Through 1936

Even though *Gibbons* had indicated that the commerce power broadly authorized regulation of intrastate activities that "affect other states," Congress seldom invoked the Commerce Clause to enact federal legislation during the 1800s. As the century neared its close, however, the proliferation of railroads and other large business enterprises triggered enactment of two major federal laws supported by the affecting-commerce theory: the Interstate Commerce Act of 1887 and the Sherman Antitrust Act of 1890.

As soon as the Sherman Act's ban on monopolization landed in the law books, federal authorities began to put it to work. An early civil action targeted acquisitions that gave a single corporation control of 98% of the nation's sugar refining business. In response to the government's demand for divestiture, the firm argued that the commerce power did not permit Congress to outlaw a monopoly in manufacture. In *United States v. E. C. Knight Co.*,[45] the Court endorsed this view. The problem, according to Chief Justice Fuller, was that "[c]ommerce succeeds to manufacture, and is not a part of it,"[46] because commerce involves "buying and selling and the transportation incidental thereto."[47] The Chief

45. 156 U.S. 1 (1895).

46. *Id.* at 12.

47. *Id.* at 14.

Justice acknowledged that "the power to control the manufacture of a given thing involves, in a certain sense, the control of its disposition."[48] He added, however, that controlling the manufacture of an item "affects [commerce] only incidentally and indirectly" or in "a secondary, and not a primary, sense."[49] In short, Congress could not control the production of refined sugar, including by busting a trust in that industry. Otherwise "congress would be invested, to the exclusion of the states, with the power to regulate, not only manufactures, but also agriculture, horticulture, stock-raising, domestic fisheries, mining; in short, every branch of human industry."[50]

Conveniently omitted from the Court's exegesis (though not from Justice Harlan's lone but prescient dissent) was any reference to *McCulloch*'s endorsement of a capacious congressional authority to develop means for carrying its enumerated powers into effect. Without saying as much, the Court

48. *Id.* at 11.

49. *Id.*

50. *Id.* at 14. Notably, this thought was not an original one. It reached back at least as far as the events that led to the nullification crisis of 1832 when South Carolina proclaimed its constitutional authority to ignore federal tariffs on imported cotton goods. Even this purported use of the federal taxing authority, theorists such as John C. Calhoun declared, was an unconstitutional attempt to promote domestic manufacture, "which was not a legitimate subject of federal concern." DANIEL A. FARBER, LINCOLN'S CONSTITUTION 59 (2003). Notably, Joseph Story attacked this view in his classic treatise on constitutional law. JOSEPH STORY, COMMENTARIES ON THE CONSTITUTION §§ 526–29 (Carolina Academic Press 1987) (original work published 1833).

rejected the idea that a congressional effort to coun-
teract monopoly pricing was "conducive" to facilitating interstate commerce in sugar and other products. Instead the Court embraced a different style of
analysis. Relying on a parade-of-horribles argument,
it forged a categorical rule designed to keep the
affecting-commerce prong of the congressional power within meaningful, judicially discernable bounds.
The rule was simple: Manufacturing (and other
forms of production) were in and of themselves
beyond the reach of congressional regulation. But
just how far did this principle extend?

The Court began to answer that question, while
simultaneously salvaging the federal antitrust laws,
in *Addyston Pipe & Steel Co. v. United States*[51] and
Northern Securities Co. v. United States.[52] In the
former case, it was enough to establish a "direct,
immediate and intended relation"[53] to interstate
commerce that the pipe-manufacturer defendants
had entered into a conspiracy for the purpose of
fixing prices for "the *future disposition* of the manufactured article."[54] In the latter case, the Court
concluded that Congress could outlaw an acquisi-
tion of corporate securities that threatened to de-
crease competition in interstate train rates because
the transaction directly affected interstate commerce.[55] A cohort of four dissenters stood ready to

51. 175 U.S. 211 (1899).

52. 193 U.S. 197 (1904).

53. *Addyston Pipe & Steel Co.*, 175 U.S. at 243.

54. *Id*. at 240 (emphasis added).

55. *Id*. at 344.

fence off securities transfers altogether from the reach of the federal commerce power, advocating in effect a categorical rule of non-regulability akin to the rule applied to manufacturing in *E. C. Knight*. Emphasizing "fact" over "form," however, the Court's majority refused to distinguish a competition-squelching consolidation by way of share transfers from a conspiracy of independent operators effected by way of contractual arrangement.[56]

Any doubt about the potential significance of the affecting-commerce prong of the commerce power fell away with the Court's decision in the *Shreveport Rate Case* (*Houston, East & West Texas Railway Co. v. United States*).[57] At issue was an order promulgated pursuant to the Interstate Commerce Act that in effect set rates charged by railroad companies for the intrastate transport of goods in an effort to counter discrimination against interstate shipments.[58] The Supreme Court upheld the order, reasoning that Congress's regulatory authority over "instruments of interstate commerce" extended to intrastate "matters having such a close and substantial relation to interstate traffic that the control is essential or appropriate to the . . . maintenance of conditions under which interstate commerce may be conducted upon fair terms."[59] The

56. *No. Secs. Co.*, 193 U.S. at 345.

57. 234 U.S. 342 (1914).

58. For example, prior to issuance of the order, "[t]he rate on furniture from Dallas to Longview, Texas, 124 miles, was 24.8 cents and that from Shreveport [in Louisiana] to Longview, 65.7 miles, was 35 cents." *Id*. at 346.

59. *Id*. at 351.

Court noted that it had previously upheld federal regulation of the equipment used on intrastate trains because of the "close relation" that the safety of intrastate traffic bore to the effective operation of rail cars moving across state lines.[60] Here too, the Court reasoned, federal regulatory authority could be "exerted to prevent the intrastate operations of such carriers from being made a means of injury to that which has been confided to Federal care."[61]

As President Roosevelt crafted his New Deal program, these precedents loomed large. "Cases such as Shreveport were encouraging; yet cases like

60. The key case was *Southern Railway Co. v. United States*, 222 U.S. 20, 27 (1911) (upholding application of a federal rule requiring the use of safe coupling devices to railroad cars employed only in intrastate journeys, albeit on tracks that covered interstate routes, because "trains on the same railroad are ... interdependent; for whatever brings delay or disaster to one, or results in disabling one of its operatives, is calculated to impede the progress and imperil the safety of other trains").

61. *Shreveport Rate Case*, 234 U.S. at 351; *see also id.* at 353 ("This is not to say that Congress possesses the authority to regulate the internal commerce of a state, as such, but that it does possess the power to foster and protect interstate commerce and to take all measures necessary or appropriate to that end, although the intrastate transactions of interstate carriers may thereby be controlled."). For a later case employing similar logic in a different setting, *see United States v. Ferger*, 250 U.S. 199, 203–05 (1919) (upholding federal prohibition on forgery of bills of lading; relying in part on the assertion that such bills "are instrumentalities of ... commerce" but also citing the "effect" on the regulated behavior and the danger that "the credit and confidence which sustains interstate commerce would ... be impaired or weakened by the unrestrained right to fabricate and circulate spurious bills ...").

Knight looked the other way."[62] It remained for the Supreme Court to say how far Congress could go in regulating local matters on the theory that they "affected" interstate commerce, and the first test came in *Railroad Retirement Board v. Alton R. Co.*[63] The issue in *Alton Railroad* was whether Congress could force interstate railroad carriers to adopt pension plans for their employees. The basic argument for constitutionality was simple: Sound retirement structures would help build employee morale, thus "promot[ing] . . . efficiency and safety in interstate transportation."[64] A five-Justice majority, however, found this argument unavailing. Justice Roberts recognized (as he had to in light of past decisions) that rules that limited railroad workers' hours and that assured them fair compensation for injuries "have a direct and intimate connection with the actual operation of the railroads."[65] Marshaling em-

62. KATHLEEN M. SULLIVAN & GERALD GUNTHER, CONSTITUTIONAL LAW 130 (14th ed. 2001).

63. 295 U.S. 330 (1935).

64. *Id*. at 364.

65. *Id*. at 369. Justice Roberts did not discuss these cases in great detail, but he did offer some comments on why other railroad-employee laws were, or might be, constitutional. A law governing labor relations in the railroad industry, for example, was constitutional because facilitating "the amicable settlement of disputes which threatened the service of the necessary agencies of interstate transportation tended to prevent interruptions of service." *Id*. at 367. And a worker's compensation program for railroad workers would be more readily sustainable than the challenged retirement law in part because "the very certainty that compensation must be paid for every injury . . . promotes and encourages precaution on the part of the employer against

pirical and commonsense arguments, however, he declared that any connection between governmentally mandated pensions and efficient interstate train service was too tenuous to sustain the legislation.[66] To this thought he added the now-familiar parade-of-horribles flourish. If the challenged retirement-payment scheme were sustained, he observed, federal mandates requiring employers to provide "for free medical attendance and nursing, for clothing, for food, for housing, for the education of children, and a hundred other matters, might with equal propriety be proposed as tending to relieve the employee of mental strain and worry."[67] Without citing the pretext language of *McCulloch*, Justice Roberts in effect invoked its principle: "Is it not apparent that [such laws] are really and essentially related solely to the social welfare of the worker, and therefore remote from any regulation of commerce as such? We think the answer is plain. These matters obviously lie outside the orbit of congressional power."[68]

The precedential significance of *Alton Railroad* was unclear from the start. The Railroad Retirement Act had been clumsily drawn, the Court's reliance on federalism principles to invalidate it came in an alternative holding, and the Court carefully distinguished a compulsory retirement program from maximum-hour and collective-bargaining laws applicable to the railroad industry. Nonethe-

accident and tends to make transportation safer and more efficient." *Id*. at 370.

66. *Id*. at 351.

67. *Id*. at 368.

68. *Id*.

less, the pretext reasoning of *Alton Railroad* hung like the sword of Damocles over other New Deal initiatives that had been enacted on an affecting-commerce theory. Would the sword fall? The answer came—as it had with regard to the scope of the in-commerce principle—in *Schechter Poultry* and *Carter Coal*.

In *Schechter Poultry,* government lawyers had not relied solely on the in-commerce theory. They also had advanced an affecting-commerce defense for federal minimum-wage laws that targeted localized work forces. "Maintaining wage distributions," the government asserted, "would provide the necessary stimulus in starting 'the cumulative forces making for expanding commercial activity,' " which in turn would revitalize the entire economy of the United States.[69] The Court responded to this effects-based argument by insisting that "[e]xtraordinary conditions do not create or enlarge constitutional power,"[70] that the Court's precedents required it to attend to "the well-established distinction between direct and indirect effects,"[71] and that the hours and wages of the Schechters' employees had "no direct relation to interstate commerce" because they concerned only "the details of defendants' management of their local business."[72]

69. *Schechter Poultry*, 295 U.S. at 550.

70. *Id.* at 528.

71. *Id.* at 546.

72. *Id.* at 548. Seeking to tie its affecting-commerce defense of the statute more directly to interstate commerce in poultry,

In *Carter Coal* the Court completed the circle by holding that Congress could not justify application of wage-and-hour rules to the nation's coal mines on an affecting-commerce rationale. In reaching this conclusion, the Court invoked both *E. C. Knight* and *Hammer v. Dagenhart* for the proposition that production was "a purely local activity," which in its nature had only an "indirect" effect on interstate commerce.[73] In a critical passage, Justice Sutherland explained:

> The distinction between a direct and an indirect effect turns, not upon the magnitude of either the cause or the effect, but entirely upon the manner in which the effect has been brought about. If the production by one man of a single ton of coal intended for interstate sale and shipment, and actually so sold and shipped, affects interstate commerce indirectly, the effect does not become direct by multiplying the tonnage, or increasing the number of men employed, or adding to the expense or complexities of the business, or by all combined. It is quite true that rules of law are sometimes qualified by considerations of degree,

the government also argued that low wages contributed to lower charges for chickens and "that the cutting of prices brings about a demoralization of the price structure," which generally inhibits commerce in poultry products. *Id.* at 548–49. Once again moved by a parade-of-horribles counterattack, however, the Court responded that "this argument proves too much." *Id.* at 549. If the federal government could control wages because of their effect on prices, then on the same theory it could "control . . . the number of employees, rents, advertising, methods of doing business, etc." *Id.*

73. *Carter Coal*, 298 U.S. at 304.

as the government argues. But the matter of degree has no bearing upon the question here, since that question is not—What is the extent of the local activity or condition, or the extent of the effect produced upon interstate commerce? but—What is the relation between the activity or condition and the effect?[74]

Put another way, it might well be that struggles over "wages, working conditions, the right of collective bargaining, etc." invite strikes and work stoppages that "greatly" affect coal prices and the resulting vibrancy of interstate commerce.[75] "But . . . the conclusive answer is that the evils are all local," and "[s]uch effect as they may have upon commerce, however extensive it may be, is secondary and indirect."[76]

Carter Coal did not resolve all questions concerning the constitutionality of New Deal reforms. The Court, for example, was careful to sidestep the simmering question whether Congress could establish federal price controls for coal sales (as opposed to wage and hour controls for coal workers) on an affecting-commerce theory.[77] From President

74. *Id.* at 308.

75. *Id.* at 304.

76. *Id.* at 304, 309.

77. The majority invalidated price-control regulations applicable to coal on the theory that these regulations—whether or not constitutional under the Commerce Clause in and of themselves—were not severable from the invalidated wage and hour regulations. In a dissenting opinion joined by Justices Brandeis and Stone, Justice Cardozo reached the constitutionality of the price rules and found no Commerce Clause problem. He reasoned

Roosevelt's perspective, however, the *Schechter Poultry* and *Carter Coal* decisions were nothing short of catastrophic. Decrying them as usurpations, the President declared to the nation that "we must take action to save the Constitution from the Court and the Court from itself."[78]

D. The New Deal Crisis, the Court–Packing Plan and the Politics of Constitutional Law

Close on the heels of *Schechter Poultry* and *Carter Coal* came the election of 1936, in which Franklin Roosevelt "achieved a victory without precedent in American politics," carrying all the states except Maine and Vermont.[79] With his political adversaries on the ropes, the President's juices were flowing. It was time to take on the one group that stood between his most ambitious New Deal goals and their successful implementation—the Supreme Court's five-Justice phalanx of Willis Van Devanter, James C. McReynolds, George Sutherland, Pierce Butler and Owen Roberts. All these jurists, with the sole exception of Justice McReynolds, had come to

that "to regulate the price for [coal sold in interstate transactions] is to regulate commerce itself," *id*. at 326 (Cardozo, J., dissenting), and that "prices for intrastate sales of coal have so inescapable a relation to those for interstate sales that a system of regulation for transactions of the one class is necessary to give adequate protection to the system of regulation adopted for the other," *id*. (Cardozo, J., dissenting). Notably, Justice Cardozo's position in time carried the day. *See* Sunshine Anthracite Coal Co. v. Adkins, 310 U.S. 381 (1940).

78. SULLIVAN & GUNTHER, *supra* note 62, at 136 (quoting Franklin D. Roosevelt, Radio Broadcast of March 9, 1937).

79. JOHN M. BLUM ET AL., THE NATIONAL EXPERIENCE 664 (1963).

the Court by way of appointment by a Republican president. By making each of them effectively unremovable, the Constitution's structural features in effect were permitting the influence of long-gone leaders such as Herbert Hoover and Warren Harding to block pursuit of the Democrats' New Deal initiatives. President Roosevelt, however, was savvy enough to recognize that the Constitution's system of checks and balances might be used not only to constrain the efforts of the nation's elected Democratic leadership but also to strike back at the actions of a Republican-oriented Supreme Court. With this thought in mind, the President set about to find a way to remove obstacles placed in his path by five men who read the Commerce Clause far more narrowly than he did.

On February 5, 1937, President Roosevelt transmitted a message to Congress. In it he asserted that the Supreme Court was laboring under a "heavy burden" and that "one of the definite duties of the Congress" is "to maintain the effective functioning of the Federal judiciary."[80] He then laid out an unprecedented proposal for institutional reform— namely, that Congress should authorize the President to appoint one additional Supreme Court Justice for each sitting Justice who was "of retirement age" but chose not to step down.[81] Enactment of the

80. Franklin D. Roosevelt, Speech: Message to Congress (February 5, 1937), *in* THE PUBLIC PAPERS AND ADDRESSES OF FRANKLIN D. ROOSEVELT, 1937 VOLUME, at 51 (1941).

81. In an effort to strengthen the President's hand even more, the proposal also provided that the President could ap-

proposed law in all its details would have permitted President Roosevelt to increase the size of the Supreme Court from nine to fifteen (assuming no resignations occurred), thereby overwhelming the five conservative jurists who had lined up against him in *Carter Coal* and other key cases.[82]

President Roosevelt's attempt to restructure the Court in his own image—particularly after being initially marketed as an aid to overtaxed Justices— stirred widespread resistance, including within the Democratic Party. Chief Justice Hughes expressed the Supreme Court's own opposition, arguing that the plan "would *not* promote ... efficiency" because "[t]here would be more judges to hear, more judges to confer, more judges to discuss, more judges to be convinced and to decide."[83] The Chief Justice made these comments, he noted, without addressing "any question of policy."[84] The Senate committee charged with assessing the President's proposal, however, had considerations of policy very much on its mind. It repudiated the plan as an "utterly dangerous abandonment of constitutional

point additional lower court federal judges according to the same age-based formula. *id.*

82. The President's proposed bill envisioned retirement at "the age of seventy years" so long as the Justice or judge had sat for at least ten years; at the time six Justices—Brandeis, Butler, Hughes, McReynolds, Sutherland and Van Devanter—met this standard.

83. SULLIVAN & GUNTHER, *supra* note 62, at 136 (quoting Letter from Chief Justice Charles Evans Hughes to Senator Burton K. Wheeler (March 22, 1937)).

84. *Id.*

principle." Explaining why, the committee observed:

> Its practical operation would be to make the
> Constitution what the executive or legislative
> branches of the Government choose to say it is—
> an interpretation to be changed with each change
> of administration. It is a measure which should
> be so emphatically rejected that its parallel will
> never again be presented to the free representa-
> tives of the free people of America.[85]

With the demise of his court-packing plan, President Roosevelt had lost a battle. Yet he stood on the brink of winning his war. While Congress labored over the court-packing proposal, the Court it targeted began to hear a new muse. In March of 1937, the Court handed President Roosevelt a major judicial victory when it upheld the National Labor Relations Act's protections of union activity, including in the manufacturing sector, in *NLRB v. Jones & Laughlin Steel Corp.*[86] This action was followed by a string of rulings hospitable to the President's New Deal philosophy. In each case, the four outliers in *Alton Railroad* and *Carter Coal* (Chief Justice Hughes and Justices Brandeis, Stone and Cardozo) found a new ally in Justice Roberts, who had joined the majority opinion in the latter case and written passionately for the Court in the former.[87] Histori-

85. *Id.* at 137.

86. 301 U.S. 1 (1937). *See generally infra* Chapter IV.

87. In this set of decisions, the Court not only moved away from the direct/indirect distinction of its earlier commerce-power jurisprudence, but also abandoned previous "freedom of conans have long debated whether the court-packing proposal launched in February of 1937 triggered, only one month later, Justice Roberts' so-called "switch in time that saved nine."[88] Whether it did or did not, however, the Court's transformation was unmistakable.[89]

What is one to glean from the extraordinary events of 1937? The overwhelming rejection of President Roosevelt's court-packing plan—a plan sent to Capitol Hill "by a President who had just received an overwhelming popular vote of confidence and who had not yet been denied in Congress any of his important demands"[90]—stands as a striking reminder of the esteem and trust the American people

tract" rulings that threatened minimum-wage and other business-regulating efforts under both state and federal law. *See generally* ROBERT G. MCCLOSKEY, THE AMERICAN SUPREME COURT 117–20 (2d ed. 1994) (revised by Sanford Levinson). Most significantly, during the same term that produced *Carter Coal*, the Court in *Morehead v. New York* ex rel. *Tipaldo*, 298 U.S. 587 (1936), had invalidated New York's minimum wage for female employees by a five-to-four vote. Yet, in *West Coast Hotel v. Parrish*, 300 U.S. 379 (1937), decided two weeks before *Jones & Laughlin Steel*, the Court again by a five-to-four vote upheld a Washington statute that likewise imposed a minimum wage for women. Once again, it was Justice Roberts who joined the majority in both cases.

88. *See, e.g.,* Michael Ariens, *A Thrice–Told Tale, or Felix the Cat*, 107 HARV. L. REV. 620 (1994); Richard D. Friedman, *Switching Time and Other Thought Experiments: The Hughes Court and Constitutional Transformation*, 142 U. PA. L. REV. 1891 (1994).

89. And any lingering possibility for a conservative retrenchment evaporated when Justice Willis Van Devanter announced his retirement from the Court on June 2, 1937.

90. MCCLOSKEY, *supra* note 87, at 113.

long have directed toward the Supreme Court. But it is equally true that "[t]he Court's recantation had helped save the day."[91] In the end, the forces unleashed by the Great Depression were "too cosmic" for even a life-tenured Supreme Court to withstand.[92] The result was a "judicial revolution" that sharply altered constitutional doctrine, particularly with respect to the scope of the commerce power.[93]

91. *Id.* at 119.

92. *Id.* at 117.

93. *Id.* at 119.

CHAPTER IV

THE COMMERCE POWER FROM **1937** TO **1985**: THE ROOSEVELT-ERA REVOLUTION

The judicial revolution of 1937 had profound implications for each of the three aspects of the congressional commerce power. Within five short years, the limiting approaches of *Hammer, Schechter Poultry* and *Carter Coal* would be things of the past. In coming decades a Court dominated by disciples of the New Deal would uphold sweeping federal legislation concerning labor relations, civil rights, environmental protection and local crime, relying primarily on a much-broadened affecting-commerce theory. Indeed, the spirit of judicial restraint became so pronounced that, for a period of nearly 60 years, the Court could not identify a single federal law that exceeded the commerce power.

A. The Channels/Instrumentalities Theory and the Commerce–Prohibiting Technique in the Post–1936 Period

In the period following 1936, the Court continued to embrace an expansive view of the congressional power over the "channels" and "instrumentalities" of interstate commerce.[1] As new technologies proliferated, so did the Court's willingness to sustain congressional regulation of such things as airplanes, telecommunications facilities and natural gas pipelines.[2] Federal statutes concerning the infrastructure of interstate trade typically were designed to keep the avenues of interstate commerce open and well-functioning. The Court, however, also strengthened Congress's ability to block interstate trade by lending new energy to the commerce-prohibiting technique. The Court's key post–1936 encounter with the theory came in *United States v. Darby*,[3] and the Court's decision in that case left no doubt that a new day for the commerce power had dawned.

Following the Court's validation of the National Labor Relations Act (NLRA) in 1937,[4] Congress quickly erected the other pillar of modern labor law, the Fair Labor Standards Act of 1938 (FLSA). That Act's constitutionality came before the Court in

1.   Perez v. United States, 402 U.S. 146, 150 (1971). *See, e.g.,* Oklahoma *ex rel.* Phillips v. Guy F. Atkinson Co., 313 U.S. 508, 523 (1941) (noting, among other things, that "Congress may exercise its control over the non-navigable stretches of a river in order to preserve or promote commerce on the navigable portions").

2.   *See, e.g.,* Consolidated Edison Co. v. NLRB, 305 U.S. 197, 213 (1938) (lumping telegraph, telephone, radio and airport operations together with railroads and shipping in discussing instrumentalities of "interstate and foreign commerce").

3.   312 U.S. 100 (1941).

4.   *See* NLRB v. Jones & Laughlin Steel Corp., 301 U.S. 1 (1937).

Darby, which involved a prosecution under each of the statute's two principal sections. The first provision, section 15(a)(1), barred transportation across any state line of goods manufactured by workers who were not paid a specified minimum wage or who were required to work more than a specified maximum number of weekly hours. The Court recognized that this attempted use of the commerce-prohibiting technique could not stand under the authority of *Hammer v. Dagenhart*[5] because goods made by underpaid workers, no less than goods made by underage workers, failed to qualify as bad "of themselves."[6] The Court dealt with this difficulty by declaring that *Hammer* "should be and now is overruled."[7] Tracking the "powerful and now clas-

5. 247 U.S. 251 (1918) (discussed *supra* Chapter III).

6. *Id*. at 272.

7. *Darby*, 312 U.S. at 117. Citing the *Lottery Case* and its progeny, the Court explained that *Hammer* "was a departure from the principles which have prevailed in the interpretation of the commerce clause both before and since the decision." *Id*. at 116–117. Particularly important among the post-*Hammer* precedents was *Kentucky Whip & Collar Co. v. Illinois Cent. R.R. Co.*, 299 U.S. 334 (1937). In that case the Court upheld a ban on interstate shipment of convict-made goods into any state in which receiving or possessing such goods was unlawful. Pointing to the Court's many prior commerce-prohibiting-technique rulings, the Court emphasized that "[t]he power to prohibit interstate transportation has been upheld ... in relation to diseased livestock, lottery tickets, commodities owned by the interstate carrier transporting them, except as may be required in the conduct of its business as a common carrier, adulterated and misbranded articles, under the Pure Food and Drugs Act, women, for immoral purposes, intoxicating liquors, diseased plants, stolen motor vehicles, and kidnaped persons." *Id*. at 346 (citations omitted). The Court sought to distinguish *Hammer* on the

sic dissent of Mr. Justice Holmes,"[8] the Court declared that exercises of the commerce-prohibiting technique would be constitutional, from that day forward, whatever the underlying motive of Congress and whether or not the transported goods were intrinsically "harmful or deleterious."[9]

The second provision at issue in *Darby*, section 15(a)(2), required employers to comply with federal wage-and-hour rules for all employees engaged in making goods for shipment across state lines. The commerce-prohibiting technique, standing alone, could not sustain this provision because it did not target interstate movements *per se*; rather, it directed its sting at workers involved in producing goods prior to their shipment. Even so, the Court sustained the provision by relying on two separate affecting-commerce rationales, the latter of which was intimately connected to the congressional ban on cross-border movements. The Court's first affecting-commerce rationale focused on "the evils ... of substandard labor conditions" and the "dislocation

ground that the law at issue in *Kentucky Whip & Collar* did not reflect only an attempt to achieve favored federal objectives, but instead entailed a congressional effort "to regulate interstate commerce so as to prevent that commerce from being used to impede the carrying out of the state policy." *Id*. at 351.

8. *Darby*, 312 U.S. at 115.

9. *Id*. at 116. The Court, moreover, has been true to its word. *See, e.g.*, Cleveland v. United States, 329 U.S. 14, 19 (1946) (upholding ban on interstate transport of women for immoral purposes as applied to man who transported woman across state lines for purposes of involving her in a polygamous marriage); United States v. Carolene Prods. Co., 304 U.S. 144 (1938) (upholding prohibition on interstate shipment of "filled" milk).

of the commerce" they brought about,[10] including by "driving down labor conditions in [other] states."[11] In addition, as the Court would later explain, "substandard labor conditions tended to lead to labor disputes and strikes" and those conditions inevitably threatened "the flow of goods in commerce" across state lines.[12]

No less significant in *Darby*—and more directly related to the commerce-prohibiting technique—was the Court's alternative basis for upholding section 15(a)(2). This alternative approach hinged on the Court's willingness to let Congress adopt "appropriate aids" to effectuating the prohibition on cross-border shipments imposed by section 15(a)(1).[13] The Court put its point this way: "Con-

10. *Darby*, 312 U.S. at 122.

11. Maryland v. Wirtz, 392 U.S. 183, 189 (1968). *See supra* Chapter III (discussing possible "race to the bottom" justification for federal regulatory controls).

12. *Wirtz*, 392 U.S. at 191. As the Court explained in *Wirtz*, this rationale applied to both suppliers and purchasers of goods in interstate commerce. *See id.; see also* Overnight Motor Transp. Co. v. Missel, 316 U.S. 572, 576 (1942) (noting, in upholding FLSA as applied to transit company employee, that "undue extension of hours, ... by inducing labor discontent [is] apt to lead to interference with commerce through interruption of work"; also adverting to problem of unfair competition and resulting "friction between production areas with different length work weeks"). Notably, by the time of *Darby*, the Court's decisions in the NLRA cases had retreated enough from the manufacturing-is-not-commerce principle that the Court could apply this broad affecting-commerce rationale to the lumber producer involved in the case. *See infra* notes 43–45 and accompanying text.

13. *Darby*, 312 U.S. at 120.

gress, having by the present Act adopted the policy of excluding from interstate commerce all goods produced for the commerce which do not conform to the specified labor standards ... may choose the means reasonably adapted to the attainment of [the] permitted end, even though they involve control of intrastate activities."[14] Although this rationale harkened back to *Hipolite Egg*'s approval of post-delivery seizures of improperly shipped goods,[15] it went a step further. Now the Court stood ready to countenance enactments that targeted *pre-shipment* activity to effectuate bans on interstate movements developed under the commerce-prohibiting technique.[16]

14.   *Id.* at 121.

15.   *See supra* Chapter III.

16.   As the Court noted in *Darby,* this sort of means-to-the-end justification for regulating pre-shipment local activity had surfaced in the pre–1937 period. Thus in *Thornton v. United States*, 271 U.S. 414 (1926), the Court had held that "Congress may require inspection and preventive treatment of all cattle in a disease infected area in order to prevent shipment in interstate commerce of some of the cattle without the treatment." *Darby,* 312 U.S. at 121. Not surprisingly, however, the Court in *Thornton* had emphasized the distinctively national nature of the problem posed by "the spread of disease from one state to another by [infected] cattle." *Thornton*, 271 U.S. at 425. The Court in *Thornton* had also pointed out that the indictment concerned regulatory efforts in a county "on the line between Georgia and Florida" and that "cattle ranged between one state and the other in that region." *Id.* at 421. *See also* Kentucky Whip & Collar Co. v. Illinois Cent. R.R. Co., 299 U.S. 334, 352–53 (1937) (reasoning that Congress could pass laws "reasonable and appropriate" for effectuating its ban on interstate shipments of convict-made goods into states where possession of such goods was unlawful and concluding that this authority authorized

Professor Gunther detected in this latter rationale a "superbootstrap suggestion" that raised
large questions about just how far Congress could
go in leveraging the commerce-prohibiting technique to regulate intrastate behavior.[17] Could Congress ban intrastate production-related activities by
all workers paid less than a specified wage (including, for example, employees in a local bakery or
sandwich shop) to effectuate the federal prohibition
on the interstate transport of goods made in violation of federal wage standards? Could Congress bar
the interstate movement of same-sex couples who
have formalized their relationships in violation of
federal standards, and then impose a nationwide
ban on same-sex marriages and unions, even if
otherwise permissible under governing state law, to
make sure that no such interstate movements occur?[18] The answers to these questions (at least
insofar as they concern the commerce power) remain unclear.[19] In the post–1936 period, however,

congressional ban on interstate shipment of all convict-made
goods not labeled in conformance with federal standards "regardless of the law of the State of destination").

17. GERALD GUNTHER, CONSTITUTIONAL LAW 143–44 (11th ed.
1985).

18. *Cf.* Cleveland v. United States, 329 U.S. 14, 19 (1946)
(noting that "[t]he fact that the regulation of marriage is a state
matter does not, of course, make the Mann Act ... unconstitutional" and that the commerce-prohibiting power "may be used
to defeat what are deemed to be immoral practices" even if the
means used "have 'the quality of police regulations' ").

19. This statement is qualified with the parenthetical observation because even entirely proper exercises of the commerce
power may be trumped by freestanding constitutional restraints,
such as those imposed by the Bill of Rights. For example, a
constitutional right of free interstate travel or a right of intimate

the Court continued to uphold regulations of intrastate activities on the ground that they had been tied to bans on cross-border movements.[20]

In *United States v. Sullivan*,[21] for example, the Court held that Congress could prohibit the movement of drugs labeled in violation of federal standards and, to effectuate that prohibition, bar postshipment relabeling in violation of those standards. In addition, the Court held that Congress could

association might well override congressional efforts (whether direct or indirect in nature) to inhibit the interstate movement of same-sex couples.

20. *See, e.g.,* United States v. Walsh, 331 U.S. 432, 437–38 (1947) (sustaining prohibition on making of false guaranty that drugs are properly labeled to "one engaged wholly or partly in an interstate business" as proper means to block interstate shipments of mislabeled drugs because, absent the prohibition, the purchaser is "more likely to engage in interstate distribution without making an independent check of the product"; upholding application of law even though wrongful sale occurred intrastate and no showing was made of purchaser's intent to resell the particular drugs out of state); Oklahoma Press Publ'g Co. v. Walling, 327 U.S. 186, 192 (1946) (upholding congressional authority to permit administrator of FLSA to issue subpoenas concerning information about whether firm is subject to the act or has violated it); Kirschbaum v. Walling, 316 U.S. 517, 526 (1942) (finding no constitutional problem in applying FLSA to elevator operators and other employees of lessor of work space used by lessees in production of goods for interstate shipment under statutory provision extending it to any person engaged in "occupation necessary to the production"); Cloverleaf Butter Co. v. Patterson, 315 U.S. 148, 154–55 (1942) (vindicating federal authority over "manufacturing processes" of "renovated butter," including by preempting state rules regarding pre-shipment seizures, as part of "appropriate means" Congress could use in connection with its ban on cross-border movements of this product).

21.   332 U.S. 689 (1948).

apply this ban on intrastate relabeling even to a pharmacist who (1) had not been involved at all in the drugs' interstate shipment; (2) had obtained the drugs in a purely intrastate purchase six months after their arrival in the state; and (3) had violated the law not by removing the label from any container shipped across state lines but instead by failing to re-affix the federally required label to separate smaller containers used in repackaging the drugs for retail transfer. Given the ban on cross-border shipments of mislabeled drugs, the majority deemed it sufficient that the law dealt with "the branding of articles that have completed an interstate shipment and are being held for future sales."[22]

The implications of *Sullivan* for future "super-bootstrapping" efforts, particularly in regulating pre-shipment conduct, remain unclear. After all, the Court in *Sullivan*, like the Court in *Hipolite Egg*, dealt with post-shipment, rather than pre-shipment, behavior. No less important, *Darby* itself is suscepti-

---

22. *Id.* at 698. The Court relied on *McDermott v. Wisconsin*, 228 U.S. 115 (1913). There the Court had confronted a federal statute that required the proper labeling of foods shipped in interstate commerce and barred the post-shipment intrastate relabeling of such foods as long as they remained "unsold." *Id.* at 131. Citing *McCulloch* and *Hipolite Egg*, the Court found this ban on relabeling a "means appropriate" to keeping "the channels of [interstate] commerce free from the transportation of illicit ... articles," *id.* at 128, because the "opportunity for inspection *en route* may be very inadequate" and the "real opportunity" for effective inspection might well only arise after delivery and prior to sale, *id.* at 136. In *Sullivan*, the Court found *McDermott* controlling notwithstanding asserted distinctions based on the defendant's intrastate repurchasing of the items and his repackaging of them prior to sale.

ble to a reading that does not authorize prohibitions on all forms of local activity on a "superbootstrap" theory. In particular, the wage-and-hour rule made applicable to local workers by section 15(a)(2) did not extend to employees engaged in any sort of production activities, but only those particular employees who were engaged in "the production of goods *for interstate commerce*."[23] The bottom line is that neither *Darby* nor its progeny unequivocally gave to Congress an unbounded ability to pass any law governing any intrastate activity on the theory that it effectuates to any extent a statutory ban on the movement of particular items or persons across state lines.[24]

23. *See also* North America Co. v. SEC, 327 U.S. 686 (1946) (observing that the Commerce Clause "permits Congress to attack an evil directly at its source, provided that the evil bears a *substantial relationship* to interstate commerce") (emphasis added).

24. In *United States v. Five Gambling Devices*, 346 U.S. 441, 445–48 (1953), the Court confronted a law in which Congress (1) outlawed cross-border shipments of gambling machines into states that had not specifically exempted themselves from the act's coverage; and (2) in an effort to effectuate this prohibition, also required all sellers of gambling devices to file monthly reports with federal authorities detailing each sale of a device. One issue presented by the case was whether the reporting requirement extended to purely intrastate sales. In considering this question, four Justices were prepared to say that the reporting provision did apply to intrastate sales and that, thus applied, it was constitutional because it helped "make effective and enforceable the interstate shipment ban" by complicating efforts to evade that ban through "straw-man transactions ... and the like." *Id.* at 459 (Clark, J., dissenting). Three Justices, however, argued that application of the law to purely intrastate transfers raised "serious constitutional questions" and accordingly interpreted the reporting requirement to apply only to interstate

In one respect, however, the post–1936 cases have expanded on the commerce-prohibiting technique and its "superbootstrapping" corollary by endorsing the view—or at least assuming—that "Congress may regulate behavior involving any object that has previously crossed a state line."[25] The well-spring of

transfers. *Id.* at 446–48 (plurality opinion of Jackson, J.). (The other two Justices did not speak to commerce-power issues because they focused instead on constitutional vagueness problems.) How would *Five Gambling Devices* come out today if the constitutional issue were squarely presented? It is almost certain that the modern Court would uphold the law, even as applied to intrastate activity, because sales transactions, whether interstate or intrastate in nature, plainly constitute "economic activity." *See infra* Chapter V (discussing the *Lopez* and *Morrison* cases). *See also* Robert L. Stern, *The Commerce Clause Revisited—The Federalization of Intrastate Crime*, 15 ARIZ. L. REV. 272, 275–76 (1973) (arguing that "[i]n retrospect, the *Gambling Devices* case would seem to have presented a pretty simple constitutional question" because "requiring all manufacturers and dealers to register and file reports as to their sales would facilitate the determination of which devices were transported interstate").

25. Donald H. Regan, *How To Think About the Federal Commerce Power and Incidentally Rewrite* United States v. Lopez, 94 MICH. L. REV. 554, 561 (1995). This notion of the commerce power apparently made its first appearance in the *United States v. Five Gambling Devices* case (discussed *supra* note 24). There, Justice Clark, writing for the only four Justices who reached the commerce power issue, found it "clearly established" that "activities local in nature may be regulated ... if local goods ... were previously in interstate commerce." *Id.* at 460 (Clark, J., dissenting). Notably, the assertion came in dicta because the challenged prohibition on intrastate possession of unreported gambling machines was tethered to a federal ban on interstate shipments of unreported machines. In addition, Justice Clark cited no authority for his broad assertion apart from *Sullivan*, which similarly involved an intrastate possession ban directly linked to an exercise of the commerce-prohibiting power.

this theory is *United States v. Bass*,[26] in which the Court read the federal statute that outlaws receipt of a gun by a felon to apply whenever the "the Government ... demonstrates that the firearm received has previously traveled in interstate commerce."[27] Similarly, in *Scarborough v. United States*,[28] the Court held that the federal ban on possession of guns by felons applies as long as the prosecution establishes "the minimal nexus that the firearm have been, at some time, in interstate commerce."[29] Although as a technical matter both *Bass* and *Scarborough* presented only questions of statutory interpretation, it seems clear that the Court in each case assumed that the statute, as interpreted, constituted a constitutional exercise of the commerce power.[30] Yet the sort of regulations sanctioned by *Bass* and *Scarborough* went beyond

26.   404 U.S. 336 (1971).

27.   *Id*. at 350.

28.   431 U.S. 563 (1977).

29.   *Id*. at 575. For a similar ruling, see *Barrett v. United States*, 423 U.S. 212, 215 (1976) (applying statute prohibiting receipt of gun "if the firearm at some time in its past had traveled in interstate commerce").

30.   In *Bass*, for example, the Court fully recognized that its approach was "not the narrowest possible reading of the statute" but nonetheless deemed that reading "consistent with our regard for the sensitive relation between federal and state criminal jurisdiction" because it "preserves as an element of all the offenses a requirement suited to federal criminal jurisdiction alone." 404 U.S. at 351. Indeed, in neither *Bass* nor *Scarborough* did the Court even note the possibility that federal regulation of gun receipt or possession premised on the gun's past movement across a state line presented a debatable constitutional point. For more on *Scarborough*, see *infra* Chapter V.

even the broad regulation of intrastate activities previously sustained in *Sullivan*. In particular, those regulations did not, from all appearances, find their justification in any congressional effort to help effectuate a ban on specified cross-border movements; rather, the prior movement of the gun in and of itself seemed, in the Court's view, to justify congressional regulation of intrastate activities concerning it. In practical effect, *Bass* and *Scarborough*—in keeping with the theme of broad congressional power that marked the post–1936 period—suggested a willingness to recognize an entirely new prong of the commerce power. Under what might be called the super-channels-of-commerce theory, the Court appeared ready to endorse congressional power to regulate intrastate activities on the ground that they concerned something that had "at some time" moved across a state line whether or not that thing remained "in" interstate commerce or was the subject of any ban on cross-border movements.

B. The In–Commerce Theory in the Post–1936 Period

In the years immediately following the judicial revolution of 1937, the Court took steps to reinvigorate the in-commerce prong of the commerce power, just as surely as it had moved to resuscitate the commerce-prohibiting technique in *Darby*. Most important, in *Currin v. Wallace*,[31] the Court invoked the in-commerce theory to uphold a federal statute

31. 306 U.S. 1 (1939).

that barred the sale of tobacco from auction houses at which farmers customarily sold products destined for interstate commerce unless the tobacco had first been inspected and graded by federal authorities. This regulatory scheme had been developed to address recurring problems, including sharp practices by sophisticated buyers and "an unusual degree of uncertainty in ... prices" that resulted from a lack of information about product quality at the time of auctioning. The Court first concluded that it was "idle to contend" that the case did not concern "sales in interstate or foreign commerce" because "[w]here goods are purchased in one State for transportation to another the commerce includes the purchase quite as much as it does the transportation."[32] The Court added that practical considerations permitted Congress to apply its program even to tobacco destined solely for intrastate uses. As the Court explained, "the transactions on the tobacco market were conducted indiscriminately at virtually the same time, and in a manner that made it necessary, if the congressional rule were to be applied, to make it govern all the tobacco thus offered for sale."[33] In short, just as *Darby* signaled that Congress could reach intrastate production activities to render effective its exercise of the commerce-prohibiting theory, *Currin* showed that Congress could reach intrastate sales activities when

32. *Id.* at 10. *See also id.* at 12 (adding that it made no difference that the required "inspection and grading of the tobacco take place before the auction" because "it is obvious that the inspection and grading have immediate relation to the sales in interstate and foreign commerce").

33. *Id.* at 32.

doing so was important to effectuate its regulation of things found to be "in" interstate commerce.[34]

Most of the Court's post–1936 in-commerce cases have focused on questions of statutory interpretation.[35] These cases typically arise because Congress has passed a number of statutes that eschew regulation on an affecting-commerce theory and instead, by their terms, apply only if the defendant has engaged "in" interstate commerce.[36] Not surpris-

34. In *Mulford v. Smith*, 307 U.S. 38 (1939), the Court relied on a similar theory in sustaining federally imposed limits on the quantities of tobacco properly sold at market, reasoning that the rule reaches interstate commerce "at the throat where the tobacco enters the stream of commerce,—the marketing warehouse." *Id.* at 47. Citing *Currin*, the Court added that: "In markets where tobacco is sold to both interstate and intrastate purchasers it is not known, when the grower places his tobacco on the warehouse floor for sale, whether it is destined for interstate or intrastate commerce. Regulation, to be effective, must, and therefore may constitutionally, apply to all sales." *Id.* Notably, the Court went on to supplement its in-commerce defense of the statute with an invocation of the commerce-prohibiting theory, reasoning that a congressional power to prohibit all cross-border movements of a product extended "a fortiori to limitation of the amount of a given commodity which may be transported in such commerce." *Id.* at 48. *See also* United States v. Rock Royal Co-op., 307 U.S. 533, 568–69 (1939) (relying largely on *Currin* and *Mulford* to uphold price regulations for both intrastate and interstate sales of milk as applied to defendants whose product "reaches the [regulated] market area through the channels of interstate commerce").

35. *See, e.g.*, Mitchell v. C.W. Vollmer & Co., 349 U.S. 427, 429–30 (1955) (holding that workers were "engaged 'in commerce'" for FLSA purposes in building a lock on the Gulf Intercoastal Waterway).

36. *See, e.g.*, FTC v. Bunte Bros., 312 U.S. 349, 355 (1941) (construing Federal Trade Commission Act to cover only activity

ingly, these cases carry forward the idea, well established in the pre–1937 context, that some local
activities lie outside the stream of commerce. In
United States v. Yellow Cab Co.,[37] for example, the
Court held that intrastate taxi trips that immediately precede or follow interstate train travel are
"too unrelated to interstate commerce to constitute
a part thereof within the meaning of the Sherman
Act" even though the stream of commerce does
reach taxi rides that take passengers from one train
station to another in the middle of an interstate
journey.[38] Notwithstanding cases such as *Yellow
Cab*, the Court has insisted that the in-commerce
theory must be viewed "in a practical sense."[39] In
Goldfarb v. Virginia State Bar,[40] for example, the
issue was whether local lawyers who conducted
residential title searches operated "in commerce"
for purposes of the Sherman Act. Without dissent,
the Court concluded that they did. Because funds
for home purchases "frequently" come from outside
the state and title examinations are a "practical
necessity" to secure financing, "a title examination
is an integral part of an interstate transaction."[41]
The regulated lawyers, in other words, had acted
"in commerce" even though they had not handled

in interstate commerce and thus excluding intrastate retail can-
dy sales from its reach).

37.   332 U.S. 218 (1947).

38.   *Id.* at 230.

39.   Goldfarb v. Virginia State Bar, 421 U.S. 773, 784 (1975).

40.   *Id.*

41.   *Id.* at 783–85.

any of the funds that gave the transaction its interstate character and had provided services only with respect to the title search and not with respect to the broader sale or financing transaction itself. By thus extending the in-commerce theory to persons on the edge of an interstate transaction, the Court created space to argue that Congress may regulate large numbers of persons caught up in local transactions that facilitate or disrupt cross-border commercial activity.[42]

Despite the post–1936 reinvigoration of the in-commerce theory, the Court has invoked it infrequently in the post-New Deal period. This state of affairs has resulted, more than anything else, from the Court's endorsement of such a broad view of the affecting-commerce theory that, at least until recently, that prong of the commerce power has provided a vehicle for sustaining almost any law that has a bearing on the flow of interstate trade. We turn now to an examination of the development of the affecting-commerce theory in the pre–1986 period.

---

42. *But cf.* McLain v. Real Estate Bd. of New Orleans, Inc., 444 U.S. 232, 244–45 (1980) (considering application of Sherman Act to alleged price fixing by realtors on an affecting-commerce, rather than an in-commerce, theory; noting, however, lower courts' distinction of *Goldfarb,* with respect to in-commerce theory, based on fact that lawyers were "necessary" for conducting title searches, whereas residential real estate sales often occur with no involvement of realtors at all).

C. The Affecting–Commerce Theory in the Post–1936 Period

1. *The National Labor Relations Act Cases.* *Schechter Poultry* and *Carter Coal* embodied efforts by the Supreme Court to put judicially enforceable restrictions on both the in-commerce and affecting-commerce aspects of Congress's supposedly limited Article I powers. The Court, however, dramatically changed course following the election of 1936, and its first sign of a transformation came in *NLRB v. Jones & Laughlin Steel Corp.*[43] That case brought before the Court the constitutionality of the NLRA as applied to an attempt to impede unionizing efforts at a plant operated by one of the nation's largest steel companies. Citing *Carter Coal*, the lower court found this application of the Act unconstitutional because it concerned only manufacturing activity. Writing for a five-Justice majority (now including Justice Roberts), however, Chief Justice Hughes overturned this ruling, reasoning that the regulated activities, though "intrastate in character," had "such a close and substantial relation to interstate commerce that their control is essential or appropriate to protect that commerce from burdens and obstructions."[44] In reaching this conclusion, the Court swept away the principle laid down 32 years earlier in *E. C. Knight* and reaffirmed one year earlier in *Carter Coal*. "[T]he fact that the

43.   301 U.S. 1 (1937).

44.   *Id.* at 37.

employees here concerned were engaged in production," Chief Justice Hughes declared, "is not determinative."[45] What mattered instead was the Court's conclusion that the "stoppage of [the steel company's] operations by industrial strife would have a most serious effect upon interstate commerce."[46]

How could the Court sidestep the authority of *Carter Coal*? That case, the Chief Justice wrote, did not control because "the Court was of the opinion that the provisions of the statute relating to production were invalid upon several grounds."[47] Chief Justice Hughes did not explain why, even assuming that alternative holdings had supported the Court's decision in *Carter Coal*, its categorical rule of excluding production from the regulatory reach of Congress should now be abandoned. On behalf of the four dissenters, Justice McReynolds could only shake his head in disbelief. "Every consideration brought forward to uphold the Act before us," he remarked, "was applicable in *Carter Coal*."[48] He then added the now-predictable parade-of-horribles warning: "Whatever effect any cause of [labor] discontent may ultimately have upon commerce is far too indirect to justify Congressional regulation. Almost anything—marriage, birth, or death—may in some fashion affect commerce."[49]

45. *Id.* at 40.

46. *Id.* at 41.

47. *Id.*

48. *Id.* at 77 (McReynolds, J., dissenting in *Jones & Laughlin Steel* and companion cases).

49. *Id.* at 99.

Non–New–Dealers rightly saw in *Jones & Laughlin Steel* a harbinger of wholesale retreat from the interventionist spirit of *Schechter Poultry* and *Carter Coal.* Chief Justice Hughes's opinion, however, offered glimmers of hope to those who disapproved of the Democrats' most far-reaching programs because some passages of the opinion suggested that the principle of the case might extend only to "far-flung" enterprises that "organize themselves on a national scale."[50] In a companion case, however, the post-switch-in-time Court revealed that it was not about to limit the principle of *Jones & Laughlin Steel* in this way. *NLRB v. Friedman–Harry Marks Clothing,*[51] like *Jones & Laughlin Steel,* involved an agency effort to remedy retaliatory discharges of union organizers under the NLRA. Unlike in *Jones & Laughlin Steel*, however, the agency's action targeted a "small clothing manufacturer with a

50. *Id.* at 41. In particular, before declaring that labor strife at Jones & Laughlin Steel's Aliquippa plant would in fact have a "direct" effect on commerce, the Chief Justice emphasized the expansive, multi-faceted character of the steel company's overall business activities. Thus, with operations that extended from "mines in Michigan and Minnesota" to "steamships on the Great Lakes" to "warehouses in Chicago, Detroit, Cincinnati and Memphis" to fabricating shops in "Long Island City, New York, and in New Orleans," this employer was a nationwide operation, *id.*, with production mills "that might be likened to the heart of a self-contained, highly integrated body," *id.* at 27. On the basis of this rhetoric, the principle of the case might have been confined to firms, such as Jones & Laughlin Steel, which "transform ... materials and then pump them out to all parts of the nation through [a] vast mechanism...." *Id.*

51. 301 U.S. 58 (1937).

minuscule share of the interstate market."[52] As
Justice McReynolds suggested in dissent, this fact
made the case tough to distinguish not only from
Carter Coal but from *Schechter Poultry* as well. The
Court's new five-Justice juggernaut, however, was
not to be denied. Offering no additional legal analysis, it declared that "for the reasons" set forth in
Jones & Laughlin Steel, any constitutional challenge to the Labor Board's intervention was "without merit."[53]

2. Wickard v. Filburn, *The Affecting–Commerce Theory and the Aggregation Technique*. The
other shoe dropped in *Wickard v. Filburn*.[54] At issue
in the case was the application of the Agricultural
Adjustment Act of 1938 to Roscoe C. Filburn, an
Ohio dairy farmer, who grew a small amount of
wheat on his land for his own family's in-home
consumption. Sued by the Secretary of Agriculture
for exceeding a federally imposed production limit,
Filburn argued that this exercise of the commerce
power offended—if anything did—both common
sense and the Constitution. The case came before
the Court in 1942, by which time President
Roosevelt had replaced all four dissenters in *Jones
& Laughlin Steel* with tried-and-true New Dealers.
Now, without a single dissenting vote, the Court
upheld the Act's application even to the Filburn
farm.

Justice Jackson began his disquisition with a
statement of principles that captured recent and

52. DAVID P. CURRIE, THE CONSTITUTION IN THE SUPREME COURT:
THE SECOND CENTURY, 1888–1986 at 237 (1990).

53. *Friedman-Harry Marks*, 301 U.S. at 75.

54. 317 U.S. 111 (1942).

seismic shifts in the law. He declared that "[t]he Court's recognition of the relevance of economic effects ... has made the mechanical application of legal formulas no longer feasible."[55] Thus "questions of federal power cannot be decided simply by finding the activity in question to be 'production' nor can consideration of its economic effects be foreclosed by calling them 'indirect.' "[56] Citing *Gibbons v. Ogden,* Justice Jackson invoked Chief Justice Marshall's "warning that effective restraints on its exercise must proceed from political rather than from judicial processes."[57] Because in this instance Congress had regulated activities that had a "substantial effect" on interstate commerce, it had not exceeded its constitutional authority.[58]

55. *Id.* at 123–24.

56. *Id.* at 124.

57. *Id.* at 120.

58. Two years after *Filburn* sealed the demise of the categorical exclusion of production from regulation under the Commerce Clause, the Court rejected another similar exclusion in *United States v. South–Eastern Underwriters Ass'n,* 322 U.S. 533 (1944). In a series of decisions dating back to 1869 the Court had held that "contracts of insurance are not commerce at all" and thus could not be regulated under the commerce power. *See, e.g.,* New York Life Ins. Co. v. Deer Lodge County, 231 U.S. 495, 510 (1913). Relying largely on *Wickard,* the Court overruled these cases in *South-Eastern Underwriters,* reasoning that "past decisions of this Court emphasize that legal formulae devised to uphold state power cannot uncritically be accepted as trustworthy guides to determine Congressional power under the Commerce Clause." 322 U.S. at 545. Because the term "commerce" has always embraced "businesses in which persons bought and sold, bargained and contracted," *id.* at 539, and the business of insurance had come to include "a continuous and indivisible stream of intercourse among the states composed of collections of premiums, payments of policy obligations, and ... countless

But how could the growing of wheat on a patch of land for one family's needs create a "substantial" impact? The answer was that, in wielding its commerce power, Congress could regulate each individual member of a group—even assuming each individual's effect on commerce was *de minimis*—so long as the activity of that individual, "taken together with that of many others similarly situated, is far from trivial."[59] In other words, for Commerce Clause purposes, the activities of Farmer Filburn did not stand alone. He and all "similarly situated" wheat growers, viewed in the aggregate, posed a substantial danger to the interstate wheat market, susceptible to a congressional corrective, because unregulated production threatened such problems as the industry-wrecking suppression of wheat prices and a proliferation of "tied up railroad cars."[60]

Lurking quietly in the background of the *Filburn* case was a question that recurs in judicial decisions that deploy this sort of aggregation approach: Just whom may Congress aggregate with whom? In *Filburn*, for example, the case for finding an effect on commerce would be easy if Congress had authority to consider the activities of all wheat growers of all sorts. The Court, however, had the option of saying that Congress could look in the aggregate only at

documents and communications," *id*. at 541—and because "Congress can regulate traffic though it consist of intangibles," *id*. at 546—the "exception of the business of insurance" from the commerce power could no longer stand, *id*. at 553.

59. 317 U.S. at 128.

60. *Id*. at 125.

those persons who grew wheat for home consumption, thus significantly narrowing the universe of actors whose actions would be assessed in gauging the relevant effect on commerce. This latter course might in theory have led to invalidation of the statute as applied in *Filburn*. After all, if very few farmers grow wheat for home use, then unlimited production by such growers, even in the aggregate, might well not have a "substantial" effect on interstate commerce.[61] In the *Filburn* case the Court dealt with this whom-to-aggregate problem by looking only at home-use wheat growers, but then finding that their activities, in the aggregate, did have the requisite "substantial" effect. Such an effect existed, the Court explained, because many growers produced home-use wheat in large quantities, which in turn influenced prices in interstate markets by affecting both supply and demand. On the supply side, such wheat "overhangs the market and if induced by rising prices tends to flow into the

61. Nor is this point only theoretical in nature. In the early 1940s, for example, Congress did not regulate home-use tobacco and cotton precisely because farmers "brought nearly all [of these products] to the tobacco warehouse or cotton gin for marketing" in the ordinary course of events. Robert L. Stern, *The Commerce Clause and the National Economy (Part Two), 1933–1946*, 59 HARV. L. REV. 883, 902 (1946). Had Congress sought to regulate tobacco or cotton grown for home use, it is possible, if not likely, that the Court would have deemed this effort unconstitutional on the ground that aggregate home use of each such crop did not substantially affect interstate pricing and product movements. At the least, as we shall see, the Court would have had to expand significantly the rationale it employed in *Wickard v. Filburn* to sustain such an exercise of the commerce power.

market and check price increases."[62] On the demand side, such wheat "supplies a need of the man
who grew it which would otherwise be reflected by
purchases in the open market."[63] In sum, the Court
reported: "This record leaves us in no doubt that
Congress may properly have considered that wheat
consumed on the farm where grown if wholly outside the scheme of regulation would have a substantial effect in defeating and obstructing its purpose
to stimulate trade therein at increased prices."[64]

The Court's abandonment of *Carter Coal* and its
embrace of aggregation analysis left no doubt that
the affecting-commerce prong of the commerce power had a long reach—so long, in fact, that the Court
would find no law beyond its grasp for the next
half-century.[65] In early post-*Jones & Laughlin Steel*
cases, for example, the Court upheld laws that
regulated intrastate activities in an effort to ensure
the effective movement of natural gas across state

62. *Id.* at 128.

63. *Id.*

64. *Id.* at 128–29.

65. *See, e.g.*, Mandeville Island Farms v. American Crystal
Sugar Co., 334 U.S. 219, 236 (1948) (repudiating *E. C. Knight*
and its production-versus-commerce distinction in an antitrust
action involving alleged conspiracy among three local sugar-beat
processors; reasoning that "the individual activity when multiplied into a general practice is subject to federal control").
Extensive consideration of the precedents of this period is provided by PAUL R. BENSON, JR. THE SUPREME COURT AND THE COMMERCE
CLAUSE, 1937–1970 (1970); Robert L. Stern, *The Commerce Clause
and the National Economy (Part One)*, 59 HARV. L. REV. 645
(1946); and Robert L. Stern, *The Commerce Clause and the
National Economy (Part Two)*, 59 HARV. L. REV. 883 (1946).

lines[66] and to protect cross-border commerce in milk.[67] In addition, the Court had no difficulty sustaining the application of federal labor laws to large numbers of intrastate employment relationships.[68] More knotty problems surfaced, however, when Congress turned to the subject at the center of state-rights struggles for most of American history—the subject of race relations.

3. *The Commerce Power and the Civil Rights Act of 1964.* When Lyndon Johnson came to the

66. Illinois Natural Gas Co. v. Central Ill. Pub. Serv., 314 U.S. 498, 509 (1942) (eschewing "in commerce" analysis, and reasoning instead that intrastate "extension of appellant's facilities ... would so affect ... distribution among the states as to be within the Congressional power to regulate those matters which materially affect interstate commerce").

67. United States v. Wrightwood Dairy Co., 315 U.S. 110, 118, 120 (1942) (upholding extension of price controls for interstate milk sales to competing intrastate milk sales lest "the effective sanction of the order will wither before the force of competition, the morale of the market will disintegrate, and this attempt at solution of the problem by the National Government will fail"; adding that "[t]he injury, and thus the power, does not depend upon the fortuitous circumstance that the particular person conducting the intrastate activities is, or is not, also engaged in interstate commerce" and that "[i]t is the effect upon the interstate commerce or its regulation, regardless of the particular form which the competition may take, which is the test of federal power").

68. *See, e.g.*, Polish Nat'l Alliance v. NLRB, 322 U.S. 643, 645–46, 648–50 (1944) (insurance company; reasoning that "practical judgment," concerning effects on interstate commerce, "the Constitution entrusts primarily and very largely to Congress, subject to the latter's control by the electorate"); NLRB v. Fainblatt, 306 U.S. 601 (1939) (small cloth-processor employer); Consolidated Edison Co. v. NLRB, 305 U.S. 197, 221–22 (1938)

presidency in 1963, following the assassination of President John F. Kennedy, racial discrimination—including in the form of outright segregation—pervaded the workplace, the restaurant and hotel industries, housing rentals and sales, and government operations in much of the United States. President Johnson responded to these conditions by throwing his support (and substantial political skills) behind the sweeping civil rights bill previously put forward by President Kennedy. A bitter legislative struggle followed as Senators and Representatives, particularly from the Deep South, attacked both the substance and the constitutionality of the proposed statute. In response, some proponents of this legislation sought to justify it as a proper exercise of Congress's power to "enforce by appropriate legislation" the guarantee of "equal protection of the laws" embodied in section 1 of the Fourteenth Amendment. Invoking supportive Supreme Court precedent, critics responded that the Fourteenth Amendment guarded against only state action and not the sort of purely private discrimination targeted by the administration's proposal.[69] In the end, Congress chose to rely primarily on its commerce power, rather than its Fourteenth Amendment enforcement power, in enacting the most significant piece of anti-discrimination legislation in American

(intrastate electric-power utility that supplied electricity to, for example, railroad facilities and broadcaster).

69. *See* The Civil Rights Cases, 109 U.S. 3, 11 (1883) (stating that "[i]ndividual invasion of individual rights is not the subject-matter of the [fourteenth] amendment").

history, the Civil Rights Act of 1964.[70]

Title II of the Act broadly prohibited discrimination on the basis of race, color, religion or national origin in any "place of public accommodation ... if its operations affect commerce."[71] The Act went on to define this term to include all hotels and motels, as well as any eating establishment that "offers to serve interstate travelers or a substantial portion of the food which [it sells has] moved in commerce."[72] In *Heart of Atlanta Motel v. United States,*[73] the Court upheld the Act's application to a motel located in downtown Atlanta, emphasizing that extensive evidence before Congress established that "discrimination by hotels and motels impedes interstate travel."[74] It did not matter to the Court that this particular business could be characterized as having a "purely local character"[75] because " 'if it is interstate commerce that feels the pinch, it does not matter how local the operation which applies the squeeze.' "[76] Nor was it of consequence that a "moral" purpose had propelled enactment of the law. As the Court explained, "that fact does not detract from the overwhelming evidence of the disruptive

70. 42 U.S.C. §§ 2000a *et seq*.

71. 42 U.S.C. § 2000b.

72. Heart of Atlanta Motel v. United States, 379 U.S. 241, 247–248 (1964).

73. *Id*.

74. *Id*. at 253.

75. *Id*. at 258.

76. *Id*. at 258 (quoting United States v. Women's Sportswear Mfg. Ass'n, 336 U.S. 460, 464 (1949)).

effect that racial discrimination has had on commercial intercourse."[77]

The Court's validation of the Civil Rights Act's application to a bustling motel, however, did not answer the question whether Congress could regulate local restaurants on the theory that they sold food that had moved across state lines. In *Katzenbach v. McClung*,[78] the Court drew on its affecting-commerce precedents to uphold this feature of the public accommodations provision as well.[79] The case involved Ollie's Barbecue, a 220–seat family restaurant in Birmingham, Alabama, which during the previous year had bought $69,683 worth of meat (constituting 46% of its total food purchases) from a local dealer who had obtained it from outside Alabama.[80] Making "no claim that interstate travelers frequented the restaurant,"[81] the Justice Department argued that the restaurant's practice of relegating black customers to a take-out counter was subject to federal regulation because it affected interstate commerce. The restaurant's owners re-

---

77. *Id.* at 257.

78. 379 U.S. 294 (1964).

79. *McClung* pre-dated cases such as *Bass* and *Scarborough*, and the Court did not consider whether the past movement of this food over state lines in and of itself justified a congressional ban on serving it in places that engaged in discrimination. *See supra* notes 25–30 and accompanying text. Questions about the scope of any "jurisdictional nexus" theory of regulation, and whether it would today support the constitutionality of the sort of law involved in *McClung,* remain unresolved. *See infra* Chapter V.

80. 379 U.S. at 296.

81. *Id.* at 298.

sponded—as had Farmer Filburn—that application of the Act to their small-time operation exceeded constitutional limits. A unanimous Court, however, found no commerce-power problem.

Building on *Darby* and *Wickard*, the Court began by articulating a deferential standard of review: So long as "the legislators, in light of the facts and testimony before them, have a *rational basis* for finding a chosen regulatory scheme necessary to the protection of commerce, [judicial] investigation is at an end."[82] It did not matter in this regard that Congress had not made "specific findings which were embodied" in the statute itself.[83] Nor, given the now-settled aggregation principle, was the operation of Ollie's Barbecue to be "viewed in isolation."[84] Rather, it sufficed that the legislative record was "replete with testimony of the burdens placed on interstate commerce by racial discrimination in restaurants."[85] Studies showed reduced spending in restaurants among African–Americans even "after discounting income differences, in areas where discrimination was widely practiced," and it was obvious that "[t]he fewer customers a restaurant enjoys the less food it sells and consequently the less it buys."[86] Still other evidence revealed that race discrimination had caused "wide unrest" that had "a depressant effect on general business condi-

82. *Id*. at 303–04 (emphasis added).

83. *Id*. at 304.

84. *Id*. at 300.

85. *Id*. at 299.

86. *Id*.

tions"; that the widespread pattern of discrimination by restaurants "had a direct and highly restrictive effect upon interstate travel by Negroes"; and that "discrimination deterred professional, as well as skilled, people from moving into areas where such practices occurred and thereby caused industry to be reluctant to establish there."[87] To be sure, there was no "direct evidence" that linked discriminatory restaurant service to an overall reduction in the "flow of interstate food."[88] (After all, most African–Americans denied meals in restaurants presumably would instead eat meals in their homes.) That fact, however, was not "a crucial matter" in light of the demonstrated "effect of such practices on other aspects of commerce."[89]

The Ollie's Barbecue case raised interesting questions about the affecting-commerce prong of the commerce power. Was it enough that race discrimination cut down on interstate shipments of restaurant food even if it did not cut down on shipment of food as a whole?[90] Could Congress have directed its regulation at a broadened group of local operators—for example, all restaurants, whether or not they received goods in interstate commerce,[91] or all

87. *Id.* at 300.

88. *Id.* at 304.

89. *Id.* at 305.

90. *Cf.* Perez v. United States, 402 U.S. 146, 153 (1971) (noting that the Court in *McClung* had considered "the effect on the flow of food in commerce to restaurants").

91. *See* Stern, *supra* note 24, at 272 (suggesting most "easily defensible" justification for result in *McClung* may be that Congress may regulate "all restaurants," whether or not they

business establishments,[92] or all establishments that served food, including social clubs[93]—on the theory that, in the aggregate, their discriminatory activities blocked interstate shipments, travel and business relocation? Could Congress constitutionally aggregate religious discrimination with racial discrimination in food service? What if the latter practice but not the former was extensive?[94]

serve interstate travelers, "because of the inevitable uncertainty as to which [restaurants] interstate travelers might choose to patronize and the fact that the discrimination in itself would discourage interstate travel"). *But cf.* Heart of Atlanta Motel v. United States, 379 U.S. 241, 275 (1964) (Black, J., concurring) (speculating that "isolated and remote lunchroom" might be beyond the reach of Congress under the Commerce Clause); Daniel v. Paul, 395 U.S. 298, 315 (1969) (Black, J., dissenting) (objecting to Congress's use of commerce power to reach snack bar at "country people's recreation center ... miles away from any interstate highway").

92. *See, e.g.*, GUNTHER, *supra* note 17, at 162 (reprinting statement of Bruce Bromley that the proposed Civil Rights Act would not reach a local barber shop).

93. *See, e.g., id.* at 160 (reprinting Senate hearings in which Attorney General Robert F. Kennedy suggested that applying the proposed Civil Rights Act to "personal or social relationships" would exceed the reach of the Commerce Clause).

94. Another question that lurked in *McClung* concerned the super-channels-of-commerce and in-commerce theories touched on earlier: Could Congress regulate the local service to local customers in a local restaurant because (regardless of all else) the food being served had previously crossed state lines and/or because it remained "in" interstate commerce? *See* Stern, *supra* note 24, at 272 (suggesting that Civil Rights Act provision involved in *McClung* was "perhaps" sustainable on the theory "that a restaurant which obtained goods from outside the state was thereby subject to federal regulation of all its practices"; adding that this theory "suggests that the slightest interstate

The Court's opinion also raised broad questions about the Justices' methods and purposes. Was the Court saying, in effect, that the gréater congressional power to regulate all restaurants included the lesser power to regulate restaurants that received food that moved in interstate commerce?[95] Was the Court—while highlighting the destructive effects of massive race discrimination on the vibrancy of the national economy—intentionally writing in an oblique style to leave itself room to put limits on the commerce power in later cases?[96] Or was the Court in effect declaring that all elements of the national economy had by 1964 become so interwoven that Congress in effect could now regulate under an affecting-commerce theory any activity that was in any way connected up with business? Whatever the answers to these questions, the drift of *McClung* was unquestionably in the direction of permitting

connection can provide an adequate basis even for a federal statute which serves a noneconomical national purpose").

95. It is worth noting in this regard that the aggregation technique invites criticism because it suggests that the more sweeping a congressional program is the more likely it is to be constitutional. In other words (and ironically), the more broadly a federal program intrudes on federalism concerns by sweeping across fields previously regulated by states, the more likely it is to survive federalism-based attack. One possible response to this argument is that built-in checks exist on gratuitous exercises of federal power. *See infra* notes 106–11 and accompanying text (discussing *Garcia* case). Another possible response is that judges may choose to break broad regulatory programs into functional sub-units for aggregation-analysis purposes. *See supra* notes 54–68 and accompanying text (discussing the *Filburn* case).

96. *See generally* CASS R. SUNSTEIN, ONE CASE AT A TIME: JUDICIAL MINIMALISM ON THE SUPREME COURT (1999).

Congress to decide for itself whether the "total incidence" of a disfavored type of behavior unduly impedes interstate commerce.[97]

4. *Local Crimes, Local Lands and the Rejection of New Categorical Limits in the Pre–1986 Period*. Notwithstanding the broad rhetoric and reach of *Heart of Atlanta Motel* and *McClung*, litigants continued to push for judicial recognition of limits on the congressional commerce power. *Hodel v. Virginia Surface Mining & Reclamation Ass'n*,[98] for example, involved a challenge to federal strip mining restrictions founded on the view that Congress could not regulate "the use of private lands within the borders of the States."[99] The unanimous Court, however, made short shrift of this attempt to engraft a new categorical limit on the Court's post-*Carter Coal* jurisprudence. As Justice Marshall explained, it was enough to support Congress's action that "many surface mining operations result in disturbances ... that burden and adversely affect commerce ... by destroying or diminishing the utility of land for commercial, industrial, residential, recreational, agricultural, and forestry purposes, by causing erosion and landslides, by contributing to floods, by polluting the water, [and] by destroying fish and wildlife habitats...."[100]

97.   379 U.S. at 301.

98.   452 U.S. 264 (1981).

99.   *Id*. at 275.

100.   *Id*. at 277 (quoting 30 U.S.C. § 1201(c)). Speaking more generally about the burgeoning field of federal environmental controls, the Court added that "the power conferred by the

In *Perez v. United States*,[101] the Court encountered another plea to forge a specialized restriction
on the affecting-commerce theory. The case involved the prosecution, under a federal statute that
broadly criminalized "extortionate credit transactions," of a local loan shark who threatened to
break the legs of a neighborhood butcher if he did
not promptly repay a $1,000 loan. Justice Stewart
seized on these facts to argue that Congress could
not, consistent with the Tenth Amendment, use the
affecting-commerce theory to regulate "local, intrastate crime" unless it showed that the outlawed
category of behavior had "interstate attributes that
distinguish it in some substantial respect from other local crime."[102] Justice Stewart, however, found
himself making this argument in lone dissent. The
majority deemed it determinative that "the loan
shark racket provides organized crime with its second most lucrative source of revenue, exacts millions from the pockets of people, coerces its victims
into the commission of crimes against property, and
causes the takeover by racketeers of legitimate businesses."[103] Moreover, even though nothing indicated that the local loan shark involved in the *Perez*
case itself had any connection to organized crime,
"a class of activities [is] properly regulated by Con-

Commerce Clause [is] broad enough to permit congressional
regulation of activities causing air or water pollution, or other
environmental hazards that may have effects in more than one
State." *Id.* at 282.

101.   402 U.S. 146 (1971).

102.   *Id.* at 157–58 (Stewart, J., dissenting).

103.   *Id.* at 156.

gress without proof that the particular intrastate activity against which a sanction was laid had an effect on commerce."[104]

In the pre–1986 march toward judicial entrenchment of a sweeping commerce power, one last chapter remained to be written. During the same period that the Court was rejecting entreaties to place internal limits on the commerce power in cases such as *Perez* and *Hodel*, the Court was also exploring whether the Constitution embodied "external" limits that sheltered "states as states" from otherwise permissible exercises of the commerce power on federalism grounds.[105] The critical juncture in this journey came in 1985, with the Court's decision in *Garcia v. San Antonio Metropolitan Transit Authority*.[106] There the Court—departing from prior state-favoring precedent—concluded that Congress could apply the Fair Labor Standards Act not only to employees of private firms, but also to police officers, firefighters and other workers engaged by state and local governments to discharge even their most central responsibilities. In reaching this conclusion, the Court reasoned that the built-in "solicitude of the national political process for the continued vitality of the States" cut against the assumption of any significant judicial role in guarding against over-reaching exercises of

104.   *Id.* at 152 (citing *Darby*).

105.   *See generally infra* Chapter VI (exploring evolution of these external constraints in both the pre- and post–1985 periods).

106.   469 U.S. 528 (1985).

the commerce power.[107] *Garcia* left no doubt that a majority of the then-sitting Court had little inclination to embrace free-standing limits on the Commerce Clause based on federalism concerns. But the underlying "solicitude of the national political process" logic of *Garcia* also indicated something more. It reinforced, and helped to justify and explain, the Court's hands-off approach toward finding "internal" limits the commerce power that had pervaded the post–1936 period.

So where did the congressional commerce power stand as of 1985? Taken as whole, the Court's rulings signaled—to say the least—that "Congress' power under the Commerce Clause is very broad."[108] Indeed, particularly in the wake of *Garcia*, many observers found reason to conclude that, as a practical matter, Congress could justify on Commerce Clause grounds any law it wished to enact. However, even while handing down decisions like *Sullivan, McClung, Perez,* and *Hodel,* the Court continued to insist that the Constitution placed some limits on the commerce power. In *Maryland v. Wirtz,*[109] for example, the Court, even while upholding an expansion of the FLSA, observed that Con-

107. *Id.* at 557. *See generally supra* Chapter II.

108. Fry v. United States, 421 U.S. 542, 547 (1975) (upholding application of federal wage controls to state employers; reasoning that law "could well result" in increased interstate commerce because "raises to state employees could inject millions of dollars of purchasing power into the economy and might exert pressure on other segments of the work force to demand comparable increases").

109. 392 U.S. 183 (1968).

gress could not "use a relatively trivial impact on commerce as an excuse for broad general regulation of state or private activities."[110] Likewise in *Garcia* itself the Court acknowledged that there existed at least some "limitation on federal authority inherent in the delegated nature of Congress' Article I powers."[111] It was against this backdrop that Chief Justice Burger announced his retirement, and President Ronald Reagan received the chance to alter the membership and jurisprudential direction of the Supreme Court.

110. *Id.* at 196 n.27.

111. *Garcia*, 499 U.S. at 550.

CHAPTER V

THE COMMERCE POWER AFTER 1985: THE REHNQUIST COURT'S RETRENCHMENT

In 1986, William H. Rehnquist became the Chief Justice of the United States, and Antonin Scalia assumed his seat as Associate Justice. In 1992, an equally significant shift in the Court's membership occurred when Clarence Thomas filled the vacancy created by the retirement of Justice Thurgood Marshall. This changing of the guard meant that the Court now included five members—Chief Justice Rehnquist and Justices O'Connor, Scalia, Kennedy and Thomas—prepared to subject claimed exercises of the federal lawmaking power to probing judicial examination. On the watch of these five Justices, the Court has expounded important limits on the Fourteenth Amendment enforcement power and taken a broadened view of "external" limits on federal regulatory authority designed to protect state autonomy.[1] At the heart of the Rehnquist Court's work, however, has been its reassessment of the contours of the commerce power itself. Because that reassessment has reinvigorated the law of federalism and raised a plethora of issues that have

1. *See infra* Chapter VI.

practical present-day importance, we pause to examine in detail the work of the Rehnquist Court
and the controversies that work has spawned.

A.   The Lopez and Morrison Decisions

On March 10, 1992, Alfonso Lopez, a twelfth-
grader in San Antonio, Texas, carried a concealed
handgun into Edison High School.[2] This episode led
to the prosecution and conviction of Lopez under
the Gun Free School Zones Act of 1990 (GFSZA),
which made it a federal crime "for any individual
knowingly to possess a firearm at a place that the
individual knows, or has reasonable cause to believe, is a school zone."[3] Mr. Lopez's appeal drew on
federalism concerns to challenge the constitutionality of the GFSZA as applied to his highly localized
act. Responding to this contention, the Court—for
the first time since *Carter Coal*—ruled that an act
of Congress exceeded its power under the Commerce Clause. The Court began its analysis by reviewing key post–1936 precedents and finding in
them a recognition that Congress could regulate
"three broad categories of activity":

> First, Congress may regulate the use of the chan-
> nels of interstate commerce. . . . Second, Congress
> is empowered to regulate and protect the instru-
> mentalities of interstate commerce, or persons or

2.   United States v. Lopez, 514 U.S. 549, 551 (1995).

3.   The Act defined a "school zone" to include any location
within 1000 feet of a school building. *See* 18 U.S.C. § 921(a)(25).

things in interstate commerce, even though the threat may come only from intrastate activities.... Finally, Congress' commerce authority includes the power to regulate those activities having a substantial relation to interstate commerce, ... *i.e.*, those activities that substantially affect interstate commerce....[4]

Because the first two categories plainly did not cover a case of simple gun possession, the only question was whether the challenged statute passed muster under the third aspect of its commerce power—namely, the affecting-commerce theory.

The Court acknowledged that Congress possessed wide-ranging authority to regulate matters that affect interstate commerce. The Court also concluded, however, that none of its post-New Deal precedents controlled the *Lopez* case because each of them involved regulation of "economic activity."[5] The Court continued:

Even *Wickard*, which is perhaps the most far reaching example of Commerce Clause authority over intrastate activity, involved economic activity in a way that the possession of a gun in a school zone does not.... Section 922(q) is a criminal statute that by its terms has nothing to do with "commerce" or any sort of economic enterprise, however broadly one might define those terms. Section 922(q) is not an essential part of a larger regulation of economic activity, in which

4. Lopez, 514 U.S. at 558–59 (citations omitted).

5. *Id.* at 560.

the regulatory scheme could be undercut unless the intrastate activity were regulated. It cannot, therefore, be sustained under our cases upholding regulations of activities that arise out of or are connected with a commercial transaction, which viewed in the aggregate, substantially affects interstate commerce.[6]

Shifting away from *Wickard*-type aggregation analysis, the Court observed that "section 922(q) contains no jurisdictional element which would ensure, through case-by-case inquiry, that the firearm possession in question affects interstate commerce."[7] The Court thus indicated that a different analysis could apply if the law included an "express jurisdictional element which might limit its reach to a discrete set of firearm possessions that additionally have an explicit connection with or effect on interstate commerce."[8] The Court also noted that the pre-enactment legislative record contained no evidence that connected guns near schools to the vitality of interstate commerce. As to this display of legislative inattentiveness, the Court observed:

We agree with the Government that Congress normally is not required to make formal findings as to the substantial burdens that an activity has on interstate commerce. But to the extent that congressional findings would enable us to evaluate the legislative judgment that the activity in question substantially affected interstate com-

6. *Id.* at 560–61.

7. *Id.* at 561.

8. *Id.* at 562.

merce, even though no such substantial effect was visible to the naked eye, they are lacking here.[9]

In the end, it was not enough that the presence of guns near schools could result in violent crimes that deter travel or generate monetary costs spread through the nation by way of "the mechanism of insurance." Nor was it sufficient that guns in schools create disruptions of student learning that "result in a less productive citizenry," which in turn undercuts "the Nation's economic well-being." The implications of these effect-on-commerce arguments were simply too much for the majority to bear. Under the government's chain-reaction logic, Chief Justice Rehnquist complained, Congress could regulate even "family law (including marriage, divorce, and child custody)" and "areas such as criminal law enforcement or education where States historically have been sovereign." In the majority's view, for example, it was intolerable to think that "Congress could mandate a federal curriculum for local elementary and secondary schools" on the theory that better instruction fosters a more energetic national economy.[10]

The dissenters' responses were predictable. Justice Souter bemoaned what he described as the majority's disregard of the "chastening experience" endured by the Court following its decisions in *Hammer, Schecter Poultry* and *Carter Coal*.[11] In particular, he worried that the majority's newly

9. *Id.* at 562–63 (citations omitted).

10. *Id.* at 564–65.

11. *Id.* at 604 (Souter, J., dissenting).

minted "non-economic activity" test would resuscitate just the sort of approach—built on woodenly
excluding specified categories of activity from congressional control under the commerce power—that
the Court had abandoned in 1937.[12] Justice Breyer
added that, even accepting the soundness of the
majority's methodology, the operation of schools
qualified as an "economic activity" because it entailed the provision of valuable educational services
at a cost of billions of dollars per year.[13] To the
latter point, the majority offered the now-familiar
"it proves too much" response. If schooling constitutes an economic activity, Chief Justice Rehnquist
observed, so does "childrearing" because it also
entails the provision of "a 'valuable service—namely, to equip [children] with the skills they need to
survive in life and, more specifically, in the workplace.' "[14]

Perhaps the most important opinion in *Lopez* was
the concurrence drafted by Justice Kennedy and
joined by Justice O'Connor. That opinion emphasized that past experience "counsels great restraint" when the Court assesses congressional invocations of its commerce power.[15] Nonetheless, the
maintenance of "two governments ... with distinct
and discernible lines of political accountability"[16]

12. *Id*. at 608.

13. *Id*. at 629 (Breyer, J., dissenting).

14. *Id*. at 565 (quoting Justice Breyer's dissent).

15. *Id*. at 568 (Kennedy, J., concurring).

16. *Id*. at 576.

remained "vital ... in securing freedom."[17] According to Justice Kennedy, "[w]ere the Federal Government to take over the regulation of entire areas of traditional state concern, areas having nothing to do with the regulation of commercial activities, the boundaries between spheres of state and federal accountability would blur and political responsibility would become illusory."[18] In short, Justices Kennedy and O'Connor took care to emphasize the limited scope of the *Lopez* holding, but their votes sufficed, for the first time in 59 years, to bring down a federal statute on the theory that it lay beyond the limits of the commerce power.

In the wake of *Lopez*, commentators predicted that the Court's five-to-four decision might well prove to be little more than a symbolic nod of the head to the Framers' rejection of unlimited federal powers.[19] The Court's decision in *United States v. Morrison*,[20] however, revealed that *Lopez* was not an isolated event. *Morrison* presented the question whether Congress could grant to the victim of gender-motivated violence a civil-damages remedy against the attacker. On behalf of the Court, Chief Justice Rehnquist acknowledged that, unlike in *Lopez*, Congress had made elaborate findings about the effects of gender-motivated battering on inter-

17. *Id*. at 578.

18. *Id*. at 577.

19. *See* Jesse H. Choper, *Taming Congress's Power Under the Commerce Clause: What Does the Near Future Portend?*, 55 ARK. L. REV. 731, 732 & n.9 (2003) (collecting authorities that predicted that *Lopez* would or might well be an "aberration").

20. 529 U.S. 598 (2000).

state commerce. Indeed, four years of congressional study had revealed that rape and related forms of violence produced massive quantities of lost work time, foregone travel and business transactions, and increased medical and other financial costs.[21] For the five-Justice majority, however, these facts did not matter. As in *Lopez*, the commerce power was not implicated because the case involved only "non-economic activity" and a misguided effort to defend a congressional enactment based on the impermissibly sweeping "cost of crime" rationale.[22] As in *Lopez*, the majority saw no proper stopping point to the government's argument because its underlying logic would allow Congress even "to regulate murder or any other type of violence."[23] As in *Lopez*, the Court also emphasized that the federal statute did not include a "jurisdictional element," connected up with "the use of the channels of interstate commerce," that "would lend support" to the argument in favor of the enactment's constitutionality.[24]

Writing for four dissenters, Justice Souter reiterated his view that, in the commerce-power field, "categorical exclusions [had] proven as unworkable in practice as they are unsupportable in theory."[25] He saw in the majority's approach—now firmly tethered to the economic/non-economic activity di-

21. *Id.* at 629–31.

22. *Id.* at 612–13; *see id.* at 615–16.

23. *Id.* at 615.

24. *Id.* at 613–14 & n.5.

25. *Id.* at 640 (Souter, J., dissenting).

viding line—an ill-conceived return to the "earlier and nearly disastrous experiment" that reached its crest in the years before *Jones & Laughlin Steel*.[26] Justice Breyer added that "in a Nation knit together by two centuries of scientific, technological, commercial and environmental change,"[27] it was wrong for the Court, and harmful for the country, to "depriv[e] Congress of the power to regulate activities that have a genuine and important effect upon interstate commerce."[28] The dissenters seemed ready to limit the significance of *Lopez* to cases in which Congress had failed to document in legislative hearings the connection between its enactments and the movement of interstate commerce. For the majority, however, the principle of *Lopez* focused on the substance of—and not just the process underlying—the challenged congressional intrusion on state prerogatives.

At the same time, the dissenters' pleas for judicial restraint did not fall on entirely deaf ears. In *Morrison*, as in *Lopez*, the Court gave no hint that it was abandoning any of its post–1936/pre–1986 Commerce Clause precedents, and it emphasized that the new limits it had placed on the affecting-commerce power were subject to important limits of their own. We turn now to the impact of *Lopez* and *Morrison* on each of the three prongs of the congressional commerce power.

26. *Id.* at 642–43 (Souter, J., dissenting).
27. *Id.* at 660 (Breyer, J., dissenting).
28. *Id.*

B. The Channels/Instrumentalities Theory and the Commerce–Prohibiting Technique After 1985

Even as the Court in *Lopez* and *Morrison* trimmed the sails of the aggregation-based affecting-commerce prong of the commerce power, it reaffirmed Congress's broad authority to regulate the "instrumentalities" and the "channels" of interstate commerce,[29] and the Court's post-*Morrison* decision in *Pierce County v. Guillen*[30] confirmed that this component of the commerce power retains a long reach. *Pierce County* concerned the constitutionality of a federal rule that excludes from evidence, in both state and federal court, certain data collected by state authorities concerning unsafe highway conditions. In upholding the rule, a unanimous Court reasoned that the evidentiary privilege it creates heightens accuracy in the reporting of highway hazards, which in turn facilitates road-safety enhancements. It followed, according to Justice Thomas, that the rule was constitutional because it both "improv[es] safety in the channels of commerce and increas[es] protection for the instrumentalities of interstate commerce."[31]

Do *Lopez* and *Pierce County* support the constitutionality of the often-invoked federal statute that criminalizes local "carjackings"? The Court could

29. *Lopez*, 514 U.S. at 558.

30. 537 U.S. 129 (2003).

31. *Id.* at 147.

uphold such a statute on the theory that the behavior it targets interferes with an instrumentality of commerce in the form of the ripped-off car. Alternatively, the Court might reason that the violent commandeering of vehicles disrupts the channels of commerce by discouraging travel and slowing down drivers confronted with gawking bystanders, resulting police chases and the like. Critics of the statute might well respond that carjackings pose no threat to or from roadways themselves and that automobiles (unlike trains and planes) primarily serve as instrumentalities of noncommercial, intrastate movement.[32] The Supreme Court has yet to consider the constitutionality of the carjacking law, but so far lower courts have consistently upheld it, often invoking the instrumentalities/channels prong of the commerce power.[33]

As cases such as *Darby* and *Sullivan* reveal, one important way in which Congress may control the "channels" of interstate commerce is through use

32. *Cf.* Perez v. United States, 402 U.S. 146, 150 (1971) (indicating that Congress could outlaw intrastate destruction of airplanes because they qualify as instruments of commerce).

33. *See, e.g.,* United States v. Bishop, 66 F.3d 569, 590 (3d Cir. 1995) (upholding statute in part on theory "that motor vehicles are instrumentalities of interstate commerce"). Of course, the carjacking statute might also be upheld on the basis of substantial-affects aggregation analysis if one views theft as an "economic activity." *See id.* at 581 (characterizing forcible taking as economic activity and reasoning that when carjackings are "replicated 15,000 or 20,000 times per year, the economic effects are indeed profound"). *Accord, e.g.,* United States v. Cortes, 299 F.3d 1030, 1033–34 (9th Cir. 2002) (collecting additional authorities).

of the commerce-prohibiting technique. Because the Court in *Lopez* in no way questioned this long-recognized power of Congress, it apparently may continue to (1) impose prohibitions on cross-border movements of goods or persons it deems objectionable and (2) limit intrastate behavior, to a substantial extent, to effectuate any such prohibition.[34] Tough questions remain, however, about how far Congress can push this so-called "super-bootstrapping" strategy. Assume, for example, that Congress responded to *Lopez* by enacting (1) Statute A, which outlaws the carrying of any gun across a state line with the intent of possessing it within 1000 feet of a school; and (2) Statute B, which undertakes to ensure the effectiveness of Statute A by outlawing the possession of any gun within 1000 feet of a school. At least under modern authorities, Statute A would pass constitutional muster as a straightforward exercise of the commerce-prohibiting technique.[35] Moreover, defenders of Statute B would be sure to argue that it is "reasonably adapted" to effectuating Statute A because, for example, it will help catch Statute A violators who might otherwise escape prosecution because of the difficulty of proving their specific-intent *mens rea*.[36]

34. *See supra* Chapter IV.

35. *See, e.g.*, United States v. Lankford, 196 F.3d 563 (5th Cir. 1999) (upholding federal statute criminalizing movement across a state line with intent to injure spouse or intimate partner); *see generally* United States v. Ballinger, 312 F.3d 1264, 1273 n.8 (11th Cir. 2002) (collecting interstate-travel prohibitions of this kind).

36. United States v. Darby, 312 U.S. 100, 121 (1941).

Even so, most lawyers will sense that coupling Statute B with Statute A will not save Statute B from invalidation. After all, Statute B replicates precisely the statute that the Court struck down in *Lopez*,[37] and the linkage between Statute A and Statute B is demonstrably tenuous because in the real world almost all Statute B violators will never have violated Statute A. These observations highlight what students of the Commerce Clause should see as the key point: After *Lopez*, no less than before it, much uncertainty marks Congress's ability to exploit the "channels of commerce" rubric through aggressive use of the super-bootstrapping technique.

The state-protective philosophy reflected in *Lopez* and *Morrison* may well drive new arguments for a narrowed view of the super-bootstrap approach and even for a rejection of the commerce-prohibiting technique itself.[38] On the other hand, the commerce-prohibiting technique has persevered since the days of the *Lottery Case*, and Congress has

---

37. Both precedent and common sense suggest that lawmakers may not achieve "indirectly" what the Constitution "directly" forecloses them from doing. *See, e.g.*, U.S. Term Limits, Inc. v. Thornton, 514 U.S. 779, 829 (1995).

38. *See, e.g.*, Donald H. Regan, *How To Think About the Federal Commerce Power and Incidentally Rewrite* United States v. Lopez, 94 MICH. L. REV. 554, 576–78 (1995) (arguing against federal "toll-gate power" embodied in the commerce-prohibiting technique); Grant S. Nelson, *A Commerce Clause Standard for the New Millenium: "Yes" to Broad Congressional Control Over Commercial Transactions, "No" to Federal Legislation on Social and Cultural Issues*, 55 ARK. L. REV. 1213, 1221–24 (2003) (arguing that some, but not all, past uses by the Court of the commerce-prohibiting technique were inappropriate).

relied on its channels-of-commerce power to enact many prohibitory statutes—including federal mail and wire fraud laws—of long-standing significance.[39] As Professor Choper has noted, however, some issues concerning the channels/instruments theory have a new vitality in the post-*Lopez* era. For example:

> Could Congress add other crimes apart from fraud to the mail and wire statutes: conspiracy to commit murder, robbery, assault, and so on? Seemingly, all it would take is one phone call in the course of planning to rob or attack a victim to make something a federal crime. Further, could Congress make it a federal offense to use the interstate highways, or any road connected to a federal road, in the commission of any unlawful act? Could Congress make it a federal crime to use the Internet, or a computer network attached to the Internet, to engage in designated misconduct?[40]

The Court may ultimately derive from the principle of *Lopez* and *Morrison* a restriction on federal authority to adopt these sorts of laws, at least when

39. *See, e.g.*, Choper, *supra* note 19, at 761. For a related invocation of this power, see *United States v. Watts*, 256 F.3d 630, 633–34 (7th Cir. 2001) (reasoning that Congress may outlaw robbery from financial institutions insured by the Federal Deposit Insurance Corporation on the theory that they "are instrumentalities and channels of interstate commerce"). *Accord, e.g.*, United States v. Spinello, 265 F.3d 150 (3d Cir. 2001) (adding that banks are "integral to the web of interstate commercial activity").

40. Choper, *supra* note 19, at 761.

Congress deals with such traditionally state-regulated subjects as murder, rape and other violent crimes. For now, however, it is important to see that the *Lopez/Morrison* principle does not speak— or at least does not speak directly—to these questions because they focus on Congress's authority to regulate the "channels" and "instrumentalities" of interstate commerce, rather than on the affecting-commerce power at issue in *Lopez* and *Morrison* themselves.

Other conundrums tied to the channels-and-instrumentalities power emanate from the Court's post–1936 endorsement of federal statutes that regulate things that have previously moved across state lines. Most significantly, in *Scarborough v. United States*,[41] the Court read a statute that targeted gun possession by felons to require "no more than the minimal nexus that the firearm have been, at some time, in interstate commerce"[42] and on this basis upheld a conviction for possession of a firearm that "was manufactured in France in the nineteenth century and was somehow later brought into Virginia."[43] Picking up on this cue, the Court in *Lopez* stressed that the GFSZA did not include an "express jurisdictional element which might limit

41. 431 U.S. 563 (1977).

42. *Id*. at 575.

43. *Id*. at 565 n.2. *See generally supra* Chapter IV. Although "the issue squarely presented in *Scarborough* concerned only the interpretation of the statute," the Court's reasoning indicated its belief that the statute, thus construed, fell within Congress's "full Commerce Clause power." LAURENCE H. TRIBE, AMERICAN CONSTITUTIONAL LAW, § 5–5, at 830 (3d ed., vol. one, 2000).

its reach to a discrete set of firearm possessions."[44]
Federal lawmakers were quick to realize the possibilities this passage created. Heeding its admonition, they reenacted exactly the same guns-near-
schools possession ban invalidated in *Lopez* with the
exception that they made that ban applicable only if
the possessed gun "has moved in or otherwise affects interstate commerce...."[45] Does this retooled
version of the GFSZA satisfy Commerce Clause
requirements? Lower courts have said that the answer is "yes" and invoked the super-channels-of-
commerce rationale in upholding both the post-
Lopez version of the GFSZA and other possession
laws that contain similar so-called jurisdictional
hooks tied to the past interstate movement of the
offending firearm.[46]

44. *Lopez*, 514 U.S. at 562.

45. Pub. L. No. 104–208 § 101(f), 110 Stat. 3009, *codified as
amended* at 18 U.S.C. § 922(q)(2).

46. *See, e.g.*, United States v. Danks, 221 F.3d 1037 (8th Cir.
1999) (upholding post-*Lopez* GFSZA). Particularly plentiful are
post-*Lopez* decisions that reaffirm the constitutionality of the
felon-in-possession law involved in *Scarborough* itself. *See, e.g.*,
United States v. Lemons, 302 F.3d 769 (7th Cir. 2002) (indicating that the nexus requirement discussed in *Scarborough* applies
to post-*Lopez* analysis of felon-in-possession law); United States
v. Singletary, 268 F.3d 196 (3d Cir. 2001) (reevaluating law of
the circuit in light of *Lopez* and *Morrison* and finding *Scarborough* still applicable to uphold felon-in-possession statute); *see
generally* Choper, *supra* note 19, at 759 n.137 (collecting circuit
court cases). Notably, courts have recognized that a "jurisdictional element" need not entail a finding that the regulated item
previously moved in interstate commerce. *See* United States v.
Faasse, 265 F.3d 475, 790 (6th Cir. 2001) (finding "explicit
jurisdictional nexus" present in child-support nonpayment stat-

It may be, however, that the Supreme Court, when given the chance, will modify the *Scarborough* rule.[47] Common sense suggests that Congress cannot save *any* otherwise unconstitutional enactment by tacking on to it *any* commerce-related "jurisdictional element."[48] It seems farfetched to think, for example, that Congress could revive the statute struck down in *Morrison* simply by requiring that the gender-motivated batterer had at some past time crossed any state line. And it seems even more farfetched to think that the Violence Against Women Act would no longer pose a problem if it operated only when the batterer had, when the assault occurred, worn or owned an article of clothing that once moved in interstate commerce.[49] The problem

ute because it reached only non-custodial parent's obligations to pay for children located in another state).

47. *See, e.g.*, Brent E. Newman, *Felons, Firearms, and Federalism: Reconsidering* Scarborough *in Light of* Lopez, 3 J. APP. PRAC. & PROCESS 671, 683–84 (2001) (expressing doubt about whether *Scarborough* remains good law). *See also* United States v. Cortes, 299 F.3d 1030, 1037 & n.2 (9th Cir. 2002) (noting that continuing "vitality of *Scarborough* engenders significant debate" but reasoning that lower courts must "follow *Scarborough* unwaveringly" until "the Supreme Court tells us otherwise").

48. *See, e.g.*, United States v. Pappadopoulos, 64 F.3d 522, 527 (9th Cir. 1995) (asserting that "Congress's power to regulate articles or goods in commerce may not permit it to regulate an item for eternity simply because it has once passed state lines"); United States v. Wilson, 73 F.3d 675, 685 (7th Cir. 1995) ("In discussing the lack of a jurisdictional element in *Lopez*, the court simply did not state or imply . . . that all statutes with such an element would be constitutional.").

49. *See* TRIBE, *supra* note 43, at 831 n.29 (providing additional extreme examples). *See also* Brannon P. Denning & Glenn H. Reynolds, *Rulings and Resistance: the New Commerce Clause*

is that giving credence to these machinations of statutory drafting could well render *Lopez* an empty letter and resurrect the very problem it attacked—the specter of a functionally unlimited congressional commerce power.[50]

Once we conclude that not every would-be jurisdictional hook will work, however, it becomes open to question whether the new GFSZA—at least in some of its applications—will pass constitutional muster. In *Lopez* itself the Court noted that the defendant had not "*recently* moved in interstate commerce" and that the challenged statute imposed

Jurisprudence Encounters the Lower Courts, 55 ARK. L. REV. 1253, 1273 (2003) (worrying about whether Congress could "evade" constitutional difficulties with the federal arson statute as applied to private residences by requiring that "some portion of the building materials used in construction had moved in interstate commerce in the past"). To be sure, the new GFSZA is potentially distinguishable from the border-crossing-clothes hypothetical because the new GFSZA's jurisdictional element focuses on a specific object—namely a gun—the possession of which is the gravamen of the criminal offense.

50. Responding to this concern, the Ninth Circuit, in *United States v. McCoy*, 323 F.3d 1114 (9th Cir. 2003), invalidated a federal ban on possession of any child pornography made with materials that had moved in interstate commerce as applied to the possession of a photograph meant for a family photo album taken with a camera and made with film that had been manufactured outside the state. Noting that the offending photograph had not itself moved across state lines (and was held solely for personal, rather than commercial, purposes and with no plans for interstate shipment), the Court reasoned that the jurisdictional hook did not save the statute because it "encompasses virtually *every* case imaginable" of possession of such materials. *Id.* at 1124 (emphasis in original). *But see id.* at 1125 n.20 (collecting cases from other jurisdictions upholding statute because of its inclusion of this "jurisdictional element").

"no requirement that ... possession of the firearm have any *concrete* ties to interstate commerce."[51] These passages provide tools for building a variety of limiting principles—for example, a requirement that the *defendant* (and not just the gun) must have crossed a state line; that the defendant must have crossed a state line *with the gun*; or that the defendant (or both the defendant and the gun, or at least the gun) must have *recently* crossed a state line.[52]

The issue whether the Court should embrace some such limiting principle brings us back to basic concerns that have driven debate about the commerce power for more than a century. On the side of rebuffing any constitutional limit on Congress's power to regulate things that have crossed state lines in the past stands the idea that thus restricting congressional power will inevitably involve the courts in the drawing of arbitrary and "political" lines. (How recent is "recent"? How concrete is

51. *Lopez,* 514 U.S. at 567 (emphasis added).

52. A related question is whether Congress can save possession laws that are otherwise not salvageable through inclusion of a moved-in-commerce jurisdictional element standing alone by utilizing the super-bootstrapping technique. For example, 18 U.S.C. § 922(g)(1) prohibits a felon from receiving a gun by way of an interstate shipment, "which certainly involves congressional regulation of the channels of interstate commerce." Denning & Reynolds, *supra* note 49, at 1272. May Congress wholly ban possession of guns by felons to ensure this ban operates effectively? May Congress at least use this effective-enforcement rationale to ban possession by felons of guns that have previously moved in interstate commerce? Put more generally, just how do the "jurisdictional hook," the commerce-prohibiting, and the super-bootstrapping aspects of the commerce power fit together in the post-*Lopez* environment?

"concrete"?) On the side of embracing such a restriction lies the indefatigable parade-of-horribles
argument that found its latest expressions in *Lopez*
and *Morrison*. (If Congress can regulate all guns
that once crossed state lines, why not all people who
once crossed state lines or people who wear clothing
that once crossed state lines?) Seeing how the Court
will sort through these matters must await another
day. For now, however, lawyers would be foolish to
assume that congressional inclusion of any "jurisdictional element" in any federal criminal statute
will automatically shelter it from successful constitutional attack.

C. The In–Commerce Theory After 1985

Drawing on the legacy of the early stockyard-
regulation cases, the Court in *Lopez* reaffirmed that
Congress may regulate "persons or things *in* interstate commerce," regardless of any post-*Lopez* limits on its power to regulate non-economic activity
on an aggregation-based affecting-commerce theory.
This "in commerce" concept—as we already have
seen—has a murky quality. (So it is that a cab ride
to a train station to start an interstate trip is not in
the stream of commerce, but a mid-trip cab ride
from one station to another is.[53]) The principle,
however, also has a long lineage, and the Court's
recent decisions confirm its persisting significance.

Most important, in *Reno v. Condon*,[54] the Court
signaled a willingness to view this power broadly,

53. *See supra* Chapter IV.
54. 528 U.S. 141 (2000).

even in the wake of *Lopez*, when it held that Congress could forbid the transfer of personal data collected by states in issuing motor vehicle licenses because such information "is a 'thin[g] in interstate commerce.' "[55] In the view of a unanimous Court, the in-commerce label fit the challenged statute because the "information which the States have historically sold is used by insurers, manufacturers, direct marketers, and others engaged in interstate commerce to contact drivers with customized solicitations." In other words, "[b]ecause drivers' personal identifying information is, in this context, an article of commerce, its sale or release into the interstate stream of business [was] sufficient to support congressional regulation," whether or not such distributions would warrant regulation under the "substantial effects" test.[56]

One wonders why the Court in *Reno v. Condon* found it necessary to invoke the in-commerce rubric. The statute, after all, focused on *sales* of data, a paradigmatic economic activity for purposes of post-*Lopez* affecting-commerce analysis. At the least, however, the Court's taking of an in-commerce approach removed the need to explore whether the regulated activity, in the aggregate, had a "substantial effect" on interstate commerce.[57] The

55. *Id.* at 148 (quoting *Lopez*, 514 U.S. at 558).

56. *Id.*

57. In addition, the statutory language extended to "disclos[ing] or otherwise mak[ing] available such data," apparently

case thus illustrates one important role that in-commerce analysis can play: It may offer an analytical shortcut for judges prepared to validate federal statutes but disinclined to explore the limits of the non-economic activity principle and other problems posed by the *Lopez/Morrison* rule.[58]

whether for profit or not. *Reno*, 528 U.S. at 144. Perhaps the Court had qualms about characterizing a statute that covered all forms of distribution as targeting an "economic activity" for purposes of *Lopez*. *See infra* note 79.

58. *See* Denning & Reynolds, *supra* note 49, at 1288 (noting potential "advantage" to courts of relying on Commerce Clause theories that permit courts "to avoid the more complicated 'affecting commerce' analysis of *Lopez*"). Similar thinking might have influenced the Court's decision in *United States v. Robertson*, 514 U.S. 669 (1995), which involved a prosecution under the Racketeer Influenced and Corrupt Organizations Act (RICO). The government in the case sought to show that the defendant had invested proceeds of criminal drug activities in an Alaska gold mine that, as required by the language of the statute, was "engaged in or affect[ed] . . . commerce." The Court sidestepped the affecting-commerce argument by sustaining the conviction on the theory that the mining business had "engaged *in* . . . inter-state commerce" by purchasing equipment in California, hiring seven workers from the lower forty-eight states, and sending $30,000 in gold outside Alaska. *Id.* at 671–72 (emphasis added). The *Robertson* case may reflect nothing more than a fact-specific ruling on a matter of statutory interpretation. Viewed through a constitutional lens, however, *Robertson* broadly suggests that Congress may regulate intrastate activity connected up with a business's operations (there, the activity of transferring money) based on a showing that other operations have an interstate character (there, the operation of buying equipment, hiring workers and shipping goods). *See generally* Deborah Jones Merritt, *Commerce!*, 94 MICH. L. REV. 674, 732–33 (1995) (claiming that Court must have considered constitutional implications of *Robertson* and that Court did not focus on interstate elements of Mr. Robertson's investment-related activities). If, for example, Congress made it a crime for a business "engaged . . . in inter-

Reno v. Condon also reveals another important feature of present-day in-commerce analysis. In *Lopez* the Court had spoken of Congress's power "to regulate *and protect* . . . persons or things in interstate commerce, even though *the threat* may come only from intrastate activities."[59] In *Reno*, however, the Court did not uphold an effort by Congress to remove a "threat" to the interstate movement of drivers' license data. Rather, the Court said in so many words that, if an item qualifies as a "thing in interstate commerce," Congress may make it a thing *not* in interstate commerce by cutting off

state commerce" to maintain possession of a gun near a school, could it constitutionally apply to Mr. Robertson if his gold-mine office sat next door to a schoolhouse, and he kept a gun in his desk? Analytical difficulties arise in evaluating this sort of hypothetical because the Court in *Robertson* ended its analysis once it found that the gold mining business had engaged in interstate commerce and never explained what relationship, if any, the regulated conduct must have with the interstate elements of the business. For this reason, the scope of Congress's power to reach intrastate activities because they are part of, or otherwise connected to, a business's interstate activities remains uncertain. *Cf.* United States v. Bird, 124 F.3d 667, 674–75 (5th Cir. 1997) (declining to uphold the federal prohibition on obstructing access to abortion clinics on an in-commerce theory because "there is no allegation or showing that, in the present case, [the clinic] ever employed physicians, treated patients, or used supplies" that had "traveled interstate"); United States v. Ballinger, 312 F.3d 1264, 1281–83 (11th Cir. 2002) (Hall, J., dissenting) (relying in part on *Robertson* and on church's dealings across state lines, including to service out-of-state members and visitors, in suggesting that court should sustain arson conviction on theory that church was engaged "in" interstate commerce).

59. *Lopez*, 514 U.S. at 558 (emphasis added). The Court then went on to cite the federal prohibition on thefts from interstate shipments as the paradigmatic exercise of this power. *See id.*

trade in it altogether.[60] No less important, Congress could exercise its commerce power in this way to achieve the essentially non-commercial purpose of protecting motor vehicle license holders from invasions of privacy. Finally, in keeping with the principle of *Currin v. Wallace*,[61] Congress could proscribe *all* transfers of driver's license data, whether interstate or intrastate in nature, apparently on the theory that data destined for intrastate uses was functionally inseparable from the great bulk of data destined for use in transactions that would cross state lines.

Even this brief discussion of the in-commerce prong of the congressional power reveals its continuing "obscurity."[62] In most modern cases, however, courts should not have to launch into speculative investigations about where streams of commerce begin and end. In *Schechter Poultry* and *Carter Coal*, for example, stream-of-commerce inquiries played a prominent role, but they did so only because of the Court's unwillingness to find

60. Applying something like the flipside of this principle, lower courts have relied on the in-commerce theory to uphold federal criminalization of the failure to pay court-ordered child support for a child who resides in another state. *E.g.*, United States v. Faasse, 265 F.3d 475, 481, 485 (6th Cir. 2001) (noting that nine circuits have reached the same conclusion; relying on *Lopez*'s recognition of power "to regulate things in interstate commerce, be they commercial or not"). *But see id.* at 500 (Batchelder, J., dissenting) (arguing that Congress may not use the in-commerce theory to "regulate the passive failure of individuals to engage in interstate commerce").

61. 306 U.S. 1 (1939) (discussed *supra* Chapter IV).

62. Regan, *supra* note 38, at 561 n.23.

that the mining and sales activities involved in those cases could "affect" interstate commerce under pre-*Jones and Laughlin Steel* constitutional principles. Even after *Lopez*, however, the Court would almost certainly uphold the regulation of those activities on an aggregation-based affecting-commerce rationale because of their intrinsically "economic" character.[63] Nonetheless, the in-commerce theory remains important. This is so, in part, because a variety of federal statutes specifically require a showing that the defendant has

63. *See supra* Chapter IV. For this reason, under modern-day law, the Court would probably never reach the in-commerce issues presented in *Carter Coal, Schechter Poultry* and other early cases. If the Court were to reach those issues, however, intervening decisions might well dictate a different result than the Court reached in each of those cases. Most significantly, the Court in *United States v. American Building Maintenance Industries,* 422 U.S. 271 (1975), asserted that the "flow of commerce" embraces "the practical, economic continuity in the *generation* of goods and services for interstate markets and their transportation and *distribution to the consumer*." *Id.* at 276 (emphasis added). Notwithstanding this broad language, the Court went on to conclude that a local janitorial business was not operating "in" commerce for purposes of the Clayton Act simply because it made local purchases of supplies that had been produced outside the state. That case, however, did not involve either the "generation" of goods for potential export (as did *Carter Coal*) or local "distribution" of non-locally-made goods for resale (as did *Schechter Poultry*). *Robertson* (*see supra* note 58) also supplies a basis for arguing that many productive activities (even if not all of them) lie in the stream of interstate commerce. In particular, it supports the claim that the in-commerce theory extends at least to any *Carter-Coal*-type case when the coal-mining (or other production) company (like Mr. Robertson's gold-mining company) brings in workers or equipment from other states and/or sends its product across state lines.

acted "in" interstate commerce. Even more important, the practical significance of the in-commerce theory is linked directly to the Court's future elaborations of *Lopez* and *Morrison*. To the extent the Court continues to rein in the affecting-commerce theory, arguments based on an in-commerce rationale will inevitably assume increasing importance.

D. The Affecting–Commerce Theory After 1985 and the "Non–Economic Activity" Rule

As we have seen, *Lopez* and *Morrison* leave in place large reservoirs of congressional power to regulate the channels and instrumentalities of interstate commerce, as well as persons and things in interstate commerce. Of no less importance, the Court's recent Commerce Clause cases—notwithstanding the limitations endorsed in *Lopez* and *Morrison*—confirm that Congress retains far-reaching authority to regulate intrastate activities on the theory that they affect interstate commerce.

To see why this is so, it is useful to recall the core components of the Court's pre–1986 affecting-commerce jurisprudence. Perhaps most important, that jurisprudence clarified that the affecting-commerce power was not limited to countering a particular subcategory of intrinsically national problems such as "races to the bottom" among states worried about enacting labor laws or environmental controls that might cause employers to relocate elsewhere.

Rather, pre–1986 cases suggested that (as one commentator put it) "Congress may regulate any behavior that affects the quantity or identity of goods or people moving across a state line."[64] The Court also supplemented this sweeping regulatory authority with a set of sub-rules that greatly strengthened Congress's hand. For example:

1. The Court would not intervene as long as Congress had a "rational basis" for finding that the activity it regulated had a substantial effect on interstate commerce.[65]

2. In calculating the existence of a substantial effect, Congress could consider the aggregate impact of entire classes of activity, regardless of whether the impact of any individual instance of the regulated activity was only "trivial."[66]

3. Congress had the power to act in effective ways to achieve its goals of protecting and encouraging interstate economic activity, including by regulating even "local acts which in themselves have no interstate nexus or effect if as a practical matter it is difficult to distinguish such transactions from others which may have some relation to interstate commerce."[67]

64. Regan, *supra* note 38, at 561.

65. Katzenbach v. McClung, 379 U.S. 294, 304 (1964) (discussed *supra* Chapter IV).

66. Wickard v. Filburn, 317 U.S. 111, 128 (1942) (discussed *supra* Chapter IV).

67. Robert L. Stern, *The Commerce Clause Revisited: The Federalization of Intrastate Crime*, 15 Ariz. L. Rev. 271, 280 (1973).

4. The Court would not second-guess congressional judgments about whether existing federal or state legislation already dealt adequately with the problem that its exercise of the commerce power purported to target.[68]

5. Congress, if otherwise permitted to act pursuant to its affecting-commerce power, could do so based on "moral," rather than economic, considerations.[69]

6. There were—at least the Court's dicta suggested—no categorical limits on the aggregation-based affecting-commerce power akin to the no-regulation-of-production limit recognized in *Carter Coal*. Rather, as the Court declared in *Wickard*: "Even if [a person's] activity be local and though it may not be regarded as commerce, it may still, whatever its nature, be reached by Congress if it exerts a substantial effect on interstate commerce, and this irrespective of whether such effect is what might at some earlier time have been defined as 'direct' or 'indirect.' "[70]

At least at this point, the impact of *Lopez* and *Morrison* on the Court's post–1936 affecting-commerce jurisprudence is limited because (1) those

68. *E.g.,* Hodel v. Virginia Surface Min. and Reclamation Ass'n, Inc., 452 U.S. 264, 283 (1981) (rejecting challenge based on assertion that means for dealing with strip mining are "redundant or unnecessary" because "effectiveness of existing laws ... is ordinarily a matter committed to legislative judgment").

69. Heart of Atlanta Motel v. United States, 379 U.S. 241, 257 (1964) (discussed *supra* Chapter IV).

70. Wickard v. Filburn, 317 U.S. 111, 125 (1942).

decisions cut back on only the last of these sub-rules, and (2) they do so only in one way—namely, by suggesting that distinctive rules apply to congressional regulation of non-economic activity.[71] In addition, the Court itself has suggested that its newfangled "non-economic activity" limitation on the affecting-commerce power might well be subject to important limitations of its own.[72] Most impor-

71. For a post-*Lopez/Morrison* reaffirmation of Congress's broad authority to regulate local economic transactions on an aggregation-based affecting-commerce theory, see *The Citizens Bank v. Alafabco, Inc.*, 123 S.Ct. 2037 (2003) (per curiam). There, the Court upheld application of Federal Arbitration Act to a dispute concerning a local commercial loan transaction entered into in part to get funds for out-of-state uses and secured in part by "goods assembled from out-of-state parts and raw materials." Emphasizing Congress's ability to focus on a "general practice," rather than "individual . . . transactions, taken alone," the Court declared that *Lopez* did not "purport to announce a new rule governing Congress' Commerce Clause power over concededly economic activity such as the debt-restructuring agreements before us now." *Id.* at 2041.

72. Throughout his opinion in *Morrison*, for example, Chief Justice Rehnquist emphasized that the challenged statute targeted "non-economic, *violent* conduct," thus providing an opening for future arguments designed to narrow the scope of the "non-economic activity" principle itself. *Morrison*, 529 U.S. at 617 (emphasis added); *see, e.g., id.* at 615 (noting that the "suppression of [violent crime] has always been the prime object of the States' police power"). The *Morrison* majority also left room for litigants to claim that proper legislative findings might support federal regulation of at least some non-economic activity when it noted that the presence of findings "is not sufficient, *by itself,* to sustain . . . Commerce Clause legislation." *Id.* at 614 (emphasis added). Building on this rhetoric, lower courts have continued to emphasize the presence or absence of significant congressional investigations and findings. *See, e.g.*, United States v. McCoy, 323 F.3d 1114 (9th Cir. 2003) (relying in part on absence of

tant, the Court in *Morrison* went out of its way to declare that "we need *not adopt a categorical rule against aggregating the effects of any non-economic activity* in order to decide these cases."[73]

At the same time, *Lopez* and *Morrison* leave no doubt that, at least for now, economic activities and non-economic activities fall into very different categories for purposes of aggregation-based affecting-commerce analysis. The most central question raised by the cases thus concerns what types of activities qualify or do not qualify as "economic" in character. What about theft?[74] What about theft, or

supportive pre-enactment findings in invalidating ban on possession of child pornography).

73. 529 U.S. at 613 (emphasis added). It also bears mention that the decisions in *Lopez* and *Morrison* do not foreclose all affecting-commerce-based regulation of non-economic activity because some such activity—possessing weapons of mass destruction, for example—might well exert a substantial effect in and of itself, even in the absence of aggregation. *See, e.g.*, United States v. Wang, 222 F.3d 234, 239 (6th Cir. 2000) (suggesting that "extortion demand of $1,540,000" might justify federal regulation on this theory).

74. *Compare* United States v. Spinello, 265 F.3d 150, 155 (3d Cir. 2001) ("robbery of a bank ... is an 'economic' activity almost by definition") *and* United States v. Gray, 260 F.3d 1267, 1274 (11th Cir. 2001) (finding that federal Hobbs Act "undeniably regulates economic activity" because "[r]obbery, even though accompanied by actual or threatened physical harm, is undeniably an *economic* crime that involves the involuntary transfer of economically valuable assets") (emphasis in original), *with* United States v. McFarland, 311 F.3d 376, 396–97 (5th Cir. 2002) (Garwood, J., dissenting from ruling of equally divided *en banc* court) (reasoning that "economic activity" is properly equated with "commercial activity" and that robbery is not commercial) *and id.* at 421 (Jones, J., dissenting) ("Of course, robbery should not be considered an economic activity" because "[t]he

sex-based violence, done for hire?[75] What about theft, or the illegal sale of drugs, for which the penalty rises dramatically if it is carried out through violent means or while in possession of a firearm?[76] What about obstructing access to local abortion clinics?[77] What about possessing drugs

dictionary defines 'economic' as 'relating to, or concerned with' the production, distribution and consumption of commodities.''). *See also* United States v. Lynch, 265 F.3d 758, 761–62 (9th Cir. 2001) (noting that, while "the forced transfer of currency or of goods" partakes of economic activity, it is also an archetypal state-law crime).

75. *See* United States v. Marek, 238 F.3d 310 (5th Cir. 2001) (upholding federal murder-for-hire statute applicable to persons who use the mails or facilities of interstate commerce); Nelson, *supra* note 38, at 1233 (arguing that "Congress may ... criminalize *all* murder for hire" because "it is a voluntary commercial transaction") (emphasis in original).

76. *See, e.g.*, United States v. Bell, 90 F.3d 318, 320–21 (8th Cir. 1996) (upholding 18 U.S.C. § 924(c)(1), which outlaws carrying a firearm "during ... any ... drug offense" on theory that federal drug statutes are constitutional under the commerce power so that § 924(c)(1), unlike the GFSZA, "is tied to interstate commerce").

77. *Compare* United States v. Gregg, 226 F.3d 253, 261—62 (3d Cir. 2000) (upholding Freedom of Access to Clinic Entrances Act largely because "intimidation of persons obtaining and providing reproductive health services ... is activity with an effect that is economic in nature" because of service-providing nature of abortion clinics; collecting extensive circuit court authority upholding the act based on similar reasoning), *cert. denied,* 532 U.S. 971 (2001), *with id.* at 270, 272 (Weis, J., dissenting) (arguing that earlier decisions give undue weight to congressional findings in light of *Morrison* and that "[t]he fact that criminal conduct may also have financial effects does not transform that activity into one commercial in nature").

with an intent to distribute?[78] And what if the intended means of drug distribution entails not a sale but a gift?[79]

Building on the economic/non-economic distinction, the Court recently interpreted the federal arson statute not to cover arson of an ordinary house (even if the homeowner has received natural gas, insurance and financing from out-of-state sources) notwithstanding prior decisions that applied the statute to the burning of business-conducting buildings.[80] Under the principle of this case, could Con-

78. *See, e.g.*, United States v. Kim, 94 F.3d 1247, 1250 (9th Cir. 1996) (sustaining conviction and implying that, unlike in *Lopez*, specific-intent *mens rea* requirement gives the possessory action an economic character); United States v. Lerebours, 87 F.3d 582, 584–85 (1st Cir. 1996). Not surprisingly, the courts have shown no hesitation about sustaining convictions for actually selling or conspiring to sell drugs. *See, e.g.*, United States v. Genao, 79 F.3d 1333, 1336–37 (2d Cir. 1996); United States v. Wacker, 72 F.3d 1453, 1475 & n.18 (10th Cir. 1995).

79. This hypothetical case starkly presents the question whether the Court in *Lopez* and *Morrison* meant to equate "economic activities" with *commercial* activities in the form of buying, selling, bartering, and transporting items as part of those transactions. Because "gifting" is not "economic activity" according to this pared-down definition, acceptance of that definition would result in treating gift making the same as gun possession for purposes of affecting-commerce analysis. Of course, acceptance of this definition would also remove other money-related activities (including theft) from the *Lopez/Morrison* "economic activity" tent. *See, e.g.*, Nelson, *supra* note 38, at 1227 (suggesting that federal anti-possession statute would be unconstitutional as applied to possessor who has intent to distribute by way of gift).

80. Jones v. United States, 529 U.S. 848, 857–58 (2000) (reasoning that houses, in contrast to commercial buildings, are not "used in" commerce, as required by statute, in part to avoid "grave and doubtful constitutional questions" that otherwise would arise because regulated area "was one of traditional state

gress constitutionally criminalize arson of a church on the theory that a place of worship is more akin to a place of business than to a place of residence?[81] If so, could Congress criminalize arson of, or even gun possession in, a school, or at least in schools operated as profit-making ventures?[82]

Because environmental laws may regulate non-commercial activities, they raise tricky questions under the *Lopez/Morrison* doctrine.[83] For example, the Endangered Species Act (ESA) prohibits the taking of certain species of animals, including

concern" and "neither the actors nor their conduct had a commercial character").

81. *Compare* United States v. Odom, 252 F.3d 1289 (11th Cir. 2001) (dismissing federal prosecution for church arson, even though congregation's leaders purchased bibles from outside the state, provided services to nonresident members, and sent money out of state for philanthropic purposes), *with* United States v. Rayborn, 312 F.3d 229 (6th Cir. 2002) (concluding that church arson was covered by statute where, among other things, the church engaged in radio broadcasts, including from and into neighboring states, and regularly collected donations from in-state and out-of-state members).

82. *See Lopez*, 514 U.S. at 629 (Breyer, J., dissenting) (asking: "Does it matter if the school is public or private, nonprofit or profit seeking? Does it matter if a city or State adopts a voucher plan that pays private firms to run a school?").

83. *Compare* Gibbs v. Babbitt, 214 F.3d 483, 506 (4th Cir. 2000) (upholding agency rule that bans taking red wolves, promulgated under Endangered Species Act, in part because "natural resource conservation is economic and commercial"), *with id.* at 507 (Luttig, J., dissenting) (asserting that "[t]he killing of even all 41 of the estimated red wolves that live on private property in North Carolina would not constitute an economic activity" and adding that, "even assuming that such is an economic activity, it certainly is not an activity that has a substantial effect on interstate commerce").

through the destruction of habitat. Destruction of wildlife habitats, however, may occur either for economic reasons (*e.g.*, to build a shopping center) or for non-economic reasons (*e.g.*, to enhance the aesthetic appearance of one's yard). Does it follow that, after *Lopez* and *Morrison*, ESA is constitutional only in its application to developers and others who engage in habitat-harming behavior as part of an investment-related endeavor?[84] An affirmative answer to this question would raise concerns about the underlying soundness of the economic/non-economic distinction. After all, whatever one's motive for habitat destruction, the harm to commerce (as well as the chain of causation that creates that harm) is exactly the same: The destruction of species threatens injury to the national economy through the disruption of ecosystems, the foreclosing of beneficial scientific discoveries, the removal of incentives for research, the reduction of tourism and the like. If Congress may seek to avoid these harms to national commerce on an affecting-commerce theory, there is reason to ask why it must do so in halfway fashion by regulating only those events that happen to spring from exchange-related behavior.[85]

84. *See* Choper, *supra* note 19, at 741.

85. *See id.* at 739. Professor Regan made much the same point when he wrote:

[I]t is easy to think up cases in which Congress's power to regulate noncommercial local behavior under the Commerce Clause should be obvious. Surely Congress can regulate private sport-hunting of migratory birds ... or backyard incinerators if they are found to emit some airborne toxic chemical that is

Application of the *Lopez/Morrison* rule to federal legislation that covers both economic and non-economic activity will present thorny issues in a variety of settings. In *Solid Waste Agency v. United States Army Corps of Engineers*,[86] for example, a landowner argued that *Lopez* and *Morrison* rendered invalid a federal rule that impeded the filling of small ponds frequented by migratory birds. The Court was able to skirt this constitutional challenge by declaring that the so-called Migratory Bird Rule exceeded the agency's statutorily delegated rule-making powers. What if, however, Congress responded to the *Solid Waste Agency* decision by enacting the Migratory Bird Rule as a federal statute so that the Commerce Clause question was starkly presented?

Writing for four members of the Court in a dissenting opinion, Justice Stevens considered the constitutional issue and found no commerce-power problem. Noting that "the discharge of fill material into the Nation's waters is almost always undertaken for economic reasons,"[87] Justice Stevens added:

> The fact that petitioner can conceive of some people who may discharge fill for non-economic reasons does not weaken the legitimacy of the Corps' jurisdictional claims. As we observed in

deposited hundreds of miles from the site of incineration.... Commerce Clause doctrine needs to be rethought, but we can rethink it better than this.

Regan, *supra* note 38, at 564.

86. 531 U.S. 159 (2001).

87. *Id.* at 193 (Stevens, J., dissenting).

> *Perez* . . ., "[w]here the *class of activities* is regulated and that class is within the reach of federal power, the courts have no power to excise, as trivial, individual instances of the class."[88]

Given the line drawn in *Lopez* and *Morrison*, it is not clear that a majority of Justices would permit federal authorities to regulate non-economically motivated pond-fillers based on this tail-of-the-dog reasoning. It is clear, however, that the constitutional case for universal application of the Migratory Bird Rule would weaken greatly if non-economic pond-filling constituted 20%, 40% or 60% of the activity the rule covered. In these circumstances, a court might go so far as to invalidate the rule *in toto* on the ground that its promulgators had improperly aggregated regulatable and non-regulatable behavior in finding the requisite "substantial effect."[89] Notably, even Alfonso Lopez had brought his firearm to school for economic purposes because he "was being paid for acting as a courier and delivering the gun to somebody else."[90] The economic character of Mr. Lopez's possessory activity, however, did not save his conviction under a statute that, on its face, assigned that fact no significance and applied almost entirely to non-economic instances of simple gun possession.

88. *Id.* at 194 n.15 (emphasis in original).

89. *See id.* at 173 (majority opinion) (expressing concern about upholding rule on commercial pond-filling rationale where rule applied generally to all "water areas used as habitat by migratory birds").

90. Regan, *supra* note 38, at 564.

Responding to these sorts of problems, lower courts have indicated that litigants might mount either facial or "as applied" challenges to federal laws said to offend the *Lopez/Morrison* principle.[91] In cases that arose prior to the Court's decision in *Jones v. United States*,[92] for example, lower courts intimated that application of the federal arson statute to the burning of non-commercial buildings would be constitutionally impermissible even though courts could continue to apply the statute to the torching of commercial structures.[93] Statutes such as this one, which seem to blend the regulation of economic and non-economic activities, bring into

91. *See generally* Denning & Reynolds, *supra* note 49, at 1262 & n.62 (citing successful "as applied" challenges).

92. 529 U.S. 848 (2000) (described *supra* note 80).

93. *See, e.g.*, United States v. Pappadopoulos, 64 F.3d 522 (9th Cir. 1995). For a kindred decision, see *United States v. Wang*, 222 F.3d 234, 238–39 (6th Cir. 2000) (sustaining as-applied challenge to Hobbs Act when used to prosecute robbery from individuals rather than "a business entity"). *See also* United States v. Faasse, 265 F.3d 475, 487 (6th Cir. 2001) (recognizing possibility of "as applied" challenge to law criminalizing nonpayment of child-support for nonresident child in "unlikely" case where custodial parent lives in same state as payor, though child does not). These cases illustrate the sort of judicial hairsplitting that courts sometimes must undertake in applying constitutional and statutory analysis in light of the "non-economic activity" test. *See, e.g.*, Nelson, *supra* note 38, at 1235–36 (urging that federal arson statute may be constitutionally applied if "the dwelling were rented" but not if it were "owner-occupied" unless the owner-occupied dwelling were insured); *see also id.* at 1231 (suggesting the Migratory Bird Rule would be constitutional as applied to commercial, but not noncommercial, fillings, and that municipality's use of pond for landfill purposes would qualify as commercial).

focus hard questions that have always lurked beneath the surface of the Court's aggregation doctrine. Three questions are of recurring importance. First, to what extent may Congress aggregate similar, but arguably distinguishable, forms of conduct in deciding whether a "substantial effect" on commerce is present?[94] Second, when may Congress enact statutes marked by "some measure of overinclusiveness for purposes of ensuring adequate enforceability" of rules that primarily target economic activity or other properly regulated behavior?[95] Third, what powers do courts possess to sever the invalid portion of a single statute enacted on an affecting-commerce rationale from other portions or applications of the statute that appear to be constitutionally unproblematic?[96] All these questions have a new urgency in light of the suggestion in *Lopez*

94. *See, e.g.*, Susan R. Klein, *Independent-Norm Federalism in Criminal Law*, 90 CAL. L. REV. 1541, 1590 (2002) (raising questions about whether medicinal marijuana growers and users may be aggregated with "the entire illegal-marijuana market" and whether that market may be aggregated with "the entire illicit-drug market"); John C. Nagle, *The Commerce Clause Meets the Delhi Sands Flower–Loving Fly*, 97 MICH. L. REV. 174, 196–97 (1998) (questioning whether Congress can protect all endangered plants and animals because their extinction, in the aggregate, threatens interstate commerce or whether Congress must aggregate on a species-by-species or some other basis).

95. Regan, *supra* note 38, at 568 (identifying possible argument for constitutionality of GFSZA on theory that (1) Congress may regulate near-school possession of guns that have moved in interstate commerce; (2) almost all guns have moved in interstate commerce; and (3) Congress therefore could pass GFSZA based on permissible-overinclusiveness theory).

96. *See, e.g.*, Nelson, *supra* note 38, at 1237 (arguing that Hobbs Act may not be constitutionally applied even to otherwise-properly-regulated thefts from business establishments because

and *Morrison* that Congress may not use its commerce power to regulate much, if not most, non-economic activity.

The Court in *Lopez* pointed to one situation in which Congress may continue to aggregate non-economic activities in exercising the affecting-commerce prong of its commerce power. In distinguishing the GFSZA from the regulatory scheme upheld in *Wickard v. Filburn,* the Court emphasized that Congress's treatment of home-grown wheat was "an essential part of a larger regulation of economic activity, in which the regulatory scheme could be undercut unless the intrastate activity were regulated."[97] These words about the *Filburn* case suggest

Congress must more carefully "identify the type of commercial activity or business being safeguarded" than it has in the present statute). *Compare* United States v. McCoy, 323 F.3d 1114 (9th Cir. 2003) (invalidating application of federal child pornography possession law where parent took pornographic photo of child for family photo album and thus "was not the typical offender feared by Congress"; eschewing argument that holding in effect required wholesale invalidation of statute), *with id.* at 1141 (Trott, J., dissenting) (reasoning that statute should be upheld, including as applied, because Congress could regulate subject matter of child-pornography industry and "the factual noncommercial nature of a single item of the commodity is immaterial"; worrying that upholding as-applied challenge logically requires invalidation of statute on its face). *Cf.* United States v. Ballinger, 312 F.3d 1264, 1274 (11th Cir. 2002) (refusing to apply federal church defacement statute to instance involving interstate travel to engage in that behavior because "[i]f Congress wants the statute to prohibit travel in the channels of interstate commerce to commit arson, then it must say so, just as it has done in [other] statutes").

97. *Lopez,* 514 U.S. at 561. *See also* United States v. Darby, 312 U.S. 100, 121 (1941) (recognizing congressional power over

that, even if growing wheat for on-farm consumption did not qualify as an economic activity, Congress could (as it did) properly regulate that activity as part of a comprehensive scheme for controlling the interstate movement of grain. In the wake of *Lopez*, lower courts have made creative use of this line of reasoning.

In *United States v. Rambo*,[98] for example, the court upheld a federal statute that outlawed (1) distributing machine guns and (2) possessing a machine gun so long as the defendant first obtained the gun following the distribution law's enactment. Noting that the law's "grandfather" provision effectively ensured that no person could illegally possess a machine gun unless he or she had been involved in its illegal distribution as a transferee, the court upheld the possession ban on the ground that it effectuated the prohibition on distribution.[99] It remains uncertain whether the Supreme Court will

"the regulation of intrastate transactions which are so commingled with or related to interstate commerce that all must be regulated if the interstate commerce is to be effectively controlled").

98. 74 F.3d 948 (9th Cir. 1996).

99. *Accord, e.g.*, United States v. Franklyn, 157 F.3d 90, 94 (2d Cir. 1998) (deeming possession ban "integral to a larger federal scheme for the regulation of trafficking in firearms"); United States v. Beuckelaere, 91 F.3d 781, 786 (6th Cir. 1996) (distinguishing *Lopez* largely on "essential part" grounds). *But see* United States v. Kirk, 105 F.3d 997, 1013–16 (5th Cir. 1997) (Jones, J., dissenting) (advocating invalidation of machine gun possession law and attacking "essential part" defense of it; distinguishing *Wickard* on the ground that it involved a federal effort to support the wheat market, while the machine-gun law seeks to "extirpate" a market).

broadly endorse, or endorse at all, this nouveau style of super-bootstrapping reasoning.[100] Doing so, however, would open the door to enactment of federal possessory crimes aimed not only at guns but also at drugs, bombs, burglary tools and other items traditionally controlled by state law.[101]

Lower courts have invoked the "essential part of a larger regulation" principle in a variety of contexts.[102] In *Gibbs v. Babbitt*,[103] for example, the

100. It is a "nouveau" style of "super-bootstrap reasoning" because it authorizes regulation of non-economic intrastate activity not to implement a ban on movements across state lines but to implement a ban on wholly *local* economic activities (here, in the form of machine gun sales) that are proscribed because, in the aggregate, they adversely affect interstate commerce. *See supra* notes 34–38; Chapters III & IV (discussing traditional "superbootstrapping" approach, based on the commerce-prohibiting technique).

101. Notably, the validation of this latter set of possession laws might not necessarily follow, even if the Court were to sustain the machine gun law. Burglary tools, for example, may be fabricated by their possessor from materials purchased in violation of no law that targets unlawful sales or distributions. In contrast, individuals almost never build their own machine guns, which thus must be obtained from another. It follows that machine guns (perhaps unlike burglary tools) bear an almost inevitable connection to the quintessentially commercial purchase-and-sale transaction.

102. *See, e.g.*, United States v. Cortes, 299 F.3d 1030, 1035 (9th Cir. 2002) (relying on "essential part" rationale in sustaining federal carjacking statute; reasoning that "[i]n addition to making carjacking a federal crime, the Act increased penalties for importing and exporting stolen cars; criminalized the operation of chop shops; provided federal funds for anti-car theft organizations; developed a national system for combating title fraud; and increased inspection at border checkpoints").

103. 214 F.3d 483 (4th Cir. 2000).

court upheld an agency ban on the hunting of 41 endangered red wolves in reliance on the "essential part" theory, reasoning that the ESA, pursuant to which the rule was promulgated, constitutes "a comprehensive and far-reaching piece of legislation that aims to conserve the health of our national environment."[104] In the spirit of *Wickard v. Filburn*, lower courts have likewise upheld federal prosecutions for growing marijuana, even if only "for personal use," reasoning that this application of the controlled substances statutes is an important part of a broad federal effort to control illicit drug trafficking across state and foreign borders.[105] These authorities reveal the potentially far-reaching scope of the "essential part" exception to the *Lopez/Morrison* "non-economic activity" rule. They also reveal something more—namely, that many lower court judges are disinclined to apply that rule expansively, at least absent a clearer signal from the Supreme Court that significant numbers of federal statutes now stand open to Commerce Clause attack.[106]

104. *Id.* at 497 (alternative holding).

105. United States v. Leshuk, 65 F.3d 1105, 1112 (4th Cir. 1995) (reasoning that "the intrastate activities regulated in the Drug Act are clearly tied to interstate commerce" and adding that "where a general regulatory statute bears a substantial relation to commerce, the *de minimis* character of individual instances arising under that statute is of no consequence").

106. *See generally* Denning & Reynolds, *supra* note 49, at 1256 (collecting "evidence from the lower courts' opinions that they are still reluctant to take *Lopez* seriously, even after *Morrison*'s clarifying opinion").

CHAPTER VI

FEDERALISM-BASED EXTERNAL CONSTRAINTS ON THE COMMERCE POWER

Lopez and *Morrison* recognize "internal" limits on the commerce power. Under the principle of those cases, because certain activities lack an adequate link to commercial affairs, they fall wholly outside Congress's enumerated power to regulate "Commerce ... among the several States." Other limits on the commerce power—derived from the Tenth Amendment, from postulates rooted in the Constitution's recognition of continuing state authority, or from both—are more aptly described as "external." Thus in *Hodel v. Virginia Surface Mining & Reclamation Association, Inc.,*[1] the Court observed that federal statutes that come "undoubtedly within the scope of the Commerce Clause" may nonetheless encounter a "constitutional barrier" rooted in principles of federalism.[2]

At least so far, the Court has applied constitutional restraints of this kind solely to federal laws that are "directed, not to private citizens, but to the

1. 452 U.S. 264 (1981).

2. *Id.* at 286 (quoting National League of Cities v. Usery, 426 U.S. 833, 841 (1976)).

States as States."[3] In *Coyle v. Oklahoma*,[4] for example, the Court confronted an effort by Congress to dictate the location of a state's capitol upon its admission to the union. In response, the Court declared that, whatever the otherwise-operative scope of Congress's Article I authority, "[t]he power to locate [a state's] own seat of government" fell within those "essentially and peculiarly state powers" beyond the reach of "an act of Congress."[5] The scope of the *Coyle* principle remains uncertain.[6] Indeed, intervening decisions have placed even its continuing efficacy in some (though probably not much) doubt.[7] There is no uncertainty, however,

3. *Id.* (quoting *National League of Cities*).

4. 221 U.S. 559 (1911).

5. *Id.* at 565. *See also id.* at 580 (adding that states are "endowed with all the functions essential to separate and independent existence").

6. May Congress, for example, require that state capitol buildings, along with other buildings, meet minimum design standards with respect to access for persons with disabilities or environmental safety? May Congress extend statutes related to the workplace—for example, mandatory retirement laws—to key state employees, such as governors, their principal advisors or state judges? *See* Gregory v. Ashcroft, 501 U.S. 452, 464 (1991) (noting that "the authority of the people of the States to determine the qualifications of their government officials may be inviolate" and thus a trump on the commerce power; interpreting federal age-discrimination act as inapplicable to state judges subject to mandatory retirement in part for this reason, so as to "avoid a potential constitutional problem").

7. *See* Garcia v. San Antonio Metropolitan Transit Authority, 469 U.S. 528, 556 (1985) (citing *Coyle* in noting that Court need not fully define "what affirmative limits the constitutional structure might impose on federal action" but also suggesting that such limits should relate to defects in the federal lawmaking

about the existence of three sets of external restraints on the commerce power that have been affirmatively recognized by the Supreme Court in the post–1985 time frame: (1) federalism-based constraints that emanate from defects in the operation

process). Uncertainty exists in part because (with the exception of *National League of Cities*, which was overruled in *Garcia* and is discussed immediately *infra*) the Court has consistently rejected *Coyle*-like challenges to federal enactments. *See, e.g.,* United States v. California, 297 U.S. 175 (1936) (rejecting constitutional challenge to application of the Federal Safety Appliance Act to state-owned railroad; reasoning in part that a "state can no more deny the [commerce] power if its exercise has been authorized by Congress than can an individual"); Oklahoma *ex rel.* Phillips v. Guy F. Atkinson Co., 313 U.S. 508, 534 (1941) (holding that "the fact that land is owned by a state is no barrier to its condemnation by the United States" including where "subsequent flooding of the land taken will obliterate [the state] boundary"); New York v. United States, 326 U.S. 572 (1946) (rejecting challenge to extension of generally applicable federal tax to state's sale of bottled water extracted from state-owned springs); Maryland v. Wirtz, 392 U.S. 183, 195–96 (1968) (citing Sanitary Dist. v. United States, 266 U.S. 405 (1925), as having "put to rest the contention that state concerns might constitutionally 'outweigh' the importance of an otherwise valid federal statute regulating commerce"). It is noteworthy, however, that in the *New York* bottled-water case two Justices found an impermissible interference with the state's "exercise of its power of sovereignty," 326 U.S. at 591 (Douglas, J., dissenting), and four others were "not prepared to say that ... an income tax laid upon citizens and States alike could be constitutionally applied to the State's capitol, its State-house, its public school houses, public parks, or its revenues from taxes or school lands." *Id.* at 587–88 (Stone, J., concurring). *See also* Fry v. United States, 421 U.S. 542, 547 n.7 (1975) (asserting that Tenth Amendment "declares the constitutional policy that Congress may not exercise power in a fashion that impairs the States' integrity or their ability to function effectively in a federal system" but concluding that federal wage controls nonetheless could be constitutionally applied to state employees).

of the national political process; (2) structural prohibitions on congressional commandeering of state legislative and executive officials to implement federal programs; and (3) restrictions on congressional authority to expose states to monetary remedies in private damages actions. In addition, the modern court has protected states against congressional overreaching by narrowly construing federal statutes that threaten to invade areas of traditional local control.

A. Garcia and the Defective–Process Principle

In *United States v. Darby*,[8] the Court left no doubt that trading money for labor was an activity subject to federal control under the commerce power. The Court also broadly declared that the "Tenth Amendment states but a truism" about the states' reservation of powers not delegated to Congress and thus added nothing to "the relationship between the national and state government as it had been established by the Constitution before the amendment."[9] In *National League of Cities v. Usery*,[10] however, the Court drew in part on the Tenth Amendment to hold that an external constraint on the commerce power blocked Congress from extending federal minimum wage protections to police

8. 312 U.S. 100 (1941) (discussed *supra* Chapter IV).

9. *Id.* at 123–24.

10. 426 U.S. 833 (1976).

officers, firefighters and other key employees of the states themselves.[11] The Court in *National League of Cities* articulated this limit in terms of prohibiting the enactment of federal laws that "directly displace the States' freedom to structure integral operations in areas of traditional governmental functions."[12] The Court, however, never again invalidated any law under the *National League of Cities* doctrine[13] and ultimately overruled that deci-

11. In reaching this conclusion, the Court overruled *Maryland v. Wirtz*, 392 U.S. 183 (1968), which had been handed down eight years earlier.

12. 426 U.S. at 852. In *Hodel v. Virginia Surface Mining & Reclamation Ass'n, Inc.*, 452 U.S. 264 (1981), the Court further refined the doctrine by declaring that it applied only when Congress (1) subjected "States as States" (as opposed to private parties), (2) to rules that "address matters that are indisputably 'attribute[s] of state sovereignty,'" and (3) did so in a way that "would directly impair their ability 'to structure integral operations in areas of traditional governmental functions.'" *Id.* at 287–88. The Court found no violation of this standard in part because the challenged federal requirement for strip-mining targeted private, rather than public, mine operators.

13. *See* EEOC v. Wyoming, 460 U.S. 226 (1983) (upholding federal age-discrimination ban as applied to state employees; distinguishing *National League of Cities* on the grounds that (1) the Fair Labor Standards Act—unlike the age-discrimination law—disrupted state budgeting by imposing direct financial burdens on states, and (2) application of the age-discrimination law threatened non-financial interests only modestly because states remained free to pursue goals of mandatory retirement rules through individualized assessments of employees' continuing fitness to do their jobs); FERC v. Mississippi, 456 U.S. 742 (1982) (rejecting challenge to federal law that required state agencies, if in place, to consider adoption of federal approaches to electric-utility regulation and ratemaking; reasoning that law did not mandate state adoption of federal rules and that process was less intrusive than outright preemption of state laws); United

sion outright in *Garcia v. San Antonio Metropolitan Transit Authority*.[14]

In scuttling the *National League of Cities* rule, the five-Justice majority in *Garcia* first claimed that intervening cases had proven the "integral operations" test to be judicially unworkable. The Court also faulted the principle as more destructive than protective of federalism values because it forced an "unelected federal judiciary" to rank the centrality of state programmatic choices.[15] Most important, the Court found that the state-autonomy values the *National League of Cities* rule sought to foster were already adequately safeguarded by the Constitution's structuring of the federal government. Articles I and II, for example, vest state officials with extensive control over the qualifications for voters in federal elections and give state legislatures exclusive authority over the manner of selecting presidential electors. In addition, the Constitution accords the nation's geographic sub-units a particularly "direct influence in the Senate, where each State received equal representation."[16] These and other state-protective features woven into the fabric of the federal government negated, in the majority's view, any need for a strong *judicial* role in guarding against unwarranted congres-

Transp. Union v. Long Island R.R. Co., 455 U.S. 678 (1982) (upholding application of federal labor regulations to state-owned railroad).

14. 469 U.S. 528 (1985).

15. *Id.* at 546.

16. *Id.* at 551.

sional intrusions on state autonomy. Put simply, *Garcia*'s five-Justice majority concluded that the Court in *National League of Cities* had "underestimated ... the solicitude of the national political process for the continued vitality of the States" because that "political process ensures that laws that unduly burden the States will not be promulgated."[17]

The Court, however, did not go so far in *Garcia* as to say that no federalism-based external limits inhibit Congress's ability to invoke the commerce power. Instead, building on the underlying rationale of its decision, the Court indicated that any judicial role in checking congressional exercises of the commerce power would have to be "tailored to compensate for possible failings in the national political process."[18] The Court has considered application of a process-centered external restraint on congressional power on only one occasion. In *South Carolina v. Baker*,[19] the Court faced a state challenge to a federal statute that removed tax-exempt status for income from "bearer bonds" (as opposed to more readily traceable "registered bonds") issued by state and local governments. In rejecting the state's argument for invalidation of this law, Justice Brennan wrote for a six-Justice majority:

> South Carolina has not even alleged that it was deprived of any right to participate in the national political process or that it was singled out in a

17. *Id.* at 556–57.

18. *Id.* at 554.

19. 485 U.S. 505 (1988).

way that left it politically isolated and powerless. Rather, South Carolina argues that the political process failed here because [the law] was 'imposed by a vote of an uninformed Congress relying upon incomplete information.' But nothing in *Garcia* or the Tenth Amendment authorizes courts to second-guess the substantive basis for congressional legislation. Where, as here, the national political *process* did not operate in a defective manner, the Tenth Amendment is not implicated.[20]

If not in *Baker*, when might *Garcia*'s defective-political-process restraint result in invalidation of a federal law that disfavors some or all of the states? Close on the heels of *Garcia*, one commentator suggested that its principle might preclude at least strong forms of congressional regulation of educational practices in light of the robust tradition of local democratic control over American schools.[21] This position, however, seems hard to square with the Court's strict focus on *procedural* defects in the federal lawmaking process in its later ruling in *Baker*.[22] A more plausible case for invoking the

20. *Id.* at 512–13 (citations omitted).

21. Andrzej Rapaczynski, *From Sovereignty to Process: The Jurisprudence of Federalism After* Garcia, 1985 Sup. Ct. Rev. 341, 416.

22. *See also Garcia*, 469 U.S. at 554 (indicating aversion to recognizing any "sacred province of state autonomy"). Of course, the principle of the *Lopez* case may now independently preclude federal regulation of many aspects of local education, particularly given the majority's unwillingness in that case to embrace Justice Breyer's characterization of school operations as an economic activity. *See supra* Chapter V. For present purposes, however,

Garcia/Baker process-curative rule might arise if "a traditionally favored group of states puts in place a procedural structure that ensures their favored position will persist" in a particular area of federal lawmaking, such as highway funding.[23] But such an abuse is hard to imagine, and none has yet come to the Court's attention. The practical reality is that the "political process" restraint considered in *Baker* will seldom, if ever, result in invalidation of federal statutes. Four years after *Baker*, however, the Court concluded in *New York v. United States*[24] that another external limit on congressional power survived *Garcia* and required invalidation of an important piece of commerce-power legislation.

B. New York, Printz and the Anti–Commandeering Principle

In *New York*, the Court confronted a complex piece of federal legislation designed to deal with the proliferating problem of radioactive waste. The portion of the statute that most troubled the Court— the so-called "take title" provision—gave each state an option concerning the handling of low-level ra-

it is critical to distinguish between the *Garcia/Baker* process-centered restriction, which focuses (at least in general) on congressional regulation of states themselves, and the *Lopez* limit on congressional authority to regulate either state or private activity of a noneconomic nature.

23. Dan T. Coenen, *A Constitution of Collaboration: Protecting Fundamental Values with Second–Look Rules of Interbranch Dialogue,* 42 WM. & MARY L. REV. 1575, 1696 (2001).

24. 505 U.S. 144 (1992).

dioactive waste generated within its borders if no sound local-waste disposal mechanism existed. The state could either (1) take possession of that waste or (2) become liable for all damages the waste might cause to waste generators because of the state's failure to do so.[25] In addressing the constitutionality of this statute, a six-Justice majority first embraced a fundamental federalism-based limit on congressional legislative authority. Congress, the Court declared, may not "commandee[r] the legislative processes of the States by directly compelling them to enact and enforce a federal regulatory program."[26] The Court then proceeded to explain why either choice afforded to states by the take-title provision amounted to an impermissible commandeering. The problem was that both the forced taking of possession and the forced provision of compensation amounted "in principle" to "a congressionally compelled subsidy from state governments to radioactive waste producers."[27] And because a "choice between two unconstitutionally coercive regulatory techniques [was] no choice at all," the take-title provision ran afoul of the anti-commandeering doctrine.[28]

The Court devoted the lion's share of its opinion in *New York* to showing why the anti-commandeering principle was mandated by constitutional history, bolstered by sound policy, and not foreclosed by

25. *Id*. at 154–55.

26. *Id*. at 161 (quoting *Hodel*, 452 U.S. at 288).

27. *Id*.

28. *Id*. at 176.

Supreme Court precedent. With regard to history, the Court pointed to Hamilton's *Federalist No. 15* and other sources in concluding that the Framers made a fundamental choice to create a federal government that would "exercise its legislative authority directly upon individuals, without employing the States as intermediaries."[29] With regard to policy, the Court worried that federal compulsion of state legislation would inevitably lead to unwelcome voter confusion. With regard to the take-title statute, for example, "it may be [that] state officials [who must enact the regulatory program] will bear the brunt of public disapproval, while the federal officials who devised the regulatory program ... remain insulated from the electoral ramifications of their decision."[30] The anti-commandeering principle, the Court continued, would ensure that the choices of government authorities remained "in full view of the public," thus allowing the proper set of decisionmakers to "suffer the consequences if the decision turns out to be detrimental or unpopular."[31]

29. *Id.* at 163–64.

30. *Id.* at 169.

31. *Id.* at 168. The Court also noted that accountability concerns operated even in a case such as this one where state governments had fully supported the federal legislation. In particular, the Court noted that it would almost always be in the interest of both federal and state lawmakers to seek to evade responsibility for siting radioactive "waste" disposal facilities because of voters' "not in my backyard" objections. The take-title provision might well, albeit unwisely, achieve this political objective by blurring the source of responsibility for governmental decisions about waste disposal. Keeping political officials properly "accountable to the voters" supported a system in which both (1) federal legislators could not evade responsibility

With regard to precedent, the Court's earlier decisions in both *Garcia* and *Testa v. Katt*[32] were not controlling here. *Garcia* was distinguishable as "a case in which Congress ... subjected a State to the same legislation applicable to private parties" because FLSA applied to both public and private employers.[33] Here, in contrast, the take-title law failed to qualify as a "generally applicable" law because it imposed duties only on state governments. In *Testa*, the Court had held that Congress may require state *judicial* officials to apply federal law. In the Court's view, however, the take-title provision's imposition of duties on state legislatures differed markedly from the imposition of duties on state courts, particularly because the Supremacy Clause specifically (and distinctively) declares that "Judges in every State shall be bound" by "the Laws of the United States."[34]

Finally, the Court emphasized that its ruling would not unduly frustrate efforts by Congress to achieve its aims, including by way of programs that involve state participation. To begin with, Congress remained free to regulate radioactive waste producers directly and to preempt disfavored state rules in that process.[35] No less important, Congress could

by forcing state legislators to adopt a genuinely federal regulatory scheme and (2) state legislators could not evade responsibility for a program they supported by seeking cover in a congressional mandate that they act. *Id.* at 182–83.

32. 330 U.S. 386 (1947).

33. *New York*, 505 U.S. at 160.

34. U.S. Const. art. VI, § 2, cl. 2.

35. *New York*, 505 U.S. at 178.

encourage adoption of congressionally favored regulatory programs by the states in either of two ways. First, it could occupy a field with its own regulatory program unless and until the state legislature passed a state law (such as the take-title provision) that Congress wanted on the books.[36] Second, Congress could encourage state adoption of congressionally favored regulations by conditioning state entitlements to federal funds on the state's taking of such action.[37] In the Court's eyes, congressional use of either "conditional preemption" or "conditional spending" programs differed in a fundamental way from an outright federal mandate like the one at issue in *New York*. As Justice O'Connor explained for the Court: "Where Congress encourages state regulation rather than compelling it, state governments remain responsive to the local electorate's preferences," and as long as the "choice remains ... with the residents of the State," the vice of commandeering is not present.[38]

New York v. United States held that Congress could not force state lawmakers to legislate, while *Testa v. Katt* held that Congress could force state courts to adjudicate cases and to apply federal law. These decisions thus left behind a basic and still unresolved question: Could Congress compel state authorities to *execute* federal statutory mandates? The Court answered this question in *Printz v. Unit-*

36. *Id*. at 167–68.

37. *Id*. at 167.

38. *Id*. at 168, 174.

ed States,[39] which concerned the constitutionality of a controversial provision of the Brady Handgun Violence Prevention Act. That provision required handgun dealers to give to a local law enforcement officer (an agent of the state, rather than the federal, government) advance notice of any handgun transfer that included the name of the proposed transferee. The local law enforcement officer then had to "make a reasonable effort" to determine whether the transfer would be lawful, including through "research in whatever State and local recordkeeping systems are available and in a national system designated by the Attorney General."[40] In light of Congress's imposition of this duty, the Court had little difficulty concluding that the Act entailed federal commandeering of state authorities because it "pressed into federal service" local law enforcement officers by "compelling [them] to execute federal laws."[41] It took 81 pages of the *United States Reports*, however, to sort through the majority's and the dissenters' conflicting arguments about whether such a mandate directed at executive, rather than legislative, officials offended the Constitution.

The majority acknowledged that "there was no constitutional text speaking to this precise question," so that "the answer ... must be sought in

39. 521 U.S. 898 (1997).

40. The Act imposed further obligations on local law enforcement officers if they chose to share with handgun dealers the results of the required investigation.

41. *Printz*, 521 U.S. at 905–06.

historical understanding and practice, in the structure of the Constitution, and in the jurisprudence of this Court."[42] As to historical understanding, the majority was impressed with "an absence of executive-commandeering statutes in the early Congresses [and] in our later history as well, at least until very recent years."[43] As to the structure of the Constitution, the majority emphasized two points. First, upholding such laws would profoundly threaten state-autonomy values by permitting Congress "to impress into its service—and at no cost to itself—the police officers of the 50 States."[44] Second, the challenged statute ran counter to the Constitution's directive that the *President*—not local law enforcement officers—"shall take Care that the Laws be faithfully executed."[45] Finally, with respect to past authority, the Court reasoned that *New York v. United States* all but disposed of the *Printz* case. In particular, the majority found that *New York*'s voter-accountability rationale logically extended to the commandeering of state executive officials:

> By forcing state governments to absorb the financial burden of implementing a federal regulatory program, Members of Congress can take credit for 'solving' problems without having to ask their constituents to pay for the solutions with higher federal taxes. And even when the States are not

42. *Id.* at 905.

43. *Id.* at 916.

44. *Id.* at 922.

45. *Id.* (quoting U.S. CONST. art. II, § 3).

forced to absorb the costs of implementing a federal program, they are still put in the position of taking the blame for its burdensomeness and for its defects.[46]

The dissenters sought to counter these arguments by pointing to Hamilton's statement in *Federalist No. 27* that the federal government could "employ" the states "in the execution of its laws" as well as assertions made by Madison and others in the ratifying conventions that state officials would collect federal taxes.[47] In the dissenters' view, the majority's reliance on a dearth of prior similar enactments proved too much because it would "undermine most of our post-New Deal Commerce Clause jurisprudence," which had sustained many federal laws that likewise lacked parallels in early enactments of Congress.[48] The dissenters expressed concern that the Court's ruling would endanger, rather than promote, state autonomy values by generating incentives for the federal government to "create vast

46. *Id.* at 930.

47. *Id.* at 945 (quoting THE FEDERALIST NO. 27 (Alexander Hamilton)). The dissenters added that: "The Court's response to this powerful evidence is weak. The majority suggests that 'none of these statements necessarily implies [that] Congress could impose these responsibilities without the consent of the States.' ... No fair reading of these materials can justify such an interpretation." *Id.* at 947 (Stevens, J., dissenting). In a history-based critique that might well also apply to the *New York* ruling, the dissenters added that it made little sense to devise state-rights limits on congressional power that apparently did not operate under even the state-favoring Articles of Confederation. *See id.* at 945–46 (Stevens, J., dissenting).

48. *Id.* at 949 (Stevens, J., dissenting).

national bureaucracies to implement its policies" with no state participation whatsoever.[49] Finally, the dissenters in *Printz*—like the dissenters in *New York*—faulted the majority for ignoring *Garcia*'s admonition that state-autonomy interests were adequately protected by the state-protective architecture of federal political institutions.[50] By 1997, however, arguments based on *Garcia* were carrying little water with the five-Justice majority that, two years earlier, had handed down *Lopez*.

How far does the external constraint recognized in the *Printz* case reach? The majority noted that it was not passing on federal statutes that "require only the provision of information to the Federal Government,"[51] and Justice O'Connor took pains to stress this point in a separate concurrence. The Court, she emphasized, was not ruling on the constitutionality of "purely ministerial reporting requirements imposed by Congress on state and local authorities,"[52] including requirements that "state and local law enforcement agencies [identify] cases of missing children to the Department of Justice."[53] In dissent, Justice Stevens wondered why collecting

49. *Id.* at 959 (Stevens, J., dissenting). The dissenters added that, in their view, the majority's accountability logic was shaky because state officials forced to implement bad federal policy would be certain to proclaim "to their constituents where the source of the misfortune lies." *Id.* at 958 n.18 (Stevens, J., dissenting).

50. *See id.* at 957 (Stevens, J., dissenting).

51. *Id.* at 918.

52. *Id.* at 936 (O'Connor, J., concurring).

53. *Id.*

information (as required by the Brady Act) was less "ministerial" than reporting information (as required by the federal missing-children law).[54] Although Justice O'Connor did not focus on the point, she seemed prepared to say that a simple reporting requirement falls outside *New York/Prince* prohibition on compelling states to "*enforce* a federal *regulatory* program." After all, a reporting requirement does not require any interaction of any kind with citizens outside the law enforcement community.[55]

Another question concerning *Printz* surfaced in *Reno v. Condon*,[56] which involved a federal law that restricted sales by the states of personal data collected in automobile license applications. This law, Chief Justice Rehnquist concluded, did not run afoul of the *Printz* prohibition, but instead was akin to the federal government's withdrawal of tax-exempt status for state-issued bearer bonds, which had been sustained by the Court in *South Carolina v. Baker*.[57] In *Condon* (as in *Baker*), the challenged law "regulate[d] state activities" and did not (as in *Printz*) "control or influence the manner in which *States regulate private parties*."[58] Nor was the law in *Condon* objectionable on the proposed alternative ground that Congress goes too far whenever "it

54. *Id*. at 955 (Stevens, J., dissenting).

55. *New York*, 505 U.S. at 161 (emphasis added).

56. 528 U.S. 141 (2000).

57. *See supra* notes 18–20 and accompanying text.

58. *Id*. (quoting South Carolina v. Baker, 485 U.S. 505, 514–15 (1988) (emphasis added)).

regulates the States exclusively."[59] To this argument Chief Justice Rehnquist responded:

The essence of South Carolina's argument is that Congress may regulate the States only by means of "generally applicable" laws, or laws that apply to individuals as well as States. But we need not address the question whether general applicability is a constitutional requirement for federal regulation of the States, because the [statute] is generally applicable. [It] regulates the universe of entities that participate as suppliers to the market for motor vehicle information—the States as initial suppliers of the information in interstate commerce and private resellers or redisclosers of that information in commerce.[60]

Another question that arose in the wake of *Printz* concerned whether Congress may force state officials to follow federal requirements in registering voters under the so-called Motor Voter Law. The Supreme Court has not considered this question, but lower courts have said "yes" because these cases do not involve the commerce power but instead concern Article I, § 4, which specifically permits Congress to override state laws concerning the "Time, Places and Manner of holding Elections for Senators and Representatives."[61] Emphasizing that

59. *Id.* at 151.

60. *Id.*

61. U.S. CONST. art. I, § 4, cl. 1. *See, e.g.,* Voting Rights Coalition v. Wilson, 60 F.3d 1411 (9th Cir. 1995); Association of Cmty. Org. for Reform Now (ACORN) v. Edgar, 56 F.3d 791 (7th Cir. 1995).

the Constitution gives state officials primary authority to oversee federal elections, these courts have reasoned that a federal power to control "the Manner" of those elections necessarily carries with it the authority to establish regulatory laws with which state officials must comply.[62]

The Motor Voter Law cases provide a powerful reminder of a basic point: External limits on congressional authority may vary in their effects from one enumerated congressional power to another. In no context is this principle more in evidence than in the set of cases to which we now turn—cases that involve congressional attempts to abrogate constitutionally grounded state immunities from judicial process.

C. Seminole Tribe, Alden and the Anti–Liability Principle

The Eleventh Amendment provides that: "The judicial power of the United States shall not be construed to extend to any [suit] commenced or prosecuted against the United States by citizens of another State, or by citizens or subjects of any Foreign State."[63] The terms of the Eleventh Amendment suggest a circumscribed reach. In par-

---

62. As Chief Judge Posner observed, the distinctive terms of the Time, Place and Manner Clause give federal authorities "the whip hand" because, under it, "Congress can ... regulate federal elections *and* force the state to bear the expense of the regulation." *ACORN*, 56 F.3d at 795 (emphasis in original).

63. U.S. Const. amend. XI.

ticular, the Amendment's text places no limit whatsoever on the most common sort of action against state governments—namely, suits in which citizens assert claims against their own states for constitutional or statutory violations. In *Hans v. Louisiana*,[64] however, the Court declared that the immunity recognized in the Eleventh Amendment extends to federal actions prosecuted against a state by its own citizens, and not only to suits brought by "Citizens of Another State ... or any Foreign State."[65] On the other hand, the Court has recognized three important limitations on the Eleventh Amendment immunity. First, in *Ex Parte Young*,[66] the Court permitted courts to hear claims to enjoin unlawful state practices (as opposed to seeking a monetary recovery) as long as the plaintiff brings suit against the responsible state official rather than the state itself. Second, the Court has held that the Eleventh Amendment does not bar actions prosecuted against a state by either another state[67] or by the federal government.[68] Third,

64. 134 U.S. 1 (1890).

65. The Court has also declared that, notwithstanding these seemingly restrictive terms, the immunity from suit extends not only to suits brought by "Citizens of ... any Foreign State," but also to suits brought by foreign states themselves. *See, e.g.*, Principality of Monaco v. Mississippi, 292 U.S. 313, 330–31 (1934).

66. 209 U.S. 123 (1908).

67. *E.g.*, South Dakota v. North Carolina, 192 U.S. 286, 315–21 (1904).

68. *E.g.*, United States v. Mississippi, 380 U.S. 128, 140–41 (1965). *See generally Principality of Monaco*, 292 U.S. at 330 (reasoning that a "waiver or consent, on the part of a State,

the Court has long insisted that the Eleventh Amendment has no application to actions for either injunctive relief or money damages brought against cities or city-like sub-units of the states.[69] Notwithstanding these limitations, *Hans* and other cases indicated that state governments themselves—at least in the absence of a clearly contrary action by Congress[70]—could invoke a sweeping immunity from federal-court money-damage actions brought against them by individual plaintiffs.

In the 1960s, Congress began to increase dramatically its regulatory role in fields such as civil rights, health care and environmental protection. As it did so, many new federal private rights of action for monetary relief found their way into the United States Code.[71] In general, these enactments raised no serious constitutional questions with regard to

which inheres in the acceptance of the constitutional plan, runs to the other States who have likewise accepted that plan, and to the United States as the sovereign which the Constitution creates").

69. *E.g.,* Mt. Healthy City Sch. Dist. Bd. of Educ. v. Doyle, 429 U.S. 274 (1977); Lincoln County v. Luning, 133 U.S. 529 (1890); Osborn v. Bank of U.S., 22 U.S. (9 Wheat.) 738 (1824).

70. *See* Atascadero State Hosp. v. Scanlon, 473 U.S. 234, 242–43 (1985) (holding that abrogation, even if permissible, requires that "Congress express this intention in the statutory language," thus making its decision to abrogate "unmistakably clear").

71. In addition, Congress extended a number of private rights of action, previously available against private firms and citizens to states and localities as well. Of particular significance, as the ensuing discussion will show, was Congress's extension of the Fair Labor Standards Act to many public employers in 1966. *See* Maryland v. Wirtz, 392 U.S. 183, 186–87 (1968).

federal power, in light of the Court's sweeping post-New Deal jurisprudence, because they focused their attention on private businesses and individuals. A large question existed, however, about whether Congress could subject *the states themselves* to a burgeoning array of federal private damage remedies notwithstanding their otherwise-operative Eleventh Amendment immunity.

A critical encounter with this question came in *Fitzpatrick v. Bitzer*,[72] which concerned a state claim of immunity in an action for money damages based on sex discrimination in violation of the Civil Rights Act of 1964. The Court upheld the congressional abrogation in this setting, emphasizing that the extension of the 1964 Act to the states reflected a proper exercise of the specialized Fourteenth Amendment power to "enforce by appropriate legislation" the guaranty of "equal protection of the laws."[73] In reaching this conclusion, the Court emphasized that the Framers of the Fourteenth Amendment, which postdated the Eleventh Amendment by seven decades, had effected a critical "shift in the federal-state balance" by placing important new "limitations on state authority."[74] The Fourteenth Amendment enforcement power, however, could not provide a constitutional basis for the great mass of federal legislation that concerned matters such as the environment, bankruptcy, patents, copyrights and unionizing efforts. A critical

72. 427 U.S. 445 (1976).

73. *Id.* at 453.

74. *Id.* at 455–56.

commerce-power question was thus squarely posed: Could Congress abrogate the states' Eleventh Amendment immunity pursuant to otherwise proper exercises of its Article I powers, including its authority to regulate interstate commerce?

In 1989, a Court not yet occupied by Justice Thomas said "yes."[75] A plurality of the Court asserted, among other things, that the Eleventh Amendment dictated only that the judicial power should not be "construed"—that is, interpreted by judges—to remove the states' immunity from suit. As a result, the plurality reasoned, the Amendment did not inhibit *congressional* action, otherwise proper under the commerce power, that exposed states to monetary remedies.[76] In 1996, however, the same five Justices who had come together a year earlier in *Lopez* (and who would again come together a year later in *Printz)* proclaimed in *Seminole Tribe v. Florida*[77] that the answer was "no." And, three

75. Pennsylvania v. Union Gas Co., 491 U.S. 1 (1989) (upholding money-damage action against state defendant unambiguously authorized by the Superfund Amendments to Comprehensive Environmental Response, Compensation, and Liability Act of 1980).

76. *Id.* at 18 (quoting U.S. CONST. amend. XI) (emphasis deleted). The opinion setting forth this default-rule approach was written by Justice Brennan, who was joined by Justices Marshall, Blackmun and Stevens. Justice White wrote separately to say, without further explanation, that "I agree with the conclusion reached by JUSTICE BRENNAN ... that Congress has the authority under Article I to abrogate the Eleventh Amendment immunity of the States, although I do not agree with much of his reasoning." *Id.* at 57 (White, J., concurring and dissenting).

77. 517 U.S. 44 (1996).

years later, in *Alden v. Maine*,[78] these same five Justices extended the state-protective principle of *Seminole Tribe* in a way that gave states sweeping substantive, and not just forum-selection, protections.

Claiming a violation of the Fair Labor Standards Act (FLSA), John H. Alden initially sued his employer, the state of Maine, in federal court. After *Seminole Tribe* was decided (and the district court properly invoked that case to dismiss the suit), Mr. Alden refiled his action in state court. Mr. Alden's argument for permitting this suit to go forward proceeded in three easy steps: (1) the Eleventh Amendment by its terms limits only the "Judicial power of the United States"; (2) *Testa v. Katt* had held that Congress could force state courts to hear federal claims;[79] and (3) *Garcia* left no doubt that the FLSA fully applied to state employers.[80] Unmoved by this chain of logic, however, the majority in *Alden* held that the *Seminole Tribe* immunity carried over to state-court litigation even in the face of a crystal clear congressional effort to render it inoperative in that context.

The Court defended its ruling with an extended argument based on "structural" reasoning and "the Tenth Amendment."[81] At the decision's heart, however, lay concerns about anomalous results. Justice Kennedy, writing for the majority, could not believe

78. 527 U.S. 706 (1999).

79. *See supra* notes 32–34 and accompanying text.

80. *See supra* notes 8–17 and accompanying text.

81. *Alden* 527 U.S. at 731–33.

that the Constitution permits "the National Government [to] wield greater power in the state courts than in its own judicial instrumentalities,"[82] and he recoiled at the thought that Congress could "turn the State against itself."[83] Justice Kennedy closed his opinion by emphasizing that the Court's decision did not render meaningless Congress's extension of FLSA to the states. After all, he explained, individual victims could still seek injunctions under *Ex Parte Young*; the United States remained able to sue both public and private FLSA violators; and the "good faith of the States" provided an additional "important assurance" that FLSA violations—even though not remediable in private damages actions—would not occur.[84] The dissenters were unimpressed by these efforts to downplay the impact of the *Alden* decision. In their view, the five Justices in the majority had not only wreaked havoc with the text of the Eleventh Amendment but had adopted an approach that "comes perilously close to legitimizing political defiance of valid federal law."[85]

The Court's ruling in *Alden*—together with its acknowledgment that the state-sovereign-immunity principle does not restrict actions brought by the United States—has left behind some vexing questions. Does the suit-by-the-United–States exception to the Eleventh Amendment permit the pursuit of "*qui tam*" damages actions, brought by private

82. *Id.* at 752.

83. *Id.* at 749.

84. *Id.* at 755.

85. *Id.* at 803 n.36 (Souter, J., dissenting).

parties in the name of the United States, for injuries inflicted by state officials on the national government?[86] Does that same exception mean (as *Alden* seems to say) that Congress may authorize suits by the United States to recover compensatory damages for the benefit of individuals injured by state statutory violations, including under FLSA? And if Congress may allow such suits, may it broadly deputize private parties' lawyers to pursue such actions on behalf of the federal government?[87]

Whatever the answers to these questions, the practical impact of *Seminole Tribe* and *Alden* has been profound, and to understand why it is useful to compare the effects wrought by these rulings with the effect of the rule of *National League of Cities* repudiated by the Court in *Garcia*. To be sure, in some important respects, the *Seminole Tribe/Alden* principle does not afford states as much protection as did the *National League of Cities* rule. In particular, employees who were altogether divested of FLSA's protections in *National League of*

86. *Compare* Vermont Agency of Natural Res. v. United States *ex rel.* Stevens, 529 U.S. 765, 787 (2000) (declining to reach question in light of statutory ruling but expressing " 'serious constitutional doubt' on that score"), *with id.* at 802 (Souter, J., dissenting) (arguing that "even if one accepts *Seminole Tribe* as controlling, the State's immunity claim would fail" in part because the *qui tam* plaintiff "is, in effect, suing as an assignee of the United States").

87. *See id.* at 802 (Souter, J., dissenting) (relying in part on fact that "the Attorney General retains significant control over a relator's action" in finding no Eleventh Amendment problem with *qui tam* actions prosecuted by private parties on behalf of the United States).

Cities because they engaged in "integral" government activities may still under current law (1) obtain injunctions for FLSA violations under the doctrine of *Ex Parte Young*[88] and (2) sue under FLSA even for monetary remedies if they work for a city, rather than the state itself.[89] On the other hand, the protections afforded by the *Seminole Tribe/Alden* immunity are in two ways much broader than the protections afforded to the states by the *National League of Cities* rule. First, *Seminole Tribe* and *Alden* shelter states not only from actions under FLSA but from the duty to pay damages for any injury—based on discrimination, pollution, patent infringement, workplace safety conditions or whatever—made actionable by Congress pursuant to its Article I powers.[90] Second, even with respect

88. *See supra* note 66 and accompanying text (discussing *Ex Parte Young* principle).

89. *See supra* note 67 and accompany text (noting principle of *Mt. Healthy* and related cases).

90. *See, e.g.,* Florida Prepaid Postsecondary Educ. Expense Bd. v. College Sav. Bank, 527 U.S. 627, 635–36 (1999) (patent infringement). This effect of *Seminole Tribe* and *Alden* follows in part from the Court's recent overruling of *Parden v. Terminal Railway Co. of Alabama State Docks Department*, 377 U.S. 184 (1964), which had recognized that states might at least sometimes "constructively" waive the Eleventh Amendment immunity when they enter a "field traditionally occupied by private persons." College Sav. Bank v. Florida Prepaid Postsecondary Educ. Expense Bd., 527 U.S. 666, 680 (1999) (overruling *Parden* and dismissing suit for alleged trademark infringement brought against state agency). Notably, Justice Blackmun also made it clear in his critical concurrence in *National League of Cities* that the rule of that case would not preclude actions against states for environmental harms. National League of Cities v. Usery, 426 U.S. 833, 856 (1976) (Blackmun, J., concurring). The *Seminole*

to FLSA, the principle of *Seminole Tribe* and *Alden* forecloses suit by each and every state employee, not only those workers engaged in the state's "integral operations."[91] No gauge exists for assessing whether, on balance, the sovereign-immunity rule of *Seminole Tribe* and *Alden* affords more protection to states than did the regulatory-immunity rule of *National League of Cities*. Plainly, however, these sovereign immunity cases—which at first blush might seem to have had only an esoteric jurisdictional quality—move far in that direction.

In the wake of *Seminole Tribe* and *Alden,* plaintiffs' lawyers quickly turned their attention to finding ways to sidestep the outcome-determinative effect of those rulings. Their main hope lay in arguing that congressional abrogations of state sovereign immunity, even if not sustainable under the Commerce Clause, qualified as proper exercises of the Fourteenth Amendment enforcement power. At least with regard to anti-discrimination laws, this theory held much promise in light of the Court's prior validation of Title VII sex-discrimination claims in *Fitzpatrick v. Bitzer*.[92] Moreover, in *Nevada Dep't of Human Resources v. Hibbs*,[93] the Court in fact drew on *Bitzer* to uphold Congress's extension to state employees of the private-damages rem-

Tribe/Alden immunity, however, plainly does preclude damages actions against states for violations of federal environmental-protection laws.

91. *Nat'l League of Cities*, 426 U.S. at 852.

92. *See supra* notes 72–74 and accompanying text (discussing Court's ruling in *Fitzpatrick v. Bitzer*).

93. 123 S.Ct. 1972 (2003).

edies created to guard against gender-based discrimination by the Family and Medical Leave Act.[94] In two other post-*Alden* cases, however, the same five Justices who formed the majorities in *Seminole Tribe* and *Alden* joined together in rejecting congressional attempts to rely on Section 5 to abrogate state immunity in actions for discrimination based on disability and age.[95] Of particular note was the Court's ruling in *Kimel v. Florida Board of Regents*[96] that Section 5 did not support Congress's

94. The Court reasoned that state-based sex discrimination was subject to heightened scrutiny under the Equal Protection Clause of Section 1 of the Fourteenth Amendment and that Congress, in applying the Act to the states, had properly wielded its Section 5 power to address the unconstitutional stereotyping of women as better suited than men for domestic caretaking.

95. *E.g.*, Board of Trustees of the Univ. of Ala. v. Garrett, 531 U.S. 356 (2001) (Americans with Disabilities Act); Kimel v. Florida Bd. of Regents, 528 U.S. 62 (2000) (Age Discrimination in Employment Act). An examination of the rationales of these decisions is beyond the scope of this book. In each setting, however, the Court relied on its holding in *City of Boerne v. Flores*, 521 U.S. 507 (1997), to the effect that exercises of the Fourteenth Amendment enforcement power must be proportional to remedying an identifiable set of equal protection or due process violations. In essence, the Court in both *Kimel* and *Garrett* found that federal statutory efforts to expose states to suit for age-based and disability-based discrimination were not proportionate efforts to remedy federal *constitutional* violations. Instead, the Court concluded that those abrogations essentially exposed states to suit for violating federal *statutory* duties that reached far beyond the states' federal constitutional obligations. The results in *Garrett* and *Kimel* (which contrasted with the result in *Hibbs*) were founded in part on the constitutional rule that renders state age and disability-based discrimination, unlike state sex discrimination, subject to only minimum equal-protection scrutiny.

96. 528 U.S. 62 (2000).

attempt to expose states to suit under the Age Discrimination in Employment Act (ADEA). Even during the heyday of *National League of Cities*, after all, the Court had held that law enforcement officers stripped of FLSA's protections under the "integral operations" principle were not stripped by that same principle of the protections afforded by the ADEA.[97] By denying relief to ADEA plaintiffs who would have faced no obstacle even under the pre-*Garcia* constraint imposed by *National League of Cities*, the Court's ruling in *Kimel* confirmed just how far the pendulum of federalism had swung in the post–1985 period.

D. Federalism Values and Statutory Interpretation

As we have seen, the Rehnquist Court has reinvigorated constitutional protections of so-called "states' rights" by invalidating federal laws under (1) the *Lopez/Morrison* non-economic-activity principle; (2) the *New York/Printz* anti-commandeering doctrine; and (3) the *Seminole Tribe/Alden* damages-immunity rule. There is, however, another and more subtle way in which the Rehnquist Court, following the lead of earlier Courts, has sheltered states from federal overreaching by way of congressional invocation of the commerce power. It has done so by employing state-protective tools of statutory interpretation.

97. *See supra* note 13 (discussing *EEOC v. Wyoming*).

The story begins in the pre-Rehnquist Court period with decisions such as *United States v. Bass*.[98] That case involved a federal statute, 18 U.S.C. § 1202(a), that imposes a criminal sanction on any convicted felon "who receives, possesses, or transports in commerce or affecting commerce ... any firearm." Emphasizing the disjunctive phrasing of the provision, the government argued that the statutory ban on receiving or possessing a gun (as opposed to its ban on transporting one) applied regardless of the gun's connection to interstate commerce.[99] The Court, however, rejected this argument, relying on two principles of statutory interpretation.

First, the Court cited the canon that "ambiguity concerning the ambit of criminal statutes should be resolved in favor of lenity" so as to foster values of fair warning and humane treatment.[100] Second, and more important for our purposes, the Court declared that "unless Congress conveys its purpose clearly, it will not be deemed to have significantly altered the federal-state balance." The Court went on to justify this principle of statutory construction by suggesting that it would enhance the proper functioning of the federal lawmaking process. Thus, "[i]n traditionally sensitive areas, such as legislation affecting the federal balance, the requirement of clear statement assures that the legislature has

98. 404 U.S. 336 (1971).

99. *Id.* at 340 n.6.

100. *Bass*, 404 U.S. at 347–49.

in fact faced, and intended to bring into issue, the critical matters involved in the judicial decision.''[101]

Commentators appropriately noted that the embrace of this rule of cautious and restrictive statutory interpretation dovetailed with the Court's then-flourishing tendency to grant near-total deference to claimed congressional exercises of the commerce power. In particular, by requiring a high level of explicitness, the *Bass* rule forced Congress to grapple in a self-conscious way with the dangers to state autonomy posed by proposed federal legislation in fields traditionally dominated by the states. By thus focusing judicial attention on the *manner* of congressional action, *Bass* reinforced the underlying notion that ultimately gave rise to the *Garcia* decision—namely, that state-autonomy interests are best protected by way of well-structured political processes rather than by cordoning off, perhaps artificially, particular areas of lawmaking from all federal control.[102]

In the years following *Garcia*, however, the Court has veered away from the restraintist philosophy that marked that decision. Given the Rehnquist Court's resuscitation of strong *substantive* protections of federalism values, does it follow that the Court should now abandon the *Bass* rule of statutory interpretation on the ground that it took hold as a doctrinal corollary of the Court's now-abandoned

101. *Id.* at 349.

102. *See, e.g.*, LAURENCE H. TRIBE, AMERICAN CONSTITUTIONAL LAW, § 6–25, at 480 (2d ed. 1988); *see generally supra* notes 12–18 and accompanying text (discussing rationale of *Garcia*).

process-oriented Commerce Clause jurisprudence? Whatever the theoretical strength of arguments along this line, the Rehnquist Court has shown no interest in abandoning this federalism-friendly canon of construction. Rather, it has expanded the reach of the *Bass* rule by applying it enthusiastically not only to criminal statutes but to civil statutes as well.[103] In effect, the Rehnquist Court has shifted from a single-barreled to a double-barreled approach in protecting state-autonomy values, vindicating those values *both* with pre-existing state-favoring rules of statutory interpretation *and* with newly recognized substantive constitutional restrictions designed to safeguard the integrity of the states. The practical consequence of this move is both evident and important. Whenever congressional action poses a discernible threat to so-called "states rights," lawyers must look for ways to advance their clients' interests both with traditional

103. *See, e.g.*, Solid Waste Agency of N. Cook County v. U.S. Army Corps of Eng'rs, 531 U.S. 159, 172–73 (2001) (refusing to read Clean Water Act to authorize agency rule that precluded filling of localized non-navigable ponds); Vermont Agency of Natural Res. v. United States *ex rel.* Stevens, 529 U.S. 765, 787 (2000) (refusing to construe False Claims Act to apply to state defendants); Gregory v. Ashcroft, 501 U.S. 452, 460–61 (1991) (refusing to read ADEA as applicable to state judges in light of their vital role in administering the state judicial system); *see also* Gonzaga Univ. v. Doe, 536 U.S. 273, 287 & n.5 (2002) (refusing to read 42 U.S.C. § 1983 to permit action for school's disclosure of information protected by the Family Educational Rights and Privacy Act of 1974; relying in part on "a tradition of deference to state and local school officials"). *See generally* Dan T. Coenen, *The Rehnquist Court, Structural Due Process and Semisubstantive Constitutional Review*, 75 S. CAL. L. REV. 1281, 1295–1303 (2002).

constitutional arguments and with arguments that draw upon federalism-driven "quasi-constitutional" rules of statutory interpretation.[104]

104. William N. Eskridge, Jr. and Philip P. Frickey, *Quasi-Constitutional Law: Clear Statement Rules as Constitutional Lawmaking*, 45 VAND. L. REV. 593 (1992).

CHAPTER VII

SOURCES OF CONGRESSIONAL AUTHORITY RELATED TO THE COMMERCE POWER

The commerce power does not exist in a vacuum. Other congressional powers crowd around it, and judicial decisions concerning these powers often have a connection to decisions under the Commerce Clause.[1] Each grant of congressional power presents complexities of its own, and a full-scale assessment of all congressional powers lies beyond the scope of this book. A full understanding of the Commerce Clause, however, requires basic knowledge about other sources of congressional authority. We shall briefly survey the (1) taxing power, (2) the spending power and (3) other powers that bear a particularly close relation to constitutional doctrine developed under the Commerce Clause.

A. The Taxing Power

In *Hammer v. Dagenhart*[2] the Court invalidated a

[1]. *See, e.g.,* New York v. United States, 505 U.S. 144, 185 (1992) (noting, in rejecting congressional power to mandate state adoption of federal programs under the Commerce Clause, alternative that Congress might induce adoption of such programs under its spending power).

[2]. 247 U.S. 251 (1918) (discussed *supra* Chapter III).

congressional effort to develop federal child-labor standards using the commerce-prohibiting technique. Within weeks an insistent Congress struck again, relying on its power to "lay and collect Taxes" to impose an excise amounting to 10% of the net annual profits of every business that used child labor. In the *Child Labor Tax Case* (*Bailey v. Drexel Furniture Co.*),[3] the Court held that Congress could not substitute this taxing-power goose for the commerce-power gander that the Court had shot down in the *Hammer* case. The problem, the Court declared, was that one "must be blind not to see" that the law's purpose was to impose a regulatory "penalty" on the employment of children.[4] For this reason, the Court concluded that the law entailed a *de facto* regulation, rather than a true tax, and thus ran afoul of the pretext principle of *McCulloch*.[5]

In the *Child Labor Tax Case*, a bundle of factors supported judicial recharacterization of the would-be tax as a regulatory penalty. In particular, (1) the law imposed a charge that (unlike most excises) targeted "a detailed and specified course of conduct" in business;[6] (2) it laid an unusually "heavy exaction" on employers who fell within its reach;[7] (3) in contravention of ordinary taxing norms, it

3. 259 U.S. 20 (1922).

4. *Id*. at 37–38.

5. *Id*. at 40. *See generally supra* Chapter II.

6. 259 U.S. at 36.

7. *Id*.

imposed this charge in blunderbuss fashion, regardless of how often the employer actually engaged in the "taxed" behavior during the year;[8] (4) it raised a duty to pay only for the "knowing" employment of children, thus marking the statute with a scienter requirement more familiar to criminal law than to tax law;[9] (5) it involved not only the Internal Revenue Service, but also the Labor Department, in federal collection efforts;[10] and (6) it did all these things in the immediate aftermath of the *Hammer* decision.[11]

This distinctive matrix of facts permitted the Court to apply its newly minted "penalty" principle narrowly in later cases, and that is exactly what the Court has done. In fact, the Court has declined to recharacterize a single federal tax as a penalty in the post–1937 period.[12] Instead, it has upheld challenged exactions on firearm dealers,[13] marijuana transfers,[14] and the operation of bookmaking businesses.[15] No less important than the outcome of these cases has been the Court's deferential tone. In

8. *Id.*

9. *Id.* at 36–37.

10. *Id.* at 37.

11. *Id.* at 39.

12. For another pre–1937 case in which the Court invalidated a would-be tax on the theory that "in actuality it constituted a penalty," see *United States v. Constantine*, 296 U.S. 287 (1935) (addressing federal "tax" that targeted only those malt liquor dealers who operated in violation of state law).

13. Sonzinsky v. United States, 300 U.S. 506 (1937).

14. United States v. Sanchez, 340 U.S. 42 (1950).

15. United States v. Kahriger, 345 U.S. 22 (1953).

United States v. Kahriger,[16] for example, the Court reasoned that "regardless of its regulatory effect, the wagering tax produces revenue"; that a tax is not "invalid because the revenue obtained is negligible"; and that a congressional "intent to curtail and hinder, as well as to tax," does not of itself render a taxing measure a penalty.[17]

Even so, the tax/penalty distinction retains vitality as a tool of constitutional discourse. Assume, for example, that following *Lopez*[18] Congress had imposed a levy of $100 on every instance of gun possession within 1,000 feet of a school. The odds are high that the Court would deem such a "tax" a disguised penalty that lay beyond the congressional commerce power in light of the *Child Labor Tax Case*.[19] The Court might say that such an exaction looks so exotic as a matter of taxing tradition that it differs in a qualitative way from the formally orthodox excises upheld in the firearms, marijuana and wagering cases. It might add, drawing directly on the *Child Labor Tax Case,* that the new law's focus on a "detailed and specified course of conduct"— possessing guns within a specified radius of a school, rather than, for example, selling or making guns or even possessing them anywhere—renders

16. 345 U.S. 22 (1953).

17. *Id.* at 27–28. *See also Sonzinsky*, 300 U.S. at 514 (suggesting that when a tax "is productive of some revenue" the Court is "not free to speculate as to the motives which moved Congress to impose it, or as to the extent to which it may operate to restrict the activities taxed").

18. *See supra* Chapter V.

19. *See supra* notes 3–11 and accompanying text.

"palpable" the law's "regulatory effect and purpose."[20] It also might assert that the law's adoption right on the heels of *Lopez* helps to reveal its regulatory aim.

The bottom line is that the Court's modern cases leave room for judicial invalidation of purported federal taxes on the ground that they (1) are not sustainable under the taxing power because they are properly characterized as penalties and not taxes and (2) are not sustainable under the commerce power because, despite their regulatory character, they do not concern "Commerce ... among the several States." What's more, exactly the same state-autonomy values that drove the decision in *Lopez* might lead the federalism-minded Rehnquist Court to reinvigorate the principle of the *Child Labor Tax Case* if and when the chance arises.[21] For now, however, the law is such that Congress may lay almost any tax it wishes to impose, even if it acts with the goal of shaping primary conduct in the real world.

B. The Spending Power

Article I, § 8 of the Constitution permits Congress to spend federal monies "for the common

20. *Child Labor Tax Case,* 259 U.S. at 37.

21. *Cf.* Department of Revenue v. Kurth Ranch, 511 U.S. 767 (1994) (relying on *Constantine,* discussed *supra* note 12, in recharacterizing state marijuana tax imposed on persons arrested for unlawful possession as punishment for double jeopardy purposes).

defense and general welfare of the United States."
As the modern proliferation of so-called conditional
spending programs reveals, Congress often uses this
power for regulatory purposes. In *United States v.
Butler*,[22] for example, the Court confronted a New
Deal program that conditioned federal subsidy payments to farmers on their compliance with federal
rules designed to limit crop production. Under the
Court's then-prevailing production-is-not-commerce
jurisprudence, Congress could not use the stick of
direct penalties to force farmers to comply with
production restrictions.[23] *Butler* presented the question whether Congress could pursue the same objective with the carrot of conditional outlays.

Relying on the *Child Labor Tax Case* and the
pretext principle of *McCulloch*, the Court invalidated the program in the same year it handed down
Carter Coal. Sounding the parade-of-horribles
theme, the Court railed against validation of the act
because it would support congressional "regulation
of all industry throughout the United States ... by
similar exercises of the same power."[24] In a dissenting opinion, Justice Stone responded that any "suggestion that [the spending power] must now be
curtailed by judicial fiat because it may be abused
by unwise use hardly rises to the dignity of argument."[25] But the majority was unmoved by his
protestations. The production-limiting subsidy pro-

22. 297 U.S. 1 (1936).

23. *See supra* Chapter III.

24. *Id*. at 75.

25. *Id*. at 87 (Stone, J., dissenting).

gram had to go because it entailed, albeit "indirectly," regulation of "a field in which the United States has no power to intermeddle."[26]

Butler's restrictive view of the spending power, however, did not last for long. In two 1937 decisions—decided within months of the Court's transformative Commerce Clause ruling in *Jones & Laughlin Steel*—the Court upheld key conditional-spending features of the Social Security Act of 1935.[27] In doing so, the Court did not purport to overrule *Butler*.[28] In each decision, however, Justice

26. *Id.* at 73. Somewhat ironically, the majority's ruling in this regard came only after it first held (in keeping with the views of Hamilton and Story, rather than Madison) that Congress's authority to spend was not limited to pursuit of "the other powers enumerated in the subsequent clauses" of Article I, § 8. As a result, the sense of the opinion was that Congress had broad authority to lay out federal monies to pursue "the general welfare of the United States" but that efforts "to purchase a compliance which the Congress is powerless to command" were subject to significant federalism-driven constraints. *Id.* at 68–70. Put another way, the Court in *Butler* saw the "spending" effort as a *de facto* "regulation" in much the same way the Court in the *Child Labor Tax Case* saw the challenged "tax" as a *de facto* "penalty." *Id.*

27. Charles C. Steward Mach. Co. v. Davis, 301 U.S. 548 (1937); Helvering v. Davis, 301 U.S. 619 (1937).

28. The law involved in *Steward Machine,* for example, conditioned employer entitlements to federal largess, in the form of tax relief, on state enactment of an unemployment compensation program that conformed to federal standards. The Court distinguished *Butler* on the grounds that: "(a) The proceeds of the tax in controversy are not earmarked for a special group. (b) The unemployment compensation law which is a condition of the credit has had the approval of the state and could not be a law without it. (c) The condition is not linked to an irrevocable agreement, for the state at its pleasure may repeal its unemploy-

Cardozo (who had dissented in *Butler*) whistled a tune that sounded very different from the theme of caution sounded in that case. As he emphasized: "When money is spent to promote the general welfare, the concept ... is shaped by Congress," and as long as "the concept be not arbitrary, the locality must yield."[29]

In the post–1936 period, the Court has upheld federal spending programs without exception.[30] In

ment law ... terminate the credit, and place itself where it was before the credit was accepted. (d) The condition is not directed to the attainment of an unlawful end, but to an end, the relief of unemployment, for which nation and state may lawfully cooperate." *Steward Mach.*, 301 U.S. at 592–93.

29. *Helvering*, 301 U.S. at 645.

30. *See, e.g.,* Fullilove v. Klutznick, 448 U.S. 448, 474 (1980) (plurality opinion) (noting that "[t]his Court has repeatedly upheld against constitutional challenge the use of this [conditional-spending] technique to induce governments and private parties to cooperate voluntarily with federal policy"; upholding statute that conditioned state access to public-works funds on using at least 10% of those funds on contracts to support minority-owned businesses); Lau v. Nichols, 414 U.S. 563, 569 (1974) (upholding application of non-discrimination requirement applicable to recipients of federal aid as applied to local school district that failed to provide English-language instruction to large numbers of non-English-speaking school-aged children of Chinese ancestry); King v. Smith, 392 U.S. 309, 333 n.34 (1968) (noting, in giving effect to federal aid-for-dependent-children rule, that "[t]here is of course no question that the Federal Government, unless barred by some controlling constitutional prohibition, may impose the terms and conditions upon which its money allotments to the States shall be disbursed"); *see also* Pennhurst State Sch. & Hosp. v. Halderman, 451 U.S. 1, 17 (1981) (noting broad precedent for conditional spending programs, and analogizing conditions to contract between federal government and recipient). For illustrative cases involving Bill of Rights–based challenges to conditional spending programs, see

Oklahoma v. United States Civil Service Commission,[31] for example, the Court upheld a program that granted money used in part to pay certain state workers on the condition that the state prohibit those workers from engaging in political campaigning. Invoking the logic of *Butler*, the state argued that this program offended the Tenth Amendment by effectively regulating local elections and structuring a state's relationships with its own employees. The Court, however, dismissed this argument without even mentioning *Butler*, emphasizing instead that claims of interference with state autonomy were overblown because the state could "adopt[] the 'simple expedient' of not yielding" to federal financial inducements.[32]

The *Oklahoma* case, unlike *Butler,* involved a federal law that conditionally offered funds to states themselves, rather than to private individuals or firms,[33] and in *South Dakota v. Dole*[34] the Court laid

Buckley v. Valeo, 424 U.S. 1 (1976) (considering, among other things, First Amendment restrictions on campaign expenditure limits as a condition to receipt of federal campaign finance funding), and *Flemming v. Nestor*, 363 U.S. 603 (1960) (upholding Social Security Act provision terminating benefits to aliens upon their deportation).

31.   330 U.S. 127 (1947).

32.   *Id*. at 143.

33.   As others have observed, "the size and range of such programs have increased considerably over years, and detailed federal conditions have proliferated." KATHLEEN M. SULLIVAN & GERALD GUNTHER, CONSTITUTIONAL LAW 219 (14th ed. 2001). So have scholarly treatments of the subject. For a sampling, see Lynn A. Baker, *Conditional Federal Spending after* Lopez, 95 COLUM. L. REV. 1911, 1939–51 (1995); and Thomas R. McCoy & Barry

down a four-step test for assessing whether such a program reaches beyond the congressional spending power. At issue in *South Dakota* was a federal statute that withheld 5% of federal highway funds from any state that permitted the purchase or public possession of alcoholic beverages by persons younger than 21 years old.[35] Even while assuming that Congress could not "legislate directly a national minimum drinking age,"[36] the Court upheld this law as a proper exercise of the spending power. According to Chief Justice Rehnquist, who wrote for an eight-Justice majority, the measure passed muster because it met each of four constitutional requirements. First, it plainly advanced the "general welfare," a subject on which "courts should defer substantially to the judgment of Congress."[37] Second, Congress had acted "unambiguously" in imposing the condition, thus properly permitting states to "exercise their choice knowingly, cognizant of the consequences of their participation" in the federal program.[38] Third, despite South Dakota's argument to the contrary, the Twenty–First Amendment did not impose "an 'independent con-

Friedman, *Conditional Spending: Federalism's Trojan Horse*, 1988 Sup. Ct. Rev. 85, 100–01.

34. 483 U.S. 203 (1987).

35. 23 U.S.C. § 158. The law withheld 5% of funds in the first year following its enactment, and 10% thereafter. *See* Pub. L. No. 105–178, 112 Stat. 107.

36. 483 U.S. at 206.

37. *Id.* at 207.

38. *Id.* (quoting *Pennhurst State Sch. & Hosp.*, 451 U.S. at 17).

stitutional bar' " that precluded enactment of this
federal legislation.[39] According to the Court, the
Oklahoma case established that this limit required
only that the spending power "not be used to induce the States to engage in activities that would
themselves be unconstitutional."[40] Because states
had undisputed authority to establish drinking
ages, in that rules of this sort do not infringe rights-
protective provisions such as the Free Speech or
Cruel and Unusual Punishment Clauses, no independent bar stood in the way of Congress's imposition of the challenged minimum-drinking-age condition.

Fourth, the Court concluded that this condition
was "reasonably calculated" to advance "the federal interest" that had given rise to the highway-
spending program.[41] Justice O'Connor, in dissent,
argued that the program violated this standard
because Congress had leveraged its funds to achieve
state enactment of a generally applicable rule of law
and had not simply specified "how the money
should be spent."[42] In the majority's view, however,
the " 'germaneness' or 'relatedness' " test[43] required only (1) identification of the purpose of the

39. *Id.* at 209 (quoting Lawrence County v. Lead–Deadwood
School Dist., 469 U.S. 256, 269–70 (1985)). Section 2 of the
Amendment specifies that: "The transportation or importation
into any state ... for delivery or use therein of intoxicating
liquors, in violation of the laws thereof, is hereby prohibited."

40. *Id.* at 210.

41. *Id.* at 209–10.

42. *Id.* at 216 (O'Connor, J., dissenting).

43. *Id.* at 209 n.3.

underlying spending program and (2) a determination that the condition was adequately "relevant" to the interest thus identified.[44] Here, the Court concluded, the purpose of the federal program was "safe interstate travel."[45] It followed, in the Court's view, that the germaneness requirement was met because the minimum-drinking-age condition fostered a salutary uniformity that cut down on dangerous driving by 18–, 19– and 20–year-olds who otherwise might take road trips to states in which they could legally drink intoxicants.[46]

South Dakota v. Dole left behind many questions. It remains unclear, for example, how close the relationship between the condition imposed by Congress and the spending program's purpose must be. In a footnote in *South Dakota*, for example, the Court declined to endorse a *"directly* related" standard because it found that that test was met on the facts of the case in any event.[47] Even harder questions concern application of the "germaneness" standard to specific conditions and programs. What if, for example, Congress conditioned entitlement to 5% of federal highway funds on state employment of dog catchers in all counties traversed by federal highways? Perhaps it would suffice to satisfy the germaneness standard that, on the face of things, these workers might keep the roads clear of wandering animals otherwise destined to cause acci-

44. *Id.* at 209.
45. *Id.*
46. *Id.* at 209.
47. *Id.* at 209 n.3 (emphasis added).

dents. Perhaps the Court would insist on empirical proof that dog-catcher employment actually enhances highway safety. Or perhaps (though it seems unlikely) the Court would find *South Dakota* wholly inapposite because a dog-catcher condition would not remove a problem distinctively tied to interstate non-uniformity and resulting risks of unsafe cross-border movements.

A final question lay between the lines of the *South Dakota* case: Would it have mattered if Congress had conditioned access to 100% of federal highway funds, rather than only 5%, on state compliance with the minimum-drinking-age condition? In the closing section of its opinion, the majority observed that a "financial inducement offered by Congress might be so coercive as to pass the point at which 'pressure turns into compulsion.' "[48] Congress had not crossed this great divide in the *South Dakota* case itself, however, because the challenged program involved only "a relatively small percentage" of only "certain federal highway funds."[49] With this talk of "compulsion," however, the Court invited future arguments that there is a fifth limit on conditional spending programs and that federal grant programs entailing 100% fund forfeitures may run afoul of a this non-coercion principle.

C. Other Powers

Recently developed limits on the commerce power have focused new attention on Section 5 of the

48. *Id.* at 211 (quoting *Steward Mach. Co.,* 301 U.S. at 590).
49. *Id.*

Fourteenth Amendment, which gives Congress authority to "enforce" the due-process and equal-protection rights created by that Amendment's Section 1.[50] In keeping with the general proposition that Fourteenth Amendment protections target "state action," Congress has drawn on this power in establishing federal remedies against state and local officials who violate Section 1 guarantees.[51] To what extent, however, does the Fourteenth Amendment, like the Commerce Clause, support congressional regulation of private persons and behavior? In *United States v. Morrison*,[52] federal authorities unsuccessfully invoked not only the Commerce Clause, but also Section 5, in arguing for the constitutionality of a congressionally created private right of action against private citizens who engage in gender-based acts of violence. In rejecting the Fourteenth Amendment theory, the Court found that even unconstitutional discrimination against women by state authorities, through invidiously selective non-enforcement of state law, could not justify creating this federal remedy against private-citizen

50. "The Congress shall have power to enforce, by appropriate legislation, the provisions of this article." U.S. CONST. amend. XIV, § 5. *See generally supra* Chapter VI (examining relationship of Fourteenth Amendment enforcement power and states' Eleventh Amendment immunity).

51. *See, e.g.,* 42 U.S.C. § 1983 (providing for private remedies "in an action at law, suit in equity, or other proper proceeding for redress" for federal constitutional violations against persons who act "under color" of state law).

52. 529 U.S. 598 (2000).

abusers. Because Section 1 of the Fourteenth Amendment "by its very terms, prohibits only state action,"[53] Congress could not use the enforcement power of Section 5 to forge remedial legislation that "visits no consequence whatever" on public officials.[54]

Might Congress have defended the statute involved in *Morrison* as a proper exercise of its power to enforce the prohibition on slavery—including slavery imposed by private persons—put in place by the Thirteenth Amendment?[55] In *Jones v. Alfred H. Mayer Co.*,[56] the Court held that a congressional ban on private race discrimination in housing sales fell within its power, derived from Section 2 of the Thirteenth Amendment, "to pass all laws necessary and proper for abolishing all badges and incidents

53. *Id*. at 621.

54. *Id*. at 626. Other passages from *Morrison*, and in particular its repudiation of the views of six Justices in *United States v. Guest*, 383 U.S. 745 (1966), suggest a narrow view of congressional power to regulate private conduct under Section 5. The majority in *Morrison*, however, continued to recognize some such power, at least where, for example, private persons conspire with public officials to deprive persons of their Fourteenth Amendment rights. *See Morrison*, 529 U.S. at 622–23.

55. U.S. CONST. amend. XIII (providing in § 1 that "[n]either slavery nor involuntary servitude ... shall exist within the United States, or any place subject to their jurisdiction" and in § 2 that "Congress shall have the power to enforce this article by appropriate legislation"). *See* LAURENCE H. TRIBE, AMERICAN CONSTITUTIONAL LAW, § 5–51, at 924 (3d ed., vol. one, 2000) (noting that "the Thirteenth Amendment differs from the Fourteenth ... in that, even absent implementing legislation, it is not subject to a state action requirement").

56. 392 U.S. 409 (1968).

of slavery."[57] Because "exclusion of Negroes from white communities [had become] a substitute for the Black Codes,"[58] which in turn had served as a substitute for legal slavery, Congress could "rationally ... determine"[59] that the law targeted a "relic of slavery" permissibly regulated by the federal government.[60]

The Court's sharp focus in *Jones* on the history of *race* discrimination provides a basis for arguing that its principle would not sustain the law concerning *sex* discrimination at issue in *Morrison* if that law were defended on Thirteenth Amendment grounds.[61] At the least, however, *Jones* supports the conclusion that a federal ban on private race-based beatings would pass muster as a proper exercise of

57. *Id.* at 439 (quoting The Civil Rights Cases, 109 U.S. 3 (1883)).

58. *Id.* at 442.

59. *Id.* at 440.

60. *Id.* at 443. From a present-day vantage point, it seems certain that Congress also had authority to pass the challenged legislation under the Commerce Clause. Because housing sales entail economic activity in a very pure sense, even post-*Lopez* principles lend powerful support to enactment of anti-discrimination laws in this area on aggregation-based affecting-commerce grounds. *See supra* Chapter V.

61. On the other hand, the Court has consistently held that the anti-slavery protections fixed by the Thirteenth Amendment extend to all citizens, not only African–Americans. *See, e.g.,* The Civil Rights Cases, 109 U.S. at 24 (stating that "[t]he thirteenth amendment has respect, not to distinctions of race, or class, or color, but to slavery"). And beatings inspired by a discriminatory animus might well be seen as having as much to do with enslavement as class-based exclusion from home ownership in certain neighborhoods.

Congress's Thirteenth Amendment-based enforcement power. Because *Morrison* leaves little doubt that such a law would fall outside the commerce power,[62] *Jones* reveals how the Thirteenth Amendment continues to play an independent role in facilitating congressional regulation of some forms of private conduct.

The treaty power, set fourth in Article II, Section 2, expands on the commerce power in a similar way.[63] The seminal case, *Missouri v. Holland*,[64] concerned a federal statute that limited the hunting of certain species of migratory birds. The Court assumed—not surprisingly, as the case arose in 1920—that this law lay beyond the congressional commerce power.[65] Nonetheless, the Court upheld the statute because the United States had previously ratified a treaty designed to protect the very birds the statute covered. It did not matter that an "earlier act of Congress that attempted by itself and not in pursuance of a treaty to regulate the killing of migratory birds within the States had been held bad."[66] Because the intervening treaty dealt with "a

62. *See supra* Chapter V.

63. See U.S. CONST. art. II, § 2 ("[the President] shall have Power, by and with the Advice and Consent of the Senate, to make Treaties, provided two thirds of the Senators present concur . . . .").

64. 252 U.S. 416 (1920).

65. *See supra* Chapter III. Of course, the power to enact such a statute under the Commerce Clause remains in doubt even under modern precedents, particularly in light of the *Lopez* "noneconomic activity" principle. *See supra* Chapter V.

66. *Id.* at 432.

national interest of very nearly the first magnitude,"[67] and the statute was "a necessary and proper means" to effectuate that treaty, there was no longer a constitutional problem.[68]

The Necessary and Proper Clause, of course, does not work in tandem only with the federal government's treaty-making power; it also invigorates congressional authority—just as it did in *McCulloch v. Maryland*—by supplementing other grants of power as well.[69] In *Kleppe v. United States*,[70] for example, the Court relied on Congress's Article IV authority to regulate federal property in sustaining limits on private interference with wild burros, including when they roamed off federal ranges onto private land. Similarly, in *Woods v. Cloyd W. Miller Co.*,[71] the Court sustained post-World War II federal rent controls as a necessary and proper means of carrying out federal war powers. Congress, the Court explained, could " 'remedy the evils which have arisen from [the war's] rise and progress,' "[72] and such an evil lay in the "deficit in housing which in considerable measure was caused by the heavy demobilization of veterans and by the ... reduction in residential construction during the period of hostili-

67. *Id*. at 435.

68. *Id*. at 432.

69. *See supra* Chapter II (discussing *McCulloch* case).

70. 426 U.S. 529 (1976).

71. 333 U.S. 138 (1948).

72. *Id*. at 141 (quoting Hamilton v. Kentucky Distilleries & Warehouse Co., 251 U.S. 146, 161 (1919)).

ties."[73]

There can be little doubt that, under modern Supreme Court jurisprudence, the Commerce Clause would support the rent control law at issue in *Woods*, as well as other statutes sustained under other powers in earlier decades.[74] If the congressional commerce power continues to contract, however, other powers will become increasingly important. Cases such as *Jones*, *Kleppe*, *Woods* and *Holland* may well provide key points of departure for arguments about congressional authority in a new post-*Lopez* world.

73. *Id.* at 142. Similarly, *Hamilton,* cited *supra* note 72, and *Jacob Ruppert, Inc. v. Caffey*, 251 U.S. 264 (1920), upheld federal prohibition acts in the period following World War I "because they conserved manpower and increased efficiency of production in the critical days during the period of demobilization, and helped to husband the supply of grains and cereals depleted by the war effort." *Woods*, 333 U.S. at 142.

74. *See, e.g., supra* notes 60–61 (discussing availability of commerce power to support legislation upheld under Thirteenth Amendment enforcement power in *Jones*).

CHAPTER VIII

UNION-PROTECTING LIMITS ON STATE LAWMAKING POWERS

Cases such as *Lopez*, *Printz* and *Alden* place limits on federal authority to protect the integrity of state governments in keeping with the Framers' vertical division of lawmaking powers.[1] This theme, however, carries with it a "flip-side" implication. It suggests that the Constitution sometimes impedes *state* lawmaking authority to protect interests in *national* unification. From early in its history, the Court has recognized these sorts of limits on state power as vital components of our constitutional order.

One set of union-preserving constitutional limits has its roots in the Supremacy Clause's requirement that federal statutes override state rules whenever the two bodies of law collide. Application of the resulting "preemption doctrine" (which is the subject of Chapter XV) hinges on judicial interpretation of discrete federal statutes. Other nation-preserving limits on state power derive not from the operation of congressional acts but from the commands of the Constitution itself. These limits on

1. *See supra* Chapter II.

state authority emanate from two sources: (1) express textual prohibitions (the subject of Chapter XIV) and (2) restrictions on state authority extrapolated from the Constitution's text, history and structure. Exploration of this latter set of limits brings us back to the first years of the Republic, the controversy over the establishment of a national bank, and the Court's seminal decision in *McCulloch v. Maryland*.[2] In that case, after all, the Court held that Maryland's taxation of the bank ran afoul of a rule "not ... stated in terms" in the Constitution but that nonetheless derived from a "fair construction" of its provisions and purposes.[3]

The principle of federal immunity from state taxation first articulated in *McCulloch* has raised tough issues of constitutional line-drawing ever since the days of the Marshall Court. In *McCulloch* itself, the Court noted that this immunity would not "extend to a tax paid by the real property of the bank, in common with the other real property within the State, nor to a tax imposed on the interest which the citizens of Maryland may hold in this institution, in common with other property of the same description throughout the State."[4] Building on this passage, more modern decisions have established that state taxes related to the operations of the federal government abridge constitutional limits only if (1) they tax federal entities "directly" or (2)

2.   17 U.S. (4 Wheat.) 316 (1819) (discussed *supra* Chapter II).

3.   *Id.* at 427.

4.   *Id.* at 436.

they "discriminate against the United States or those with whom it deals."[5] Under the first of these limits—the so-called "legal incidence" requirement—a state property tax imposed on the Reconstruction Finance Corporation offends the Constitution because it falls on an "arm" of the federal government itself, and this is the case even if a private lessee has agreed to reimburse the government for any state taxes it must pay.[6] In contrast, states may tax the income of private contractors derived from work on federal construction projects, and this is the case even if the federal government must absorb the cost of the tax because it has promised to indemnify the contractor for any state-imposed levies.[7] These cases confirm what the name of the "legal incidence" test implies: Judicial inquiry focuses on who bears legal responsibility for the

5. California State Bd. of Equalization v. Sierra Summit, Inc., 490 U.S. 844, 848–50 (1989) (upholding application of state sales tax to bankruptcy liquidation sale because the tax creates an obligation of the bankruptcy estate, "not of the Federal Government," and the tax applies generally to in-state sales so that "[t]here is no claim ... that the tax discriminates against bankruptcy trustees").

6. Rohr Aircraft Corp. v. San Diego, 362 U.S. 628 (1960).

7. *See, e.g.,* United States v. California, 507 U.S. 746 (1993) (holding that an agreement by the federal government to indemnify contractor's costs does not create an immunity for the contractor from taxation); United States v. New Mexico, 455 U.S. 720 (1982) (upholding state tax on federal contractors who managed federal government's atomic laboratories); James v. Dravo Contracting Co., 302 U.S. 134 (1937) (allowing state tax on gross receipts of contractor that built locks and dams for the federal government to the extent that contractor's activities occurred in the taxing state).

tax, not on who as a practical matter will shoulder its burden.

The non-discrimination component of the tax-immunity doctrine, like the legal-incidence component, centers on core notions that lack complexity. Thus, just as surely as a state may extend generally applicable income taxes to private contractors who work on federal government projects,[8] it may likewise apply a generally applicable income tax to federal government employees.[9] A state, however, may not impose its income tax exclusively on federal employees or on some subset of federal employees, such as military personnel.[10]

In applying these overarching principles, courts sometimes encounter knotty problems of characterization. In *Davis v. Michigan Department of Treasury*,[11] for example, former federal government workers mounted a discrimination-based attack against a Michigan income tax exemption made applicable only to the retirement income of former state and local government employees. In assessing

8. *See supra* note 7.

9. *See* Graves v. People of State of New York *ex rel.* O'Keefe, 306 U.S. 466 (1939). A statute enacted in the wake of *Graves*, 4 U.S.C. § 111, now specifically provides for this result. The Court in *Davis v. Michigan Dept. of Treasury*, 489 U.S. 803 (1989), noted that the statutory rule is "coextensive with the prohibition against discriminatory taxes embodied in the modern constitutional doctrine of intergovernmental tax immunity." *Id.* at 813.

10. *See* Barker v. Kansas, 503 U.S. 594 (1992) (invalidating state's uneven treatment of former federal military personnel in taxation of retirement benefits).

11. 489 U.S. 803 (1989).

the federal retirees' challenge, the Court confronted a conundrum: Was the proper point of reference for assessing the discrimination claim the state's treatment of the favored class of former state and municipal workers (in which case the existence of uneven treatment of federal retirees was obvious) or the state's treatment of the much larger group of non-government retirees who, like the federal retirees, received no advantage whatsoever from the challenged exemption (in which case no discrimination existed)? Justice Stevens opted for the latter view, urging that "[t]he fact that a State may elect to grant a preference ... to a small percentage of its residents does not make the tax discriminatory in any sense that is relevant to the doctrine of intergovernmental tax immunity."[12] He also argued that, even if constitutionally problematic discrimination somehow inhered in the Michigan taxing scheme, that discrimination was justifiable because a state should have the same power to compensate its own former workers by lowering their state-imposed tax obligations as it has to compensate them by raising their state-awarded benefit payments.[13]

An eight-Justice majority, however, found Justice Stevens's arguments unpersuasive. Writing for the Court, Justice Kennedy reasoned that increased benefits differed from decreased taxes in a constitutionally significant way because state grants of the former, but not of the latter, "would result in

12. *Id.* at 821.
13. *Id.* at 823.

higher federal income tax payments."[14] Nor was the majority persuaded by Justice Stevens's there's-no-discrimination-in-the-first-place rationale. In its view, "it does not seem too much to require that the State treat those who deal with the [federal] Government as well as it treats those with whom it deals itself."[15]

The Court has immunized federal government operations not only from burdensome state taxation but from intrusive state regulations as well. In *Johnson v. Maryland*,[16] for example, a unanimous Court cited *McCulloch* in holding that a state could not apply a generally applicable drivers' license law to a federal postal employee. The Court acknowledged that the state might well be able to subject mail carriers to "for instance, a statute or ordinance regulating the mode of turning at the corners of streets."[17] The licensing law was unacceptable, however, because it "requires qualifications in addition to those that the [federal] Government has pronounced sufficient."[18] This principle of federal regulatory immunity has generated few Supreme Court decisions, and its present-day scope remains uncertain.[19] Settled law, however, establishes one

14. *Id.* at 814 n.4.

15. *Id.*

16. 254 U.S. 51 (1920).

17. *Id.* at 56.

18. *Id.* at 57.

19. *See, e.g.,* North Dakota v. United States, 495 U.S. 423, 454 n.3 (1990) (plurality opinion for four Justices by Stevens, J.) (indicating, in keeping with modern tax-immunity precedents,

important limit on both the regulatory and tax immunities: Courts may find no undue interference with federal operations if federal law itself authorizes what the state has chosen to do.[20]

The Court has grappled with governmental tax and regulatory immunities for nearly 200 years.[21] This long stream of cases, however, illustrates just one manner in which the Court has reined in state lawmaking powers through the implication of na-

that "[a] state regulation is invalid only if it regulates the United States directly or discriminates against the Federal Government or those with whom it deals"); *id.* at 454 n.3 (separate opinion for four Justices by Brennan, J.) (agreeing that "state taxes and regulations are subject to the same restrictions under the federal immunity doctrine" but adding that "[r]egulations ... present a wider range of possibilities for interference with federal activities than do taxes"). *See generally* LAURENCE H. TRIBE, AMERICAN CONSTITUTIONAL LAW, § 6–34, at 1223–25 (3d ed., vol. one 2000).

20. *See* 2 JEROME R. HELLERSTEIN & WALTER HELLERSTEIN, STATE TAXATION ¶ 22.06, at 22–58 (3d ed. 2002).

21. Notably, the Court initially not only protected the operations of the federal government from state taxation, but also protected state operations from federal taxation in a parallel fashion. *See* Collector v. Day, 78 U.S. (11 Wall.) 113 (1870) (leading case; reasoning that "in this respect ... the State is as sovereign and independent as the general government"). In cases such as *South Carolina v. Baker*, 485 U.S. 505 (1988), however, the Court veered away from this position. In particular, while not rejecting altogether the notion of state tax immunity, the Court noted that "at least some nondiscriminatory federal taxes can be collected directly from the States even though a parallel state tax could not be collected from the federal government." *Id.* at 523. As Professor Tribe has observed: "Whether the rebirth of a vigorous jurisprudence of states' rights [exemplified by Rehnquist Court decisions like *Lopez* and *Seminole Tribe*] might yet portend a parallel rebirth of symmetrical intergovernmental immunities ... remains to be seen." TRIBE, *supra* note 19, § 6–33, at 122.

tion-preserving constitutional principles. In *Crandall v. Nevada*,[22] for example, the Court relied largely on *McCulloch* in holding that states could not tax travel across their borders even though "no express provision of the Constitution" addressed this subject.[23] As then-Associate Justice Rehnquist would explain more than a century later, the ruling reflected "the theme that the power to obstruct totally the movements of people is incompatible with the concept of one Nation."[24] Similarly, in *Saenz v. Roe*,[25] the Court held that states may not— consistent with goal of fostering national cohesion— award fewer welfare benefits to short-term than to long-term state residents.[26] Extrapolating largely from the Citizenship Clause of the Fourteenth Amendment,[27] the Court declared that the Constitu-

22. 73 U.S. (6 Wall.) 35 (1868).

23. *Id*. at 48.

24. Nevada v. Hall, 440 U.S. 410, 441 (1979) (Rehnquist, J., dissenting) (adding that "the constitutional framework demanded that the tax be proscribed lest it sap the logic and vitality of the express provisions"). The principle of *Crandall* may find support today in the express, though opaque, prohibitory language of the Privileges or Immunities Clause of the Fourteenth Amendment. At the time of the *Crandall* decision, however, the Fourteenth Amendment had not yet been ratified. *See also* United States v. Guest, 383 U.S. 745, 758 (1966) (suggesting that right to free interstate movement may have been "conceived from the beginning to be a necessary concomitant of the stronger Union the Constitution created").

25. 526 U.S. 489 (1999).

26. *Id*. at 511.

27. "All persons born or naturalized in the United States, and subject to the jurisdiction thereof, are citizens of the United

tion "does not provide for, and does not allow for, degrees of [state] citizenship based on length of residence."[28]

A recognition of implied nation-protecting limits on state authority also underlay the Court's much publicized decision in *U. S. Term Limits, Inc. v. Thornton.*[29] The central issue in the case was whether states could establish term limits (or other qualifications apart from the age, citizenship and duration-of-residence requirements specified in Article I, § 2, cl. 2 and § 3, cl. 3) for members of

States and of the State wherein they reside." U.S. CONST. amend. XIV, § 1.

28. *Saenz,* 526 U.S. at 506 (quoting Zobel v. Williams, 457 U.S. 55, 69 (1982) (Brennan, J. concurring)). In *Zobel* the Court reached a conclusion parallel to the one in *Saenz* when it invalidated an Alaska program that allocated government oil revenues to state citizens on the basis of how long they had resided in the state. Although the majority opinion (written by Chief Justice Burger) rested this result on the Equal Protection Clause, two concurring opinions (one by Justice Brennan and one by Justice O'Connor) explored other sources of this "principle of free interstate migration." *Id.* at 67. Notably, the Court in *Saenz* relied not only on the Citizenship Clause but also on the Privileges or Immunities Clause of the Fourteenth Amendment, which provides that "[n]o state shall make or enforce any law which shall abridge the privileges or immunities of citizens of the United States." U.S. CONST. amend. XIV, § 1. To the extent that prohibitions on interstate migration (or more temporary travel) are mandated by either the Equal Protection or the Privileges or Immunities Clause, those prohibitions might well be characterized as express, rather than implied, limitations on state authority. Either way, however, the Court's application of strict scrutiny in these settings has been motivated not so much by a notion of individual rights as by a vision that the American states are closely bound together by an overarching principle of nationhood.

29. 514 U.S. 779 (1995).

Congress. A four-Justice minority insisted that the power to impose term limits was "reserved" to the states by the Tenth Amendment in light of the Constitution's failure to allocate that power to the national government or to block its exercise by the states in express terms.[30] Tracking the view of Justice Story, however, the majority concluded that "no state can say that it has reserved what it never possessed" and that states could not have fixed qualifications for federal-government officers before that government had come into being.[31] The majority added that historical evidence confirmed the Framers' design to make exclusive the restrictions on eligibility specified by Article I's Qualifications Clauses. This approach to those provisions, in the majority's view, also comported with the "fundamental principle" that citizens of the United States should be able to "choose whom they please to govern them" free from state interference.[32]

Cases such as *McCulloch, Saenz* and *U. S. Terms Limits* reflect doctrines built, at least in part, on inferences drawn from constitutional provisions located outside Article I, § 8, such as the Supremacy, Citizenship, and Qualifications Clauses. The Commerce Clause and its companion Article I provisions, however, give rise to another question: To what extent may courts extrapolate limits on state authority from affirmative grants of legislative au-

30. *Id.* at 845 (Thomas, J., dissenting, joined by Chief Justice Rehnquist and Justices O'Connor and Scalia).

31. *Id.* at 802.

32. *Id.* at 783.

thority to the federal government? In *Sturges v. Crowninshield*,[33] Chief Justice Marshall articulated a principle that has guided deliberations on this question ever since: "Whenever the terms in which a power is granted to Congress, or the nature of the power, require that it should be exercised exclusively by Congress, the subject is as completely taken away from the State Legislatures, as if they had been expressly forbidden to act on it."[34] This thought has spawned important limits on state legislative authority in such areas as Native American law[35] and foreign affairs.[36] The most important im-

33. 17 U.S. (4 Wheat.) 122 (1819).

34. *Id*. at 193.

35. *E.g.*, New Mexico v. Mescalero Apache Tribe, 462 U.S. 324, 334 (1983) (noting that Court has "rejected a narrow focus on congressional intent to pre-empt state law as the sole touchstone" for finding that state rules are displaced by federal concerns with regard to Native American tribal sovereignty).

36. *E.g.*, Zschernig v. Miller, 389 U.S. 429, 432 (1968) (invalidating state law that limited inheritance by citizens of some foreign nations because it was "an intrusion by the State into the field of foreign affairs which the Constitution entrusts to the President and the Congress"). *See generally* TRIBE, *supra* note 19, § 4–5, at 656–57 (collecting additional cases). For an illustrative modern case in which this argument was raised, see *Crosby v. National Foreign Trade Council*, 530 U.S. 363, 381 (2000) (invalidating state restriction on state agencies' dealings with firms that do business with Myanmar; relying on preemption rationale and noting lack of need to "get into any general consideration of limits of state action affecting foreign affairs," but citing "exclusive national power"). *See also* American Ins. Ass'n v. Garamendi, 537 U.S. 1100 (2003) (recognizing that state choices must sometimes yield to federal policy on foreign relations in invalidating state law concerning insurance-related matters for Holocaust survivors as incompatible with foreign policy in this field as

plied limit on state power, however, has taken shape in the hundreds of decisions in which the Supreme Court has applied the so-called dormant Commerce Clause principle. Rooted in the grant of the commerce power to Congress, the Court's dormant Commerce Clause doctrine, more so than any other facet of its constitutional jurisprudence, has put the brakes on the "centrifugal forces of localism"[37] that persistently threaten the "retarding and Balkanizing [of] American commerce, trade and industry."[38]

reflected in executive agreements and statements by high-level executive-branch officials).

37. Ernest J. Brown, *The Open Economy: Mr. Justice Frankfurter and the Position of the Judiciary*, 67 YALE L.J. 219, 222 (1957).

38. Duckworth v. Arkansas, 314 U.S. 390, 400 (1941) (Jackson, J., concurring).

Chapter IX

The Dormant Commerce Clause Principle and its Purposes

What is this strange creature that courts and commentators call the "dormant Commerce Clause"? The term captures in a shorthand way an idea that is easy to state in the abstract but hard to apply in practice: Sometimes courts invalidate state laws simply because the Commerce Clause exists. In other words, some state legislation runs afoul of the Commerce Clause, or limiting principles implied from it, even though Congress has not affirmatively exercised its commerce power to preempt that legislation. The law falls simply because the Commerce Clause is there, albeit in its dormant—that is, unexercised—state.

A. The Goals of the Dormant Commerce Clause Principle

Not surprisingly, the core purpose of the dormant Commerce Clause principle lies in safeguarding the "Commerce ... among the several States" that lay at the heart of the Framers' concerns.[1] In keeping

1. U.S. Const. art. I, § 8, cl. 3. *See generally supra* Chapter II. Some scholars have suggested that the traditional depiction of

with this aim, the Court has invalidated state laws that either "discriminate against"[2] or impose an "undue burden"[3] on interstate commerce. The difficulty is that the words "discriminate," "burden" and (most of all) "undue" are notoriously opaque. Their application thus requires courts to make tough contextual judgments as they work their way through an endless stream of cases involving every imaginable form of state law.

Some cases pose few difficulties. The Court, for example, has recognized from the outset that the protective tariff—which taxes goods imported into, but not goods produced within, the tariff-imposing state—constitutes a paradigmatic violation of the dormant Commerce Clause rule. Such a law, as the Court explained in *West Lynn Creamery, Inc. v. Healy*,[4] "violates the principle of the unitary national market by handicapping out-of-state competitors, thus artificially encouraging in-state production

widespread protectionism under the Articles of Confederation is greatly exaggerated. *See, e.g.*, Edmund Kitch, *Regulation and the American Common Market, in* REGULATION, FEDERALISM, AND INTERSTATE COMMERCE (A. Tarlock ed. 1981). It at least seems true, however, that the Framers themselves viewed the problem of state-fostered protectionism as acute and that they responded to this concern in forging the Constitution and the Commerce Clause. *See, e.g.*, Donald H. Regan, *The Supreme Court and State Protectionism: Making Sense of the Dormant Commerce Clause*, 84 MICH. L. REV. 1091, 1114 n.55 (1986).

2. City of Philadelphia v. New Jersey, 437 U.S. 617, 628 (1978).

3. Dean Milk Co. v. City of Madison, 340 U.S. 349, 353 (1951).

4. 512 U.S. 186 (1994).

even when the same goods could be produced at lower cost in other States."[5] The Court, however, could not adequately enforce the principle that "our economic unit is the Nation" simply by invalidating protective tariffs.[6] To begin with, tariffs "are so patently unconstitutional that [the] cases reveal not a single attempt by any State to enact one."[7] No less important, laws other than tariffs may prove equally disruptive of "the unitary national market" that the dormant Commerce Clause principle protects.[8] Common examples include export restrictions placed on goods much in demand in other states and discriminatory taxes, other than tariffs, that disadvantage interstate business operations. Since before the Civil War, the Court has grappled with how to evaluate these and many other types of state laws under the principle that our nation constitutes a "federal free trade unit" subject to judicial protection even in the absence of preemptive congressional action.[9]

What values have driven this judicial enterprise? In a famous opinion, Justice Jackson explained that the dormant Commerce Clause principle has enhanced our national "prosperity" by contributing to the "material success" of the United States—perhaps "the most impressive in the history of com-

5. *Id.* at 193.
6. H. P. Hood & Sons v. Du Mond, 336 U.S. 525, 537 (1949).
7. *West Lynn Creamery*, 512 U.S. at 193.
8. *Id.*
9. *Hood*, 336 U.S. at 538.

merce."[10] At least five reasons rooted in economic theory suggest why the "national common market,"[11] safeguarded by the dormant Commerce Clause principle, has had these wealth-maximizing effects. First, common markets facilitate the specialization of labor, and resulting efficiencies, by channeling productive activities to those persons within the free-trade unit best able to engage in them. Second, common markets drive down prices by expanding the number and vitality of competing sellers able to serve any given locality. Third, common markets increase overall wealth within the trading unit by lessening any subunit's ability to cast onto its neighbors costly externalities in the form of pollution, road wear, accidents and the like. Fourth, common markets cut down on unpredictable and disruptive "trade wars" marked by continuing rounds of retaliation and reciprocal retaliation. Finally, common markets reduce transaction costs by replacing systems of *ad hoc* interstate diplomacy with one central authority charged with guarding the good of all.[12]

10.   *Id.* at 536–38.

11.   Hunt v. Washington State Apple Adver. Comm'n, 432 U.S. 333, 350 (1977).

12.   To say that the dormant Commerce Clause principle has economic purposes, however, is not to say that it provides a general license for invalidating all inefficient state laws. It would almost certainly be inefficient, for example, if a city spent all its money to erect an ugly statue of King Kong in the middle of a beautiful woodland park. Such an action, however, does not entail the sort of obstruction to cross-border commerce, or the sort of imposition of externalities on outsiders, that are the concerns of the dormant Commerce Clause. *See generally* Regan,

The dormant Commerce Clause principle responds not only to economic considerations but also to political realities. In his pathbreaking book, *Democracy and Distrust*,[13] John Hart Ely argued that a central purpose of judicial review is to correct defects in political processes that cause governments to take action that harms "discrete and insular minorities" and others who are "politically powerless."[14] This "representation-reinforcement approach to judicial review,"[15] which has roots in *McCulloch v. Maryland,* helps to explain the dormant Commerce Clause principle.[16] As the tariff example shows, that principle focuses on action by state authorities designed to advance the well-being of "insider" residents at the expense of "outsider" interest groups that are not well-represented within the local polity. Put another way, a strengthened judicial role may well make sense in this context because "to the extent that the burden falls on economic interests without the state, it is not likely to be alleviated by those political restraints, which are normally exerted on legislation where it ad-

supra note 1, at 1126 (noting that terms such as "national common market," "free trade" and "free movement of goods" are inherently ambiguous and require efforts to refine precisely what values they reflect).

13. JOHN HART ELY, DEMOCRACY AND DISTRUST: A THEORY OF JUDICIAL REVIEW (1980).

14. *Id.* at 76 (quoting United States v. Carolene Prods. Co., 304 U.S. 144, 152 n.4 (1938)); *see also id.* at 83.

15. *Id.* at 88.

16. *See id.* at 83–84 (discussing dormant Commerce Clause); *id.* at 85–86 (discussing *McCulloch*).

versely affects interests within the state."[17]

Finally, the dormant Commerce Clause principle aims at fostering national "solidarity."[18] The Framers of the Constitution—George Washington foremost among them—recognized the dangers that the post-Revolutionary period posed to the very survival of states only loosely knit together by the Articles of Confederation. During the Revolution, a sense of union had sprung from the shared purpose of pursuing independence—a purpose that brought Virginians, New Yorkers and Rhode Islanders together at places such as Saratoga, Kings Mountain and Valley Forge. In a time of peace, however, national leaders had to find other means to build a strong, single people. Their vision for doing so lay in constructing a polity bound together by free travel and free trade within national borders—a union that would be liberated from the economic rivalries that had marred its recent past and that in the future would become indivisible through an energetic and common pursuit of commerce.[19]

17. McGoldrick v. Berwind–White Coal Mining Co., 309 U.S. 33, 45–46 n.2 (1940). For a critique of the use of representation-reinforcement theory in dormant Commerce Clause cases, at least as a dominant theme, see Regan, *supra* note 1, at 1160–63. For a defense of one form of representation-reinforcement-related analysis in this context, see Mark Tushnet, *Rethinking the Dormant Commerce Clause*, 1979 WIS. L. REV. 125.

18. *Hood*, 336 U.S. at 535.

19. Notwithstanding these considerations, there is no shortage of criticism of the dormant Commerce Clause principle. *See, e.g.*, Julian N. Eule, *Laying the Dormant Commerce Clause to Rest*, 91 YALE L.J. 425 (1982); Richard D. Friedman, *Putting the Dormancy Doctrine Out of its Misery*, 12 CARDOZO L. REV. 1745

Students of the dormant Commerce Clause must take care not to lose the forest for the trees. For
(1991); Patrick C. McGinley, *Trashing the Constitution: Judicial Activism, the Dormant Commerce Clause, and the Federalism Mantra*, 71 OR. L. REV. 409 (1992); Martin H. Redish & Shane V. Nugent, *The Dormant Commerce Clause and the Constitutional Balance of Federalism*, 1987 DUKE L.J. 569; *see also* DAVID P. CURRIE, THE CONSTITUTION IN THE SUPREME COURT: THE FIRST HUNDRED YEARS 1789–1888, at 234 (1985). In particular, Justices Scalia and Thomas have roundly criticized the doctrine, although at least Justice Scalia has reconciled himself to some applications of it based on its deep precedential roots. *See, e.g.,* Camps Newfound/Owatonna, Inc. v. Town of Harrison, 520 U.S. 564, 610–20 (1997); Am. Trucking Ass'ns v. Smith, 496 U.S. 167, 202 (1990) (Scalia, J., concurring); Tyler Pipe Indus. v. Washington State Dep't of Revenue, 483 U.S. 232, 260 (1987) (Scalia, J., concurring in part and dissenting in part). Critics of the dormancy doctrine tend to focus on (1) the lack of an express textual endorsement of it; (2) the absence of focused historical evidence from the Constitutional Convention and Ratification Convention in its favor; (3) the doctrine's purported clash with the Import–Export Clause, U.S. CONST. art. I, § 10, cl. 2, and other constitutional provisions that seem to presuppose state power to regulate commercial matters; (4) a claimed absence of need for the doctrine given Congress's power to preempt commerce-inhibiting state laws; and (5) the potential for judicial overreaching that the doctrine is said to create. Defenders of the dormancy doctrine rely in large part on (1) the claim of an accepted understanding during the founding period that government powers (or at least powers to "regulate") were often, if not ordinarily, in their nature exclusive; (2) the distinctively national character of the power to regulate interstate commerce (particularly given its conjunction with congressional power to regulate foreign and Indian commerce); (3) the historical centrality of the Framers' concerns about state-imposed tariffs and kindred barriers to cross-border trade; (4) the importance of judicial policing of discrete programs in this field, and Congress's long-standing acceptance of that judicial role, in light of ever-present competing demands for congressional attention; and (5) arguments from *stare decisis* based on (a) 150 years of the doctrine's operation, resulting in extensive reliance on it, and (b) Congress's accepted ability to overturn judicial applications of the doctrine that strike it as

newcomers to constitutional law, the Court's jurisprudence in this area sometimes lacks the built-in
fascination of First Amendment, right-to-privacy or
equal-protection doctrine. Problems may be exacer-
bated by the intricacy of the dormant Commerce
Clause case law (though constitutional rules concerning freedom of speech and other personal rights
are, in actuality, no less complex). Recalling the
core aims of the dormancy doctrine, however,
should remove any doubts about the importance of
this subject. That principle—probably more so than
any other in constitutional law—has given life to
the notion that the very "salvation" of America lies
"in union and not division."[20]

B. Basic Dormant Commerce Clause Doctrine

The dormant Commerce Clause principle has
deep roots in American law. In *Gibbons v. Ogden*,[21]

wrong-minded. As ensuing discussions will reveal, strong judicial
proponents included Justices Story, Cardozo and Jackson. A
partial response to Justice Scalia's criticisms appears in Mark V.
Tushnet, *Scalia and the Dormant Commerce Clause: A Foolish
Formalism?*, 12 CARDOZO L. REV. 1717 (1991). Other treatments
that lend support to the doctrine include LAURENCE H. TRIBE,
AMERICAN CONSTITUTIONAL LAW, § 6–2 (3d ed., vol. one, 2000);
Albert Abel, *The Commerce Clause in the Constitutional Convention and in Contemporary Comment*, 25 MINN. L. REV. 432 (1941);
and Ernest J. Brown, *The Open Economy: Justice Frankfurter
and the Position of the Judiciary*, 67 YALE L.J. 219, 222 (1957).

20. *Hood*, 336 U.S. at 532 (quoting Baldwin v. G.A.F. Seelig,
Inc., 294 U.S. 511, 523 (1935)).

21. 22 U.S. 1 (1824) (discussed *supra* Chapter II).

Chief Justice Marshall did not have to pass on the principle, but he volunteered that there was "great force" in the argument for it.[22] The Great Chief Justice (writing for a unanimous Court) again seemed to assume that a state law could be "repugnant to the power to regulate commerce in its dormant state" in *Willson v. Black-Bird Creek Marsh Co.*[23] even though, as in *Gibbons*, the issue was not squarely posed.[24] Joseph Story wholeheartedly endorsed the dormant Commerce Clause principle and reported, following Marshall's departure from the Court, that he had always been a true believer in the principle as well.[25]

Chief Justice Marshall's successor, Roger B. Taney, took a different view. He embraced the notion that state laws could not run afoul of the Constitution's grant of the commerce power, "unless they came in conflict with a law of Congress."[26] But Chief Justice Taney never gathered a majority for his position. In 1849, the Court for the first time (albeit in a clutter of seriatum opinions) deemed "a state's action violative of the Commerce Clause"

---

22. *Id.* at 209. In a separate concurrence, Justice Johnson did recognize the dormant Commerce Clause principle, opining that the power to regulate interstate commerce vested in Congress "must be exclusive." *Id.* at 227.

23. 27 U.S. (2 Pet.) 245, 252 (1829).

24. The Court did not have to rule on the existence *vel non* of the dormancy doctrine because it found that the challenged law was, in any event, a proper state police-power measure.

25. Mayor of New York v. Miln, 36 U.S. (11 Pet.) 102, 161 (1837) (Story, J., dissenting).

26. The License Cases, 46 U.S. (5 How.) 504, 579 (1847).

even "in the absence of a relevant federal statute."[27] Two years later, the Court came together in
Cooley v. Board of Wardens[28] (with even Chief Justice Taney now joining the majority opinion) to
declare that the grant of the commerce power in
and of itself barred some state legislation by rendering congressional power "exclusive" as to "subjects
. . . in their nature national."[29]

From the days of *Cooley*, the Supreme Court has
never looked back. In case after case, the Court has
applied the dormant Commerce Clause principle to
invalidate scores of state laws. At the same time,
the vocabulary of the dormant Commerce Clause
has evolved greatly from its first stirrings in the
eras of Marshall and Taney. In *Cooley*, for example,
the Court drew a largely unhelpful line between
matters "in their nature national" and matters
"local and not national."[30] Thereafter, in sustaining

27. TRIBE, *supra* note 19, § 6–4, at 1047 n.6 (discussing The
Passenger Cases, 48 U.S. (7 How.) 283 (1849), in which the
Court struck down charges placed on ship masters arriving from
out-of-state ports to defray or guard against possible costs associated with incoming passengers).

28. 53 U.S. (12 How.) 299 (1851).

29. *Id.* at 319. Six Justices joined the opinion articulating
this position. Two Justices dissented on the ground that the
Court not only should have recognized an implied limit on state
lawmaking authority, but also should have invalidated the har-
bor-pilotage law that the majority found, on the facts, to concern
a local matter properly subject state control. *Id.* at 321–25
(McLean, J., joined by Wayne, J., dissenting).

30. *Id.* at 319. *Accord, e.g.,* Wabash, St. Louis & Pac. Ry. Co.
v. Illinois, 118 U.S. 557, 577 (1886) (striking down state railroad
rate rule as applied to intrastate portion of interstate shipment
based on the local-national distinction).

state legislation that required testing for engineers who worked on trains operating in interstate commerce, the Court distinguished between laws that "directly" affect interstate commerce and laws that affect that commerce only "indirectly."[31] For the next 40 years, the Court continued to use the local/national standard and the direct/indirect distinction in applying the dormant Commerce Clause rule.[32] With ever-increasing insistence, however, legal-realist critics condemned these tests as unduly conclusionary and subject to judicial manipulation. As a consequence, beginning with opinions such as then-Associate Justice Stone's dissent in *Di Santo v. Pennsylvania*,[33] the Court moved away from "doing little more than using labels"[34] and embraced the more transparent evaluation of state and national interests that dominates dormant Commerce Clause

31. Smith v. Alabama, 124 U.S. 465, 474 (1888) (discussing relevant principles); *id.* at 482 (upholding law because it "affects transactions of commerce among the States ... only indirectly, incidentally, and remotely").

32. *E.g.,* Southern Ry. Co. v. King, 217 U.S. 524, 531 (1910); Silz v. Hesterberg, 211 U.S. 31, 40–41 (1908) ("That a state may not pass laws directly regulating foreign or interstate commerce has frequently been held in the decisions of this court. But ... laws passed by the States in the exertion of their police power, not in conflict with laws of Congress upon the same subject, and indirectly or remotely affecting interstate commerce, are nevertheless valid laws."). Many cases decided during this period involved state laws related to railroads. For a detailed examination of these cases, see James W. Ely, Jr., *"The railroad system has burst through State limits": Railroads and Interstate Commerce, 1830–1920*, 55 ARK. L. REV. 933, 937–60 (2003).

33. 273 U.S. 34 (1927).

34. *Id.* at 44 (Stone, J., dissenting).

discourse today.[35]

The Court's many modern decisions set out an overarching structure—complete with great chambers, meandering side halls, and nooks and crannies—for evaluating dormant Commerce Clause cases. At the center of this edifice stands the principle that broadly prohibits laws that *discriminate on their face* against interstate commerce. Facial discrimination takes many forms. States may check the inflow of commerce with taxes or regulatory laws that exclude incoming goods and services. Alternatively, they may block the outflow of commerce by imposing export bans or other hoarding measures that favor in-state over out-of-state buyers.[36] The Court has taken a hostile view of all these acts of overt discrimination, subjecting them to a "virtually *per se* rule of invalidity."[37]

The dormant Commerce Clause prohibition, however, does not stop at outlawing the most patently protectionist measures. The Court has declared that even a facially neutral state law will encounter strict scrutiny if (1) its protectionist tendencies are so apparent that it is functionally indistinguishable from a tariff or other facially discriminatory rule; (2) the law was adopted because of a protectionist purpose; or (3) the law has intolerable "extraterri-

35. The seminal academic treatment was Noel T. Dowling, *Interstate Commerce and State Power,* 27 VA. L. REV. 1 (1940).

36. For numerous other examples of facial discrimination, see *infra* Chapter X.

37. City of Philadelphia v. New Jersey, 437 U.S. 617, 624 (1978).

torial" effects. The Court's most controversial strategy for checking commerce-disrupting state regulation, however, lies in its use of the so-called "*Pike* balancing test."[38] In applying this test, the Court weighs the burden the challenged state law places on interstate commerce against the benefits it generates in advancing health or other public-welfare interests properly pursued by the state. The state law is subject to invalidation under *Pike* analysis, however, only if the burden it imposes on commerce is "*clearly excessive* in relation to the putative local benefits."[39]

To make matters even more complicated, the Court has recognized a host of exceptions to these dormant Commerce Clause rules. Thus states may adopt even the most blatantly discriminatory measures if they involve (1) actions to which Congress has consented; (2) affirmative cash subsidization; or (3) behavior by the state in its capacity as a "market participant."[40] As if this crazy quilt were not complex enough, the Court has developed important limitations on each of these exceptions—what we might well call "exceptions to the exceptions"—that keep them from excessively eroding the dormant Commerce Clause rule.

38. Oregon Waste Sys., Inc. v. Department of Envtl. Quality, 511 U.S. 93, 100 (1994) (identifying test set forth in Pike v. Bruce Church, Inc., 397 U.S. 137 (1970)).

39. Pike v. Bruce Church, Inc., 397 U.S. 137, 142 (1970) (emphasis added). *See generally infra* Chapter XI.

40. Reeves, Inc. v. Stake, 447 U.S. 429, 440 (1980). All these exceptions are discussed *infra* Chapter XII.

Finally, the Court has devised a specialized approach for applying the dormancy doctrine to state tax laws, as opposed to state regulatory measures. Under the methodology laid out in *Complete Auto Transit, Inc. v. Brady*,[41] a state may impose a tax affecting interstate commerce only if that tax (1) does not discriminate against interstate commerce; (2) falls on an activity that has a "substantial nexus" to the taxing state; (3) is fairly apportioned; and (4) bears a proper relation to the benefits the taxpayer receives from the state. Not surprisingly, subtlety marks each prong of the *Complete Auto Transit* standard.

This introduction to the dormant Commerce Clause principle reveals, if nothing else, its doctrinal complexity. What's more, this summary understates that complexity because the Court sometimes structures its analysis in ways that do not fit neatly within this framework. The Court may, for example, refer loosely to both discriminatory purpose and effect.[42] It may combine *Pike* balancing and extraterritoriality analysis.[43] Or it may even revert to *Cooley*'s local-versus-national rhetoric.[44] Perhaps most important, the Court's reliance on *de facto* discrimination largely predated development of the modern *Pike* test so that it remains uncertain, in

41. 430 U.S. 274, 279 (1977).

42. *See, e.g.,* Baldwin v. G.A.F. Seelig, Inc., 294 U.S. 511, 522 (1935).

43. *See, e.g.*, Edgar v. MITE Corp., 457 U.S. 624 (1982).

44. *See, e.g.*, Bob–Lo Excursion Co. v. Michigan, 333 U.S. 28, 37–40 (1948).

the modern era, exactly how the Court's decisions concerning facially neutral laws fit together.

For those inclined to see a cup half empty, this depiction of elaborate doctrinal pathways may inspire a gloomy sense that dormant Commerce Clause law is a hopeless muddle. For those inclined to see the cup half full, however, there is another message to hear. The intricacy of the dormant Commerce Clause reflects the complexity of life, especially as it has been encountered across many generations by different combinations of Supreme Court Justices. Even more important, that intricacy gives rise to a simple yet critical truth: Lawyers who encounter a state law that genuinely imperils interstate commerce can almost always find at least one way, and often more, to mount a strong argument against it. Doctrinal elaborateness has spawned a rich vocabulary that thoughtful lawyers can use to represent the interests of their clients and that thoughtful jurists can invoke to protect the needs of the nation.

CHAPTER X

THE RULE AGAINST DISCRIMINATION

The core of the modern dormant Commerce Clause principle lies in its prohibition of state laws that discriminate against interstate commerce. But when, exactly, is unlawful discrimination present? The Court has indicated that state laws may run afoul of the dormancy doctrine because they are (1) facially discriminatory; (2) discriminatory in effect; or (3) discriminatory in purpose. The Court has also said that discriminatory laws may survive constitutional attack if the state can show that they provide the only means for achieving an important state goal. In only one case, however, has the Court found that a discriminatory state regulation met this exacting standard. In sum, in the dormant Commerce Clause context, judicial scrutiny that is " 'strict' in theory" is, for all practical purposes, "fatal in fact."[1]

1. Gerald Gunther, *The Supreme Court, 1971 Term—Foreword: In Search of Evolving Doctrine on a Changing Court: A Model for the Newer Equal Protection*, 86 HARV. L. REV. 1, 8 (1972) (employing this phrase in regard to equal-protection-based strict scrutiny).

A. Facial Discrimination

The most frequently applied component of the anti-discrimination rule is its ban on state and local laws that discriminate on their face against interstate commerce. In *City of Philadelphia v. New Jersey*,[2] for example, the Court invoked the dormant Commerce Clause principle to invalidate a New Jersey statute that prohibited all deliveries of out-of-state solid waste for handling by in-state landfills. The Court seemed to see the case as one involving a ban on the *importation* of out-of-state waste products, which the Court found to be "articles of commerce."[3] Others might have seen the law as involving a prohibition on the *exportation* of in-state waste-disposal services. Either way, the law ran afoul of the "virtually *per se* rule of invalidity" applicable when a law "overtly blocks the flow of interstate commerce at a State's borders."[4]

1. *Facially Discriminatory Export Restrictions.* Facially discriminatory restrictions on state exports may take many forms, but the paradigmatic case involves the "export embargo."[5] In *Pennsylvania v. West Virginia*,[6] for example, the Court encountered a state law that permitted private firms to export natural gas only after local needs were satisfied. In

2. 437 U.S. 617 (1978).

3. *Id.* at 627.

4. *Id.* at 624.

5. Donald H. Regan, *The Supreme Court and State Protectionism: Making Sense of the Dormant Commerce Clause*, 84 MICH. L. REV. 1091, 1199 (1986).

6. 262 U.S. 553 (1923).

dissent, Justice Holmes saw no reason "to prevent a State from giving a preference to its inhabitants in the enjoyment of its natural advantages."[7] The majority, however, offered powerful reasons for concluding that the dormancy doctrine negated state authority to impose this sort of export restriction:

> If the states have such a power a singular situation might result. Pennsylvania might keep its coal, the Northwest its timber, the mining states their minerals. And why may not the products of the field be brought within the principle? ... To what consequences does such power tend? If one state has it, all states have it; embargo may be retaliated by embargo, and commerce will be halted at state lines.[8]

In more recent cases, the Court has blocked state efforts to hoard local minnows,[9] electricity[10] and water.[11] The Court also has held that a state may not overtly reserve for its own residents either services supplied by private firms within the state[12]

7. *Id.* at 602.

8. *Id.* at 599. For a doctrinal precursor, see *West v. Kansas Natural Gas Co.*, 221 U.S. 229 (1911) (invalidating Oklahoma pipeline regulation that effectively barred interstate transfer of all locally produced natural gas).

9. Hughes v. Oklahoma, 441 U.S. 322 (1979).

10. New England Power Co. v. New Hampshire, 455 U.S. 331 (1982).

11. Sporhase v. Nebraska, 458 U.S. 941 (1982). For a further treatment of *Sporhase*, see *infra* note 50.

12. Camps Newfound/Owatonna, Inc. v. Town of Harrison, 520 U.S. 564 (1997) (invalidating tax break afforded only to tax

or business investment opportunities that exist there.[13]

2. *Facially Discriminatory Import Restrictions.* Facially discriminatory state import restrictions also come in many shapes and sizes. In *Welton v. Missouri,*[14] for example, the Court invalidated a Missouri licensing tax levied only on peddlers of goods made in other states. In many later cases the Court has followed the lead of *Welton* by invalidating state laws that similarly disfavor the importation of out-of-state or services[15] or goods.[16] The

exempt entities, here privately operated summer camps, that direct most of their work toward state residents).

13. Lewis v. BT Inv. Managers, Inc., 447 U.S. 27 (1980) (invalidating state law that facially discriminated against out-of-state firms with regard to opportunities to acquire or operate local investment-advisory and trust-related businesses).

14. 91 U.S. (1 Otto) 275 (1875).

15. Boston Stock Exch. v. State Tax Comm'n, 429 U.S. 318 (1977) (invalidating added increment of tax imposed on stock transfers unless effected through local brokers).

16. *E.g.,* Wyoming v. Oklahoma, 502 U.S. 437 (1992) (invalidating Oklahoma law that effectively reserved 10% of coal purchases by state's electric generating plants to coal mined in Oklahoma); New Energy Co. v. Limbach, 486 U.S. 269 (1988) (striking down tax exemption afforded to locally produced, but not non-locally produced, ethanol); Polar Ice Cream & Creamery Co. v. Andrews, 375 U.S. 361 (1964) (invalidating Florida regulations that required milk distributors in Pensacola area to purchase all Class I milk from local producers unless local production became inadequate); Hale v. Bimco Trading, Inc., 306 U.S. 375 (1939) (invalidating Florida law that imposed significant inspection charges on foreign, but not local, cement). Reciprocity provisions purportedly designed to encourage free cross-border trade do not save import-impeding state laws from invalidation. In *Great Atlantic & Pacific Tea Co. v. Cottrell,* 424 U.S. 366

principle of these cases is broad and clear: States may not "discriminat[e] in favor of goods, wares, and merchandise which are the growth, product, or manufacture of the State, and against those which are the growth, product, or manufacture of other states or countries."[17]

3. *Facial Discrimination and In–State Processing Requirements.* A recurring form of regulation that runs afoul of the ban on facially discriminatory laws involves so-called "in-state processing requirements."[18] In *Dean Milk Co. v. Madison,*[19] for example, a Chicago-area milk distributor challenged an ordinance adopted by Madison, Wisconsin. The ordinance required the bottling of all milk sold in Madison within five miles of the city's central

(1976), for example, the challenged measure stipulated that milk from other states could come into Mississippi only if those states authorized the importation of Mississippi milk. The Court invalidated this inhibition on importation from non-reciprocating states because "Mississippi may not use the threat of economic isolation as a weapon to force sister states to enter into even a desirable reciprocity agreement." *Id.* at 379. In effect, the Court declared that the proper response to import-impeding neighbors was to initiate legal actions under the dormant Commerce Clause—not to engage in just the sort of legislative retaliation the Framers had found intolerable. *Accord*, Sporhase v. Nebraska *ex rel.* Douglas, 458 U.S. 941, 958 n.18 (1982) (asserting that "reciprocity requirement cannot, of course, be justified as a response to another State's unreasonable burden on commerce").

17. Bacchus Imports, Ltd. v. Dias, 468 U.S. 263, 271 (1984) (deeming unconstitutional Hawaii tax statute that discriminated against alcoholic beverages manufactured outside the state).

18. South–Central Timber Dev., Inc. v. Wunnicke, 467 U.S. 82, 93 n.8 (1984).

19. 340 U.S. 349 (1951).

square in a purported effort to facilitate effective inspections to protect the health of local milk drinkers. Because the law erected "an economic barrier protecting a major local industry against competition from without the state," it could not stand as long as "the Court could identify reasonable nondiscriminatory alternatives, adequate to conserve legitimate local interests."[20] Unfortunately for Madison, the Court found that such alternatives existed because, for example, the city could send its inspectors to more distant bottling facilities and then charge their operators for any extra travel costs. Having concluded that Madison's rule was not "essential" for the protection of local health interests, the Court declared it unconstitutional.[21]

Dean Milk is illustrative of many cases that invalidate state laws because "they bar the import of the processing service" or (to put much the same point another way) "hoard a local resource [for] the benefit of local businesses that treat it."[22] According to

20. *Id.* at 354.

21. *Id.* at 356.

22. C & A Carbone, Inc. v. Town of Clarkstown, 511 U.S. 383, 392 (1994). *See* South–Central Timber Dev., Inc. v. Wunnicke, 467 U.S. 82 (1984) (invalidating regulation requiring Alaskan timber to be processed within state prior to export); Pike v. Bruce Church, Inc., 397 U.S. 137 (1970) (invalidating state law insofar as it required local packaging of Arizona-grown cantaloupes prior to removing them from the state); Toomer v. Witsell, 334 U.S. 385 (1948) (invalidating South Carolina law requiring the unloading, packing and stamping of shrimp caught within the state prior to export); Foster–Fountain Packing Co. v. Haydel, 278 U.S. 1 (1928) (invalidating Louisiana statute prohibiting export of shrimp unless heads and hulls were removed in

the Court's most recent decisions, such overt discrimination renders in-state processing mandates subject to the "rule of virtual *per se* invalidity" laid down in *City of Philadelphia*.[23] Those decisions also establish that this strong presumption of invalidity applies whether the challenged law favors a group of local processors, as in *Dean Milk,* or only a single local processor that is given a monopoly position. The latter situation arose in *C & A Carbone, Inc. v. Town of Clarkstown*,[24] which concerned a rule that required delivery of all solid waste within a town to a specific privately owned "transfer station." In the view of several Justices, because a single facility could exert less influence in favor of adopting protectionist legislation than a cabal of local operators, it made sense to reduce the intensity of judicial review when the state gives a single in-state firm a monopoly position in handling specified work.[25] The majority disagreed, however, because in its view:

> [T]his difference just makes the protectionist effect of the ordinance more acute. In *Dean Milk,* the local processing requirement at least permitted pasteurizers within five miles of the city to compete. An out-of-state pasteurizer who wanted

Louisiana); Johnson v. Haydel, 278 U.S. 16 (1928) (invalidating similar Louisiana oyster processing law); Minnesota v. Barber, 136 U.S. 313 (1890) (invalidating Minnesota law requiring all meat sold in-state, regardless of origin, to be inspected in-state).

23. *E.g., South-Central Timber Dev. Inc.,* 467 U.S. at 100; *see also Carbone,* 511 U.S. at 392.

24. 511 U.S. 383 (1994).

25. *Id.* at 411, 416–17 (Souter, J., joined by Rehnquist, C.J., and Blackmun, J., dissenting).

access to that market might have built a pasteur-
izing facility within the radius. The flow control
ordinance at issue here squelches competition in
the waste-processing service altogether, leaving
no room for investment from outside.[26]

The majority in *Carbone* was also unimpressed with
the town's justification for its forced-use rule. According to local officials, granting a monopoly position to the transfer station served the purpose of
assuring its financial viability. As in *Dean Milk*,
however, the majority found that a less restrictive
alternative was available because the town could
subsidize the facility's operations without forcing
local residents to forego all business with out-of-
state waste handlers.

B.   Facially Neutral Laws and Discrimination in Effect

States can violate the dormant Commerce Clause
with protectionist measures that are either stark or
subtle in form. Before developing its modern *Pike*
balancing formula, the Court dealt with problematic
state laws unmarked by facial discrimination
through use of analogistic reasoning. In effect, the
Court declared that some laws, although not overtly
discriminatory, so closely parallel statutes that concededly violate the Constitution that those laws are
likewise subject to judicial invalidation. The leading

26. *Id.* at 392.

decision in this line of cases is *Baldwin v. G.A.F. Seelig, Inc.*[27]

Baldwin arose after New York established minimum price levels for milk sold by in-state dairy farmers. To help ensure this program's success, the state also stipulated that dealers who bought milk from out-of-state producers for resale in New York could not pay them less than the statutorily specified minimum amount. Even though this feature of the program gave the minimum price rule a uniform operation, a unanimous Court found it unconstitutional. The Court's reasoning was multifaceted. At its core, however, lay the thought that the law operated like a protective tariff in that it deprived efficient out-of-state sellers of the opportunity to undersell in-state competitors. The analogy constructed by the Court was imperfect. After all, the law challenged in *Baldwin*—unlike a true tariff— was not a tax, did not generate funds for the state treasury, provided much-desired price increases for some nonresident dairy farmers, and (most important) did not discriminate against anyone. It was precisely this set of factual differences, however, that revealed the potency of the Court's it's-enough-like-a-tariff analogistic technique. Because the state had "set up what is equivalent to a rampart of customs duties," its law was unconstitutional despite its seemingly neutral character.[28]

Just two years after *Baldwin*, the Court signaled that its *de facto* tariff rationale had important lim-

27.   294 U.S. 511 (1935).

28.   *Id.* at 527.

its. In *Henneford v. Silas Mason Co.*,[29] the Court faced the argument that so-called compensatory use taxes violate the tariff-likeness principle recognized in *Baldwin*. States that impose sales taxes typically also impose compensatory use taxes, which have the effect of extending the same burden created by the locally imposed sales tax to non-local purchases of goods brought back into the state for local use. In finding Washington's compensatory use tax constitutional in *Silas Mason*, Justice Cardozo reasoned that the incidence of the regulation in *Baldwin* fell on out-of-state sales, whereas the incidence of the use tax fell on the in-state use of goods.[30] This distinction seems questionable, however, because the law in each case targeted a person returning to the state with goods purchased elsewhere. The Court also asserted that in *Silas Mason*, unlike in *Baldwin*, "[e]quality is the theme" of the statute.[31] Yet this attempted distinction also had a hollow ring because the "theme" of the same-minimum-price law invalided in *Baldwin* seemed to be "equality" as well.

29. 300 U.S. 577 (1937).

30. This aspect of the Court's reasoning in *Baldwin* and *Silas Mason* raises questions about how far states may go in adopting regulations with "extraterritorial" effects. Notably, the Court has continued to cite *Baldwin* as a case that involved a law marked by problems of extraterritoriality. *See* West Lynn Creamery, Inc. v. Healy, 512 U.S. 186, 193–94 (1994); Healy v. The Beer Inst., Inc., 491 U.S. 324, 336 (1989); Milk Control Bd. v. Eisenberg Farm Prods., 306 U.S. 346, 353 (1939). The subject of extraterritoriality is considered *infra* Chapter XI.

31. *Silas Mason*, 300 U.S. at 583.

The most powerful distinction between the two programs probably lay in how closely each of them resembled a protective tariff. The key point is that the compensatory use tax—unlike the minimum milk-price law—did not inhibit out-of-state sellers' ability to engage in efficiency-based price competition. Rather, the compensatory use tax simply removed an artificial state-created disadvantage under which local sellers would otherwise have to labor due to the operation of a sales tax that could and did reach only in-state transactions. For this reason—far more so than for the reasons emphasized by Justice Cardozo—the compensatory use tax fell outside *Baldwin*'s *de facto* tariff principle.

The Court in *Baldwin* never suggested that analogy-based discriminatory-effects reasoning extended only to tariff-like state measures, and in *H. P. Hood & Sons v. DuMond*[32] the Court took much the same approach to a state law that served to hoard an in-state product. At issue in *Hood* was an order by the New York Commissioner of Agriculture and Markets that blocked the opening of a milk-receiving station near the city of Troy, New York. The Commissioner denied the permit under a state law that prohibited the licensing of any station that would "tend to a destructive competition in a market already adequately served" or otherwise harm "the public interest."[33] In the view of the Supreme Court, however, the license denial amounted to

32.   336 U.S. 525 (1949).

33.   *Id.* at 527 n.3.

unconstitutional hoarding because the Commissioners acted in response to concerns that a new receiving station would divert milk needed by purchasers in the immediate Troy area to purchasers in Boston, Massachusetts.

The dissenters found fault with the majority's readiness to condemn the state's action as inherently protectionist in nature. Focusing on the facial neutrality of the statute (rather than on the particular agency action taken pursuant to it), Justice Black urged that state regulators would be equally bound to protect milk buyers in Boston or other areas outside New York if in the future a milk processor proposed to open a station that would divert needed milk away from them. Without saying as much, the majority deemed the New York law unlikely to produce such evenhanded results. A New York law administered by a New York Commissioner was unlikely to protect Massachusetts milk buyers against competing demands made by New York milk consumers who voted in New York elections.[34] In short, the facially neutral licensing law, as applied in *Hood*, too closely resembled a facially discriminatory hoarding measure to pass constitutional muster.

34. *See* Vincent Blasi, *Constitutional Limitations on the Power of States To Regulate the Movement of Goods in Interstate Commerce, in* 1 COURTS AND FREE MARKETS: PERSPECTIVE FROM THE UNITED STATES AND EUROPE 195 (T. Sandalow & E. Stein eds., 1982) (noting possibility that "state laws are to be invalidated if they grant enforcement officials too much discretion to make judgments that might be influenced by hostility to out-of-state interests").

Following the pattern of *Baldwin* and *Silas Mason*, however, the Court in *Hood* was quick to emphasize limits on the *de facto* hoarding principle it had recognized and applied. In particular, the Court reaffirmed *Milk Control Board v. Eisenberg Farm Products Co.*,[35] in which it had upheld the application of a Pennsylvania minimum price rule to sales of milk made by Pennsylvania dairy farmers for shipment outside the state. Challengers of the law argued that it violated the dormancy doctrine because it greatly disrupted local producers' abilities to compete successfully in out-of-state markets. The Court, however, found this argument unavailing, distinguishing *Baldwin* (which also concerned a minimum price law) on the ground that the challenge in *Eisenberg* focused on state regulation of instate, rather than out-of-state, behavior.

There is reason to question the outcome in *Eisenberg*. After all, one reason to promote a national common market is to protect local buyers by facilitating price competition from out-of-state products; yet the rule challenged in *Eisenberg* plainly impeded price competition between local milk and Pennsylvania milk in non-Pennsylvania markets.[36] No less

35. 306 U.S. 346 (1939).

36. For similar reasons, one might question the correctness of *Parker v. Brown*, 317 U.S. 341 (1943), in which the Court upheld a similar effort by California to elevate the price of locally grown raisins and thus "prevent the demoralization of the industry." *Id.* at 367. Professor Tribe has suggested that the ruling in *Parker* is best explained as reflecting the Court's "substantial deference to *congressional* agricultural policy." LAURENCE H. TRIBE, AMERICAN CONSTITUTIONAL LAW, § 6–30, at 1196 n.13 (3d ed., vol. one, 2000) (emphasis added). There was no finding in *Par-*

important, from a policy perspective, a troubling asymmetry seems to mark *Baldwin* and *Eisenberg*, particularly in light of the Court's more recent declaration that state authorities "may not insist that producers *or consumers* in other States surrender whatever competitive advantages they possess."[37] On the other hand, it is a stretch to view *Eisenberg* as a hoarding case in the mold of *Hood*. From all appearances, Pennsylvania was not trying to hoard milk for local consumers, who in fact were disadvantaged by the law in its overall effect by way of increased prices.[38] Rather, the law seemed genuinely to be aimed at fostering stability for a fragile industry, and—as the Court concluded—there was plausibility in the state's assertion that "uniform

ker, however, that Congress had specifically consented to enactment of the California price-support program, and it is open to question whether the sort of "quasi-consent" logic extracted from the case by Professor Tribe would carry water today in light of later recognized clear-statement requirements. *See infra* Chapter XII (discussing rejection of similar argument in *Maine v. Taylor*).

37. Brown–Forman Distillers Corp. v. New York State Liquor Auth., 476 U.S. 573, 580 (1986) (emphasis added). In particular, the Pennsylvania law may have deprived prospective out-of-state buyers of the chance to capitalize on efficiencies they had achieved by purchasing large quantities of milk from local producers, who were barred from selling at volume-discount prices by the minimum-price law.

38. The absence of a hoarding motive, standing alone, would have been determinative for Professor Regan. *See* Regan, *supra* note 5, at 1259 (arguing that key to *Eisenberg* is that even though the minimum-price rule helped "Pennsylvania milk producers at the expense of out-of-state distributors and consumers," it did not protect New York producers vis-à-vis non-New York producers or New York distributors and consumers vis-à-vis their counterparts in other states).

operation of the statute locally would be crippled and might be impracticable" if an exemption for out-of-state sales were put in place.[39] In short, *Eisenberg* was a tricky case. It is therefore not surprising that the Court found violations of the dormancy doctrine, albeit under the now-abandoned direct-indirect test, in earlier cases that involved similar minimum-price rules.[40]

39. *Id.* at 353. In particular, state legislators had reason to worry that the entire system of price supports would come to ruin as buyers for in-state resale pretended to purchase milk for out-of-state resale so they could pay sub-minimum prices, especially given the fact that only "a small fraction of the milk produced ... in Pennsylvania [was actually] shipped outside the Commonwealth." *Id.* Professor Tribe has suggested that the presence of a predominance of local buyers for the price-regulated product may have been the decisive factor in the case, perhaps because local consumers would logically oppose a law that increased prices for their milk unless powerful justifications for its enactment existed. TRIBE, *supra* note 36, § 6–8, at 1075. *But see* Regan, *supra* note 5, at 1258 (questioning significance of this fact). In this same vein, Professors Nowak and Rotunda have suggested that the Court properly upheld the law challenged in *Eisenberg* because it "involved an inner political check." JOHN E. NOWAK & RONALD D. ROTUNDA, CONSTITUTIONAL LAW, § 8.9, at 331 (2000). These commentators fail to note, however, that a similar consumer-based "check" on enactment of a minimum-price law did not save its application to out-of-state sellers in *Baldwin*. Moreover, Professors Nowak and Rotunda themselves question the Court's seeming reliance on the large-local-consumer-base rationale in *Eisenberg* on the ground that the preponderance of local sales may well have resulted from the minimum-price law itself. *Id.* at 330. Finally, a rationale that focuses on the small amount of exported milk stands in tension with *Parker* (*see supra* note 36) because there the Court validated state-imposed price-support rules for raisins even though the vast majority of consumers of this product were located outside the state.

40. *See* Lemke v. Farmers' Grain Co., 258 U.S. 50 (1922); Shafer v. Farmers' Grain Co., 268 U.S. 189, 201 (1925) (striking

As the preceding discussion shows, the Court has not restricted its application of strict scrutiny under the dormant Commerce Clause principle to those cases that involve facially discriminatory laws. To be sure, *Baldwin* and *Hood* are well-aged cases. More modern decisions, however, continue to suggest that an ill-defined set of facially neutral state laws will trigger scrutiny more exacting than deferential *"Pike* balancing" review if their effects are distinctively or obviously destructive of interstate commerce.[41] The contours of this feature of dormant Commerce Clause doctrine remain under-developed. Whatever those contours might be, however, cases both new and old suggest that the Court will apply heightened scrutiny to state laws if they produce a "discriminatory effect."[42]

C. Facially Neutral Laws and Discriminatory Purpose

Another murky branch of dormant Commerce Clause doctrine suggests that legislatures may not

down North Dakota law that regulated prices paid by interstate buyers of local grain because the regulations "directly interfere[d] with and burden[ed] interstate commerce").

41. The leading case is *Hunt v. Washington State Apple Advertising Commission*, 432 U.S. 333 (1977), in which the Court found that the "practical effect" of a facially neutral law gave rise to the sort of "discrimination" that placed "the burden ... on the state" to justify the law. *Id.* at 353.

42. Minnesota v. Clover Leaf Creamery Co., 449 U.S. 456, 471 n.15 (1981).

enact even the most facially neutral laws if they do so because of a "discriminatory purpose."[43] In most cases the Court has assumed this principle rather than applied it.[44] Moreover, in some cases, including *Baldwin*, the Court has adverted to problematic state purposes only in combination with condemnatory references to a law's discriminatory effects.[45] Even so, it seems clear enough that some laws run afoul of a purpose-centered prohibition, which gives rise to three main questions: (1) What is a discriminatory purpose?; (2) How should courts go about the business of characterizing state purposes?; and (3) How does one prove that an allegedly improper purpose was the actual purpose that drove the government's decision?

1. *Identifying Discriminatory Purposes*. Sometimes it will be clear that the legislative motive underlying a state law qualifies as discriminatory for dormant Commerce Clause purposes. Any court, for example, would look hard at a facially nondiscriminatory statute preceded by a preamble that proclaims the state's purpose of "promot[ing] its own economic advantages by curtailment or burdening of interstate commerce."[46] For much the

43. *Id.*

44. *See Wash. State Apple Adver. Comm'n,* 432 U.S. at 352–53.

45. *Baldwin*, 294 U.S. at 522, 527.

46. *Hood*, 336 U.S. at 532. The statute in *Hood* did not include such a preamble, but the Court invalidated the state action in that case in part because it detected such a discriminatory purpose. *See also* Hale v. Bimco Trading, Inc., 306 U.S. 375, 380 (1939) (noting that state's asserted interest of neutralizing

same reason, tax breaks specifically designed to promote local industries, even if superficially neutral, usually will violate the dormant Commerce Clause principle.[47] Other cases pose trickier problems. For example, in *Cities Service Gas Co. v. Peerless Oil & Gas Co.*,[48] the state fixed a minimum price for the sale of natural gas extracted in the state to curtail demand, thus "preventing rapid and uneconomic dissipation of one of [the state's] chief natural resources."[49] Was this law marked by a discriminatory purpose of hoarding? The Court said "no," reasoning in effect that the law constricted gas sales "whether destined for interstate or intrastate consumers" in a way reasonably designed to conserve a scarce resource for both classes of buyers in the future.[50]

"the competitive effect of foreign cement in the Florida market" amounts to "a candid admission that the very purpose of the statute is to keep out foreign goods").

47. *See* Bacchus Imports, Ltd. v. Dias, 468 U.S. 263, 271 (1984) (invalidating a wholesaling tax preference afforded to okolehao, a specialty drink made from an indigenous plant, primarily because "the purpose of the exemption was to aid Hawaiian industry"). Significant complexity, however, marks constitutional restrictions concerning state tax-based business development incentives. *See generally infra* Chapter XIII.

48. 340 U.S. 179 (1950).

49. *Id.* at 187.

50. *Id.* at 188. In *Sporhase v. Nebraska ex rel.* Douglas, 458 U.S. 941 (1982), the Court went a step further. It concluded that, in the unique context of groundwater regulation, states could take steps "to conserve and preserve *for its own citizens* this vital resource in times of severe shortage." *Id.* at 956 (emphasis added). Even this specialized recognition of a seeming right to hoard, however, did not totally exempt state water-transfer re-

Cities Service illustrates that not all "economic" purposes are protectionist or discriminatory, despite loose language in some opinions that suggests otherwise.[51] Common sense confirms the same conclusion, because innumerable state laws that guard against road wear, unfair trade practices, monopolization, and even theft have economic purposes entirely proper for states to pursue. It is a *protectionist* purpose—not an economic purpose—that brings the anti-discrimination rule into play.[52]

2. *Characterizing State Purposes*. As courts apply purpose-centered rules that focus on state protectionism, a subtle question may arise: How should one *characterize* the purpose with which the legislature has acted? In *Buck v. Kuykendall*,[53] for example, the Court found an impermissible purpose in the state's refusal to license the operation of a Portland-to-Seattle "auto stage line" on the ground that the route applied for was already adequately served. Justice McReynolds stood ready to uphold

strictions from dormant Commerce Clause attack. In particular, the dormancy principle bars essentially gratuitous state water-transfer restrictions—for example, when they operate "[e]ven though the supply of water in a particular well may be abundant, or perhaps excessive, and even though the most beneficial use of that water might be in another State...." *Id.* at 958.

51. *See Hood*, 336 U.S. at 526, 535 (endorsing broad state authority to protect the "health and safety" of residents, but finding fault with license denial that would "protect and advance local economic interests").

52. *See* City of Philadelphia v. New Jersey, 437 U.S. 617, 624 (1978) (associating "virtually *per se* rule of invalidity" with "simple economic protectionism").

53. 267 U.S. 307 (1925).

the state's action because, in his view, the state's purpose was to avert the risk that "chaotic conditions will quickly develop" on the highways.[54] For the rest of the Court, however, the permit denial violated the dormancy principle because the state's "primary purpose is not regulation with a view to safety or to conservation of the highways, but the prohibition of competition."[55]

A similar problem lurked quietly in *Hood,* in which the Court discerned "an avowed purpose ... of curtailing the volume of interstate commerce to aid local economic interests."[56] In a sense, this description was apt because in fact New York sought nondisruption of the City of Troy's milk supply. Given the statutory scheme's ostensible aim of protecting all milk buyers (including buyers located outside the state), however, the Court could have characterized the licensors' purpose in a very different way. It might have said, for example, that New York's design was to protect, in even-handed fashion, stability of access for all buyers of New York milk, whether located in New York or elsewhere.

These sorts of characterization problems pervade all areas of constitutional law that take into account a challenged law's real or purported aims. In *Hood,* for example, it seemed open to the Court to charac-

54. George W. Bush & Sons Co. v. Maloy, 267 U.S. 325 (1925) (McReynolds, J., dissenting in both *Buck* and its companion case).

55. *Buck,* 267 U.S. at 315.

56. *Hood,* 336 U.S. at 530–31.

terize the state's purpose as "protectionism as to local buyers," "equal application of a milk-access-nondisruption rule," "safeguarding health," "safeguarding infant health," or even "saving helpless babies from disease or death caused by disrupted access to a vital source of nutrition." The manner in which state interests are cast—narrowly or broadly, approvingly or pejoratively—inevitably shapes the application of legal rules that hinge on what those purposes are.

3. *Proving and Finding Unlawful Purposes.* For decades judges and scholars have bemoaned the difficulties of discerning legislative purpose. The key problems are well-known. Different legislators vote for different reasons, including reasons that may have nothing to do with policy choices but that focus instead on achieving compromise or getting reelected. In the usual case, identifying even a single legislator's purpose, much less the shared purpose of scores of legislators, involves a difficult exercise in mind reading. And any rule of purpose inevitably requires some form of nose counting to see if enough legislators acted with a wrongful *mens rea*. Must a majority of legislators have a bad motive? A substantial number? One legislator standing alone?

These and other complexities have led analysts to argue against purpose-driven analysis both inside and outside the dormant Commerce Clause field.[57]

57. *See, e.g.*, Kenneth Karst, *The Costs of Motive–Centered Inquiry*, 15 SAN DIEGO L. REV. 1163 (1978) (noting problems with motive review in race-discrimination context). *See generally* Dan

Although the Court sometimes seems receptive to these pleas, it has generally turned them away.[58] Instead, at least in the dormant Commerce Clause field, the Court has considered legislative purpose but done so cautiously, looking almost exclusively to formal legislative materials or outright concessions in assessing whether an improper motivation tainted an otherwise permissible lawmaking act.[59] In *Bacchus Imports*, for example, the Court relied on assertions made by the state's own Supreme Court—which in turn relied on published committee reports of the state legislature—in finding that the purpose that lay behind a challenged tax exemption for a product made from the roots of an indigenous Hawaiian plant was "to aid Hawaiian industry."[60] In keeping with this theme of caution, the

T. Coenen, *A Constitution of Collaboration: Protecting Fundamental Values with Second–Look Rules of Interbranch Dialogue*, 42 Wm. & Mary L. Rev. 1575, 1757–59 (2001) (collecting many authorities, including Supreme Court opinions, that question purpose-centered doctrines for, among other things, the reasons set forth above).

58. *See id.* at 1759–64.

59. *Cf.* Village of Arlington Heights v. Metropolitan Hous. Dev. Corp., 429 U.S. 252, 268 n.18 (1977) (noting that in equal-protection purposive-discrimination cases "[p]lacing a decisionmaker on the stand is . . . 'usually to be avoided' "). The classic defense of recognizing (and recognizing only) a purpose-centered approach to the dormant Commerce Clause principle (at least for cases other than those involving taxes or transportation) is Donald H. Regan, *The Supreme Court and State Protectionism: Making Sense of the Dormant Commerce Clause*, 84 Mich. L. Rev. 1091 (1986).

60. 468 U.S. at 271. *Cf.* Maine v. Taylor, 477 U.S. 131, 150 (1986) (finding "weak evidence of legislative intent" in "com-

Court has yet to focus exclusively on purpose in invalidating a state law under the dormant Commerce Clause. In *Bacchus Imports*, for example, the Court also emphasized the highly discriminatory effect of the exemption, which "applie[d] only to locally produced beverages."[61] Even so, the purpose doctrine remains part of the judicial "tool kit," ready for use when lawyers can successfully demonstrate that a facially neutral law reflects protectionist goals.

D. Limits (and Non–Limits) on the Anti–Discrimination Rule

In applying the anti-discrimination rule, the Court has fashioned a series of sub-rules that refine that principle and generally accord it a broad scope. To begin with, the Court has held that a law's ultimate aim, even if unobjectionable, will not save a statute otherwise marked by impermissible discrimination. In *City of Philadelphia v. New Jersey*,[62] for example, the parties debated at length whether the underlying goal of New Jersey's waste-exclusion law was, on the one hand, to safeguard the economic interests of in-staters or, on the other hand, to effectuate beneficial environmental protection. For the Court, however, this debate was beside the point because "the evil of protectionism can reside

ments . . . made by a state administrative agency long after the statute's enactment").

61. *Bacchus Imports*, 468 U.S. at 271.

62. 437 U.S. 617 (1978).

in legislative means as well as legislative ends."[63] The Court has also made it clear that discrimination in favor of some, rather than all, in-state consumers or industry members suffices to trigger strict judicial scrutiny. In *Bacchus Imports*, for example, the fact that the statute favored only local fruit wine and okolehao producers, while treating local sake and fruit liqueur makers no better than their out-of-state competitors, did not stop the Court from discovering a constitutional violation.[64] Applying much the same principle, the Court has held that both the anti-discrimination rule and the dormant Commerce Clause in general apply to local governments (which are sub-units of state governments) no less than they apply to state governments themselves.[65] In *Fort Gratiot Sanitary Landfill, Inc. v. Michigan Department of Natural Resources*,[66] for example, the Court held that the dormant Commerce Clause does not permit a local government to exclude out-of-state garbage by subjecting it to a ban on intra-county disposal of out-of-county waste.

Two arguments might be offered for refusing to equate city- or county-based discriminatory rules with the sort of statewide ban invalidated in *City of Philadelphia*. First, a statewide ban (at least typically) will have more sweeping effects than a local prohibition. The case law, however, provides a

63. *Id.* at 626.

64. *See Bacchus Imports,* 468 U.S. at 265.

65. *Dean Milk* and *Carbone,* which are discussed *supra* notes 19–26, are important decisions in this line of authority.

66. 504 U.S. 353 (1992).

ready response to this point, because the Court has declared on many occasions that there is "no *de minimis* defense" to constitutional challenges based on the anti-discrimination principle.[67] The second argument for distinguishing statewide discrimination from localized discrimination has roots in the representation-reinforcement theory that helps support the dormancy doctrine as a general matter.[68] A comparison of *City of Philadelphia* and *Fort Gratiot* again reveals the critical point. In *City of Philadelphia*, the law ultimately adopted by New Jersey did not disadvantage any in-state generators of waste; thus in-state waste generators had no reason to lobby against enactment of the law (or for its repeal), thereby providing indirect (or "virtual" or "surrogate") representation of the out-of-state waste generators that the law disadvantaged. In *Fort Gratiot*, however, all in-state waste generators, except the relatively few waste generators located in the discrimination-practicing county, suffered the same fate as banned out-of-state waste generators. As a result, those disadvantaged in-staters might well have provided indirect representation of harmed out-of-staters' interests, thus reducing the

67. Camps Newfound/Owatonna, Inc. v. Town of Harrison, 520 U.S. 564, 581 n.15 (1997); *accord, e.g.,* Oregon Waste Sys., Inc. v. Department of Envtl. Quality, 511 U.S. 93, 100 n.4 (1994) ("our precedents ... clearly establish that the degree of a differential burden ... on interstate commerce ... is of no relevance to the determination whether a State has discriminated against interstate commerce"). *See generally* Christine A. Klein, *The Environmental Commerce Clause,* 27 HARV. ENVTL. L. REV. 1, 50 (2003) (noting absence of a "*de minimis* exception").

68. *See supra* Chapter IX.

chances that the law would be enacted in the first place in the absence of a genuinely good justification for it.

The Court, however, has never embraced this sort of surrogacy logic to shelter local—as opposed to statewide—discrimination from dormant Commerce Clause attack. Perhaps the Court believes that out-of-county state residents are poor substitutes for out-of-state residents in the world of intra-county politics; after all, county officials have accountability only to the county residents who actually elect them. To be sure, in-state victims of county-based discrimination may, at least in theory, seek relief from the state legislature and thus could indirectly represent nonresidents' interests in this way. The Court, however, may believe that it is simply too unlikely that disadvantaged state residents will seek or get relief in the statehouse from burdensome local laws. Or it may suspect that residents of in-state County A often will go along with discrimination by in-state County B in the belief that County B residents will return the favor if County A later decides to adopt a discriminatory program of its own. Whatever the Court's reasoning, its rule is clear: "a state (or one of its political subdivisions) may not avoid the strictures of the Commerce Clause by curtailing the movement of articles of commerce through subdivisions of the state, rather than through the state itself."[69]

Assuming the anti-discrimination principle applies, it puts into operation a "virtually *per se* rule

69. *Fort Gratiot*, 504 U.S. at 361.

of invalidity."[70] The accuracy of this description finds support in post-*City of Philadelphia* cases because application of the "virtually *per se* rule," in the 25 years since it was first unveiled, has led to judicial validation of only one discriminatory state law. The case that produced this result was *Maine v. Taylor,*[71] in which the issue was whether Maine's wholesale ban on the importation of baitfish violated the dormancy doctrine. Reiterating basic rules, the Court declared that the sort of facial discrimination present in the Maine statute triggered "the strictest scrutiny," under which "the burden falls on the State to demonstrate both that the statute 'serves a legitimate local purpose,' and that this purpose could not be served as well by available nondiscriminatory means."[72] In applying this test, the Court looked to the voluminous record developed at trial and the district court findings based on it. The key finding was that no effective means existed for achieving the state's goal of protecting its native baitfish population from non-native parasites except to exclude, in all-out fashion, potentially parasite-infested out-of-state minnows. Because inspections and more targeted importation bans were unworkable—and the "abstract possibility" of later "developing acceptable testing procedures" did not qualify as an "adequate" alternative—the Court concluded that the state had no practical choice

70. City of Philadelphia v. New Jersey, 437 U.S. 617, 624 (1978).

71. 477 U.S. 131 (1986).

72. *Id*. at 138.

except to retain the challenged program.[73] In dissent, Justice Stevens declared that there was "something fishy about this case" because "[a]mbiguity about dangers and alternatives should actually defeat, rather than sustain, the discriminatory measure."[74] For the eight-Justice majority, however, it sufficed to sustain the statute that the district court's findings with regard to these matters were not "clearly erroneous."[75]

Maine v. Taylor is an exceptional, indeed extraordinary, case. In *City of Philadelphia*, for example, the Court readily found that New Jersey could adequately protect its interests in land preservation and leachate reduction by limiting, in a source-neutral fashion, the overall volume of waste disposed in the state, rather than by excluding only out-of-state trash.[76] In many other cases, just as in *City of Philadelphia*, the Court has pointed to a similarly "less restrictive alternative" in striking down facially discriminatory measures.[77] In short order, we will consider exceptions to the dormancy

73. *Id.* at 147.

74. *Id.* at 152.

75. *Id.* at 146.

76. *City of Philadelphia*, 437 U.S. at 626.

77. *See, e.g.,* Hughes v. Oklahoma, 441 U.S. 322, 337–38 (1979) (finding outright ban on exportation not "the least discriminatory alternative," but in fact the most discriminatory approach, for seeking to conserve the local minnow population; citing possible alternative of putting catch limits on licensed minnow dealers and emphasizing that the challenged law was "not a 'last ditch' attempt at conservation after nondiscriminatory alternatives have proved unfeasible").

doctrine, including its anti-discrimination rule.[78] There can be no doubt, however, that when the "virtually *per se* rule" does apply, the challenged state law almost always winds ends up in the constitutional dust bin.

78.   *See infra* Chapter XII.

CHAPTER XI

FACIALLY NEUTRAL LAWS, THE PIKE BALANCING TEST AND EXTRATERRITORIALITY PROBLEMS

As we have seen, the Court has closely scrutinized state laws that discriminate against interstate commerce on their face, in their effect or in their purpose. The Court, however, has not stopped here in its effort to protect the federal common market. Recognizing that interferences with that market may take "ingenious" forms,[1] the Court has provided that a statute that "regulates evenhandedly" may fall victim to the dormancy doctrine.[2] In 1970, the modern iteration of this approach was set forth by Justice Stewart in an opinion for a unanimous Court. As stated in *Pike v. Bruce Church, Inc.*:

> Where the statute regulates evenhandedly to effectuate a legitimate local public interest, and its effects on interstate commerce are only inciden-

[1] Best & Co. v. Maxwell, 311 U.S. 454, 455 (1940). *See also* Hunt v. Washington Apple Adver. Comm'n, 432 U.S. 333, 350 (1977) (insisting that dormant Commerce Clause principle must go beyond "the rare instance where the state artlessly discloses an avowed purpose to discriminate against interstate goods") (quoting Dean Milk Co. v. City of Madison, 340 U.S. 349, 354 (1951)).

[2] Hughes v. Oklahoma, 441 U.S. 322, 336 (1979).

tal, it will be upheld unless the burden imposed on such commerce is clearly excessive in relation to the putative local benefits.... If a legitimate local purpose is found, then the question becomes one of degree. And the extent of the burden that will be tolerated will of course depend on the nature of the local interest involved, and on whether it could be promoted as well with a lesser impact on interstate activities.[3]

3. Pike v. Bruce Church, Inc., 397 U.S. 137, 142 (1970). Notably, some constitutional analysts—Justices Black and Scalia most prominently among them—have criticized the style of judicial balancing reflected in the *Pike* test. *See, e.g.*, Bendix Autolite Corp v. Midwesco Enters., 486 U.S. 888, 895–98 (1988) (Scalia, J., concurring). *See generally* Earl M. Maltz, *How Much Regulation Is Too Much—An Examination of Commerce Clause Jurisprudence*, 50 GEO. WASH. L. REV. 47, 58–64 (1981). Critics of balancing tend to emphasize problems of judicial competence and the risk that balancing inevitably and improperly injects judges into a policy-making role. Justice Black, for example, suggested that courts should invalidate only those laws that "discriminate" against interstate commerce, J. D. Adams Mfg. Co. v. Storen, 304 U.S. 307, 330 (1938) (Black, J., dissenting), lest the judiciary assume the mantle of a "super-legislature." Southern Pac. Co. v. Arizona *ex rel.* Sullivan, 325 U.S. 761, 788 (1945). A leading advocate of the modern balancing approach, Professor Noel Dowling, offered this response:

Discrimination is a delusively simple term. How overreaching must a state measure be to merit condemnation as discriminatory? It seems apparent that in answering this question the Court must make the same sort of value judgment that it has been making in performing its broader protective function. Discrimination exists or not, depending upon whether there is an economic justification for the difference in treatment which the state accords interstate commerce. Only by an evaluation of all the facts and circumstances can such an issue be decided by the Court.

In this chapter, we look at the Court's use of this so-called *Pike* balancing formula, first in the transportation context and then in other cases, as well as the Court's related ban on laws that have undue extraterritorial effects.

A. Balancing and the Transportation Cases

The Court moved cautiously in its initial brushes with balancing analysis under the dormancy doc-

Noel T. Dowling, *Interstate Commerce and State Power—Revised Version, in* SELECTED ESSAYS ON CONSTITUTIONAL LAW: 1938–1962 at 280, 290. *See generally* Noel T. Dowling, *Interstate Commerce and State Power,* 27 VA. L. REV. 1 (1940) (broadly defending balancing methodology).

Professor Regan, like Justice Black, has taken a dim view of dormant Commerce Clause balancing and advocates instead that courts should invalidate only those state laws marked by a protectionist purpose (at least outside the transportation and taxation contexts). Donald H. Regan, *The Supreme Court and State Protectionism: Making Sense of the Dormant Commerce Clause,* 84 MICH. L. REV. 1091, 1102–07, 1131, 1141 (1986). He acknowledges, however, that "courts engaged in judicial review balance frequently" outside the dormant Commerce Clause context. *Id.* at 153. He also recognizes that judicial assessment of "protectionist effect" provides proper "evidence" of protectionist purpose, *id.* at 1137, and that such evidence also is present if "the law seems to achieve nothing, or even very little, in the way of its articulated purpose ... or in the way of any plausible permissible purpose," *id.* at 1132–33. *See also id.* at 1137 ("effect is often the best evidence of purpose"); *id.* at 1225 (recognizing that "issues of permissible benefits and less restrictive alternatives are relevant to direct motive review"). Professor Regan's classic work provides a powerful argument for purpose-centered dormant Commerce Clause review. His unstinting endorsement of using effect-centered evidence to demonstrate protectionism, however, may be seen as supporting the structured effect-cen-

trine. In *Bradley v. Public Utilities Commission*,[4]
for example, the Court sustained Ohio's refusal to
authorize a new motorized common-carrier service
between Cleveland and western Michigan. Signaling
a deferential approach, the Court acceded to the
state's argument that the affected highway was "so
badly congested by established motor vehicle operations that the addition of the applicant's proposed
service would create and maintain an excessive and
undue hazard ... to safety."[5] This fact, the Court
noted, distinguished its earlier decision in *Buck v.
Kuykendall*,[6] in which the Court had invalidated a
similar license denial because the state had relied
primarily on economic, rather than safety-centered,
concerns.

The Court again sounded a theme of deference in
*South Carolina State Highway Department v. Barn-
well Bros.*,[7] in which the issue was whether South
Carolina could enforce motor vehicle width and
weight limits that kept 80–90% of the nation's
trucks off the state's roads. Although the district
court found a constitutional violation, the Supreme
Court reversed, deeming it sufficient that there was
a "rational basis" for the state's judgment that its
tered style of "balancing" analysis (self-limited by the clearly-
excessive-burden requirement) set forth in the *Pike* test.

4.   289 U.S. 92 (1933).

5.   *Id*. at 93–94.

6.   267 U.S. 307 (1925).

7.   303 U.S. 177 (1938).

regulations reduced highway accidents.[8] The Court bolstered its analysis by noting that "[u]nlike the railroads, local highways are built, owned, and maintained by the state."[9] It also drew on representation-reinforcement analysis when it added that "the fact that [the regulations] affect alike shippers in interstate and intrastate commerce in large number within as well as without the state is a safeguard against their abuse."[10]

In *Southern Pacific Co. v. Arizona ex rel. Sullivan*,[11] however, the Court shifted gears and used a balancing methodology to invalidate a facially neutral Arizona train-length law. The Court began by emphasizing that dormant Commerce Clause analysis must turn on "the relative weights of the state and national interests involved."[12] As to the federal-interest side of the balance, there was "no doubt that the Arizona Train Limit Law impose[d] a serious burden on ... interstate commerce" in that Arizona stood alone in limiting passenger trains to 14 cars and was one of only two states that limited freight trains to 70 cars.[13] Because of these distinctively restrictive features, the Arizona law in effect required either the costly breaking up of long trains before they entered Arizona or the costly rerouting of those trains to avoid the state. In measuring the

8. *Id*. at 192.

9. *Id*. at 187.

10. *Id*.

11. 325 U.S. 761 (1945).

12. *Id*. at 770.

13. *Id*. at 773.

resulting burden on interstate commerce, it mattered to the Court that 95% of Arizona's rail traffic was interstate in nature; that the Arizona train-length rules cost the Southern Pacific Company alone about $1 million per year; that the rules necessarily delayed many cross-border deliveries; and that the "practical effect" of the law was to control "train operations beyond the boundaries of the state" because practicalities required the reconfiguration of trains as far away as El Paso, Texas, and Los Angeles, California.[14]

On the state-interest side of the balance, the Court placed the trial court's findings "that the Arizona law had no reasonable relation to safety" and in fact "made train operation more dangerous."[15] Although the Arizona Supreme Court had not accepted these factual determinations, the U.S. Supreme Court was persuaded that any safety advantage gained by shortening trains was effectively "offset by the increase in the number of accidents resulting from the larger number of trains when train lengths are reduced."[16] The Court deemed it significant that the primary safety problems associated with long trains—so-called slack-action accidents—were "relatively the same" in Arizona as in Nevada, which handled "substantially the same amount of traffic" without regulating train lengths at all.[17]

14.   *Id.* at 775.

15.   *Id.*

16.   *Id.*

17.   *Id.* at 778.

The Court's opinion also revealed how judges could use balancing analysis to sidestep troublesome precedent. The Court distinguished earlier cases upholding state laws that required locomotive headlights and full train crews both (1) because those laws genuinely "removed or reduced safety hazards" and (2) because they created no "substantial interference with the interstate movement of trains" because railroad companies could readily adapt to them.[18] In a similar vein, *Barnwell* was distinguishable not only because it involved government-maintained highways but also because its stringent width and weight rules fell on intrastate and interstate truckers alike. In contrast, as Chief Justice Stone explained in *Southern Pacific*, "the burden of [Arizona's train-length] regulation falls on interests outside the state" so that it was "unlikely to be alleviated by the operation of those political restraints normally exerted when interests within the state are affected."[19]

The Court in *Southern Pacific* emphasized that a state could not avoid the restraints of the dormant Commerce Clause by "simply invoking the convenient apologetics of the police power."[20] Rather, "the decisive question is whether in the circumstances the total effect of the law as a safety measure in reducing accidents and casualties is so slight and problematical as not to outweigh the national interest in keeping interstate commerce free from

18. *Id*. at 779.

19. *Id*. at 765 n.2.

20. *Id*. at 780.

interferences which seriously impede it."[21] The Arizona law flunked this test because it generated "at most a slight and dubious" safety advantage while "preventing the free flow of commerce by delaying it and by substantially increasing its cost and impairing its efficiency."[22]

The Court's decisions in *Barnwell* and *Southern Pacific* raised an intriguing question: Did the Court mean to erect a never-to-be-breached distinction between facially neutral state road laws and facially neutral state train laws for dormant Commerce Clause purposes? In *Bibb v. Navajo Freight Lines, Inc.*,[23] the Court answered this question with a resounding "no" by invalidating an Illinois law that required trucks to use "contour" mudguards even though almost all states authorized (and in some instances required) the use of "straight" mudguards. In *Raymond Motor Transportation, Inc. v. Rice*,[24] the Court again found that a motor vehicle law—this one a Wisconsin statute that limited truck lengths to 55 feet—went beyond the constitutional pale. *Raymond*, however, was of limited precedential significance because the state had offered no evidence whatsoever in opposition to the challengers' case that 65–foot double-trailer trucks were as safe as 55–foot single-trailer trucks and that the exclusion of 65–foot "doubles" from Wisconsin imposed massive burdens on interstate commerce.

21. *Id.* at 775–76.

22. *Id.* at 779.

23. 359 U.S. 520 (1959).

24. 434 U.S. 429 (1978).

The predictable sequel to *Raymond* came in *Kassel v. Consolidated Freightways Corp.*[25] At issue was Iowa's general prohibition on trucks exceeding 60 feet in length, including 65–foot doubles. Applying *Pike* balancing analysis, Justice Powell (writing for four Justices) conceded that Iowa in *Kassel* (unlike Wisconsin in *Raymond*) had offered some evidence of a safety justification. He also found record support, however, for the district court's conclusion that 65–foot doubles were, all things considered, as safe as the 55–foot singles and the 60–foot doubles that Iowa law permitted. Turning to the other side of the balance, Justice Powell concluded that the law placed a heavy burden on interstate commerce. In particular, because all other western and midwestern states authorized the 65–foot doubles that Iowa excluded, the Iowa law increased both costs and accidents as shippers added highway miles by circumventing Iowa or used a greater number of trucks to carry goods through the state. Finally, the law raised suspicions because it created a burden that fell "disproportionately on out-of-state residents and businesses."[26] This problem was magnified because the statute included exemptions (including for Iowa truck manufacturers and for all truck traffic to or from certain Iowa cites located near state lines) that "secure to Iowans many of the benefits of large trucks while shunting to neighboring states many of the costs associated with their

25. 450 U.S. 662 (1981).

26. *Id.* at 676.

use.''[27] Considering all these matters, Justice Powell concluded that the Iowa law, as applied to 65–foot double-trailer trucks, ran afoul of the dormancy doctrine under the balancing principle of the *Pike* case.

Justice Brennan (who was joined by Justice Marshall) declined to join Justice Powell's plurality opinion even though he agreed that the Iowa law offended constitutional requirements. In Justice Brennan's view, the Powell opinion had "ask[ed] and answer[ed] the wrong question" because judicial second-guessing of legislative judgments "in the field of safety" was to be avoided at almost all costs.[28] The problem with the law, according to Justice Brennan, lay in its impermissibly discriminatory purpose.[29] Here, Justice Brennan reasoned, there was sufficient evidence that the law's "actual purpose" was "protectionist" in nature because the Governor admitted vetoing a previously enacted 65–foot-double law on the ground that it "would benefit only a few Iowa-based companies while providing a great advantage for out-of-state trucking firms ... at the expense of our Iowa citizens."[30] Justice Brennan emphasized that impermissible protectionism was not limited to disadvantaging out-of-state businesses; in his view, the nation-preserving purposes of the dormancy doctrine dictated that foisting the financial and safety costs of road use on

27. *Id.*

28. *Id.* at 679, 686 (Brennan J., concurring).

29. *See generally supra* Chapter X.

30. *Id.* at 685.

other states constituted impermissible protectionism as well.[31]

In dissent, then-Associate Justice Rehnquist (writing for three members of the Court) criticized the plurality's willingness to "compare safety benefits to commerce costs" and, in particular, to consider "incremental safety benefits from prohibiting 65–foot doubles as opposed to 60–foot doubles."[32] Justice Rehnquist argued that states must be free to enact length rules; that these rules necessarily involve numerical cutoffs, and that "[l]ines drawn for safety purposes will rarely pass muster if the question is whether a slight increment can be permitted without sacrificing safety."[33] In advocating this view, Justice Rehnquist did not pause to consider that the particular increment involved in *Kassel* was fraught with practical consequences, given the widespread authorization in the West and Midwest of 65–foot trucks but the absence of any similar allowance of, for example, 70– or 75–foot vehicle lengths. He did note, however, that, unlike in *Raymond*, Iowa had offered evidence that 65–foot-long trucks pose distinctive safety dangers, because, among other things, a "65–foot vehicle exposes a passing driver to visibility-impairing splash and spray during bad weather for a longer period than do the shorter trucks permitted in Iowa."[34]

31. *Id*. at 686.

32. *Id*. at 697 (Rehnquist J., dissenting).

33. *Id*.

34. *Id*. at 694 (Rehnquist J., dissenting).

The 4–2–3 decision in *Kassel* reflected genuine differences of opinion. The three opinions in the case, however, also shared much common ground. Each opinion started from the premise that safety-based highway laws warrant a "strong presumption of validity."[35] All the Justices also agreed, however, that claimed safety justifications will not always support validation of commerce-burdening legislation. Most interestingly, all the opinions in the case, although proceeding from different points of reference, embraced much the same formula for assessing road-safety measures. The concurring Justices proclaimed a willingness to jettison such laws if the safety benefit they created was "illusory, insubstantial, or nonexistent."[36] The dissenters likewise stood ready to step in if the state's safety justification was "illusory" or "demonstrably trivial."[37] And even Justice Powell's opinion seemed to endorse an approach under which state road laws would pass muster, at least as a general rule, only if the state's safety justifications were "not illusory."[38]

Taken as a whole, these opinions lend support to a specialized version of the *Pike* balancing test in highway safety (or perhaps all safety) cases. On this view, whenever a safety justification for a facially neutral regulation is more than "insubstantial," "trivial" or "illusory"—presumably a very easy

35. *Id.* at 670 (Powell, J.), 685 (Brennan, J., concurring), 690 (Rehnquist, J., dissenting).

36. *Id.* at 681 n.1 (Brennan, J., concurring).

37. *Id.* at 692, 697 n.8 (Rehnquist, J., dissenting).

38. *Id.* at 670 (Powell, J.).

standard for any safety-based law to meet—the case is at an end. To be sure, judges might sometimes fudge in applying this test by characterizing a state safety interest as "illusory" because a heavy burden on commerce hangs in the balance. Alternatively, judges might find some special reason not to apply the strong rule of deference in a particular case—as the plurality in *Kassel* itself may have done because of the state's adoption of suspiciously self-serving exemptions from the supposedly general 60–foot rule. In the end, it is not clear just what route the Court will take with cases like *Kassel* in the future. Read together, however, the Court's opinions strongly suggest that courts, as a rule, should apply a distinctly deferential version of the *Pike* test to highway-safety cases.

Kassel raises many interesting questions. Would the exact same truck-length law have survived constitutional challenge if it had been imposed by, say, Massachusetts or Maine? (Conceivably yes, given the law's lesser impact on interstate commerce because all New England states, and several nearby states as well, prohibited the use of 65–foot doubles.[39]) Would the Court have sustained an Iowa ban on 70–foot doubles? (Almost certainly yes, given the hypothesized rule's far lesser impact on interstate commerce and the greater safety problems it likely would address.) Does *Kassel*'s invalidation of a truck-safety regulation indicate that the result in *Barnwell* is no longer good law? (Probably no, because the weight-and-width statute at issue in

39. *See id.* at 688 (Rehnquist, J., dissenting).

Barnwell, though burdensome to interstate commerce, seemed to have something more than an "insubstantial" or "illusory" safety justification.[40]) Whatever the answers to these questions, *Kassel* reveals that the dormant Commerce Clause is alive and well in the road regulation context.

B.   Facially Neutral Laws Outside the Transportation Context

Both *Raymond* and *Kassel* revealed the Court's openness to dormant Commerce Clause balancing and generated opinions that relied on the *Pike* formula. Two qualifying points about the *Pike* test, however, merit mention before we turn to judicial balancing in non-transportation cases. First, *Pike* itself presented an odd case in which to set forth a standard for assessing neutral rules because it involved the application of a state statute that, under present-day analysis, appeared to entail overt discrimination.[41] Second, despite referring often to the

40. *See Barnwell*, 303 U.S. at 192–96 (detailing safety and road-maintenance evidence; noting, for example, with respect to the state's width rule, that many South Carolina roads were too narrow to accommodate two 96–inch trucks and that "as the width of trucks is increased it obstructs the view of the highway").

41. In *Pike*, Arizona required a cantaloupe grower to package its product in crates within the state so that state authorities could ensure that those crates indicated the Arizona origins of the product. From a present-day vantage point, the operation of the Arizona law thus seemed to discriminate against interstate commerce by imposing an in-state processing requirement on the grower. *See supra* Chapter X. At the time of the decision,

Pike test, the Court has expressly relied on that test only once in invalidating a clearly nondiscriminatory state law outside the road-safety context.[42] Even

however, the Court had not yet fully developed its modern analytical structure for dormant Commerce Clause cases or characterized all in-state-processing requirements as inherently discriminatory. For a probing analysis of *Pike*, including with regard to whether it was truly a discrimination case, see Regan, *supra* note 3, at 1209–20.

42. The one exception is *Edgar v. MITE Corp.*, 457 U.S. 624 (1982), in which five Justices joined (in Part V.B of the opinion) to invoke the *Pike* test in invalidating a state tender-offer statute. Because the Court in *Edgar* incorporated a brand of extraterritoriality analysis into its assessment of the state-interest side of the balancing equation, the case is discussed *infra* as part of a broader treatment of extraterritoriality concerns. Apart from *Edgar*, the Court has sometimes applied or alluded to *Pike*'s balancing methodology in striking down seemingly discriminatory state laws. For example, in *Lewis v. BT Investment Managers, Inc.*, 447 U.S. 27 (1980), the Court drew on the *Pike* test in striking down a state law that overtly discriminated between instate and out-of-state entities with regard to their ability to operate local investment-advisory businesses. Another post-*Pike* case that involves balancing analysis is *Bendix Autolite Corp. v. Midwesco Enters., Inc.*, 486 U.S. 888 (1988), in which the Court invalidated a rule that subjected a foreign corporation to indefinite tolling of all statutes of limitations unless it appointed an agent for general service of process, including with respect to actions over which the State could not otherwise exert personal jurisdiction. The Court—albeit without citing *Pike*—concluded that "the burden imposed on interstate commerce by the tolling statute exceeds any local interest that the state might advance." *Id.* at 891. The Court, however, also observed along the way that "the Ohio statute imposes a greater burden on out-of-state companies than it does on Ohio companies," *id.* at 894, thus suggesting that in its view the statutory scheme was discriminatory in nature. *See id.* at 898 (Scalia, J., concurring) (concluding that statute was "on its face discriminatory" against foreign corporations). *See also* Great Atl. & Pac. Tea Co. v. Cottrell, 424 U.S. 366, 375–77 (1976) (applying *Pike* test to Mississippi law

so, the Court has never questioned the *Pike* formula, and one post-*Pike* case—*Hunt v. Washington State Apple Advertising Commission*[43]—invalidated a facially neutral state law using an analysis that so closely paralleled *Pike*-based review that it provides a worthy illustration of the Court's continuing openness to dormant Commerce Clause balancing.

In *Washington State Apple Advertising Commission,* the Court confronted a law passed by North Carolina, a leading apple-producing state, that prohibited the use of closed apple containers that bore any grade other than the U.S. Department of Agriculture (USDA) quality designation. This law was challenged by growers from Washington, another leading apple-producing state, because they had developed their own grading system, which they routinely used in marking packages that contained their apples. The challengers first argued that the North Carolina law reflected nothing more than a thinly veiled effort to block competition from Washington apples. The Court, however, found it unnecessary to "ascribe an economic protection motive to the North Carolina legislature."[44] Instead, it ruled that a proper balancing of state and national interests showed that the law, although facially neutral, impinged unduly upon interstate commerce.

On the state-interest side of the ledger, the Court found little that counted. North Carolina argued

that conditioned access to local milk market on neighboring state's reciprocal agreement to admit Mississippi milk).

43.   432 U.S. 333 (1977).

44.   *Id.* at 352.

that its law reduced confusion. The Court, however, gave little credence to this proffered justification because (1) closed containers were typically purchased by sophisticated resellers, rather than consumers in need of protection; (2) removal of the Washington grade deprived the very buyers the state supposedly was protecting of potentially useful information; and (3) the risk of confusion created by inclusion of local grade marks, even to unsophisticated consumers, was small and speculative in any event.[45] The Court also emphasized that North Carolina could protect its claimed interests with less restrictive alternatives, including "by permitting out-of-state growers to utilize state grades only if they also marked their shipments with the applicable USDA label."[46]

On the other side of the ledger, the law put such a burden on Washington apples that it had the "practical effect" of "discriminating" against them.[47] So it was because (1) the law raised costs for Washington producers by forcing them to segregate crates destined for North Carolina from crates bound elsewhere; (2) the law stripped away from the Washington apple industry "advantages it has earned for itself through its expensive inspection and grading system"; and (3) the law effectively "downgraded" high-quality Washington apples to the next lower designation supplied by the cruder

45. *Id.* at 353–54.
46. *Id.* at 354.
47. *Id.* at 350.

USDA system.[48] The cumulative effect of these considerations led the Court to invalidate the facially neutral North Carolina labeling law. Even the dissenters in *Kassel* (with the exception of Justice Rehnquist, who did not participate in the case) joined a unanimous opinion finding an affront to the dormant Commerce Clause principle.

In several later cases, the Court has subjected facially neutral laws to *Pike* balancing analysis but found no constitutional violation.[49] In *Minnesota v. Clover Leaf Creamery Co.*,[50] for example, the Court upheld a state-imposed ban on the sale of milk in plastic nonreturnable containers. The challengers asked the Court to balance the law into oblivion, emphasizing that the resin used to make plastic jugs came entirely from outside the state, while the pulpwood used to make substituted paperboard con-

48. *Id.* at 351.

49. *See, e.g.*, Northwest Cent. Pipeline Corp. v. State Corp. Comm'n, 489 U.S. 493 (1989) (rejecting challenge to generally applicable Kansas measure that encouraged natural gas production by canceling rights of firms that were dilatory in taking contracted-for shipments); Arkansas Elec. Co–op. Corp. v. Arkansas Pub. Serv. Comm'n, 461 U.S. 375, 395 (1983) (specifically citing *Pike*'s "clearly excessive" test in upholding state's rate regulation of local power wholesaler, notwithstanding prior authority under Court's direct-indirect jurisprudence barring such regulation); *see also* Huron Portland Cement Co. v. City of Detroit, 362 U.S. 440 (1960) (upholding nondiscriminatory pollution-control law as applied to ships operating in interstate commerce); Breard v. Alexandria, 341 U.S. 622 (1951) (discussed *infra* Chapter XIII). A particularly significant case in this line is *Exxon Corp. v. Governor of Maryland*, 437 U.S. 117 (1978), which is discussed *infra* note 81.

50. 449 U.S. 456 (1981).

tainers constituted a major in-state product. The Court, however, declined to find the resulting burden on interstate commerce "clearly excessive" in relation to Minnesota's "substantial state interest" in mitigating energy consumption, the generation of solid waste and the depletion of the non-renewable resources used in making plastic.[51] Along the way, the Court characterized the burden imposed by the law on interstate commerce as "relatively minor" because (1) it advantaged out-of-state pulpwood producers; (2) in-state plastic container producers and users suffered its effects; and (3) both the out-of-state and in-state paperboard carton industry would benefit in ways difficult to measure. The Court also dismissed two purportedly adequate less-restrictive alternatives. First, "banning all nonreturnables" did not present a reasonable option because such a law would have had even more burdensome effects on interstate commerce than did the challenged statute.[52] Second, a program of "providing incentives for recycling" did not offer a workable alternative because it was "less likely to be effective."[53] Finally, the Court returned to the representation-reinforcement theme sounded in its earlier decisions. Noting that the law adversely affected a number of local interest groups, the Court emphasized that "the existence of major in-state interests adversely affected by the Act is a powerful safe-

51. *Id.* at 473.

52. *Id.*

53. *Id.* at 473–474.

guard against legislative abuse."[54]

C. Extraterritoriality

One line of argument that recurs in dormant Commerce Clause cases focuses on the vice of "extraterritorial regulation."[55] Identifying extraterritoriality problems is a tricky business because states seldom regulate activities with no intrastate attributes whatsoever; rather, constitutional difficulties arise when regulations that address local concerns have ripple effects on how firms conduct business in other jurisdictions. In *Brown-Forman Distillers Corp. v. New York*,[56] for example, the Court dealt with a law that required liquor producers to certify that the price they charged for any product in New York did not exceed the price certified at the outset of the month as the lowest price that would be

54. *Id.* at 473 n.17.

55. Healy v. The Beer Inst., Inc., 491 U.S. 324, 332 (1989). Extraterritoriality arguments are also sometimes founded on Due Process Clause of the Fourteenth Amendment. In State Farm Mut. Auto Ins. Co. v. Campbell, 123 S.Ct. 1513 (2003), for example, the Court significantly limited the extent to which a state could justify the award of large sums of punitive damages based on allegations of wrongful conduct that previously occurred in other states. The relation between due-process and dormant Commerce Clause requirements with regard to state regulatory programs is not well developed. In at least some state tax cases, however, the so-called nexus limitation developed under the dormant Commerce Clause has been given a longer reach than the extraterritoriality restriction imposed by the Due Process Clause. *See infra* Chapter XIII.

56. 476 U.S. 573 (1986).

charged for that product during that month any-where in nation. In the Court's view, this state-created analogue of most-favored-nation trading status improperly projected state authority into oth-er states. The problem was that "[o]nce a distiller has posted prices in New York, it is not free to change its prices elsewhere in the United States during the relevant month."[57] Because "the 'prac-tical effect' of the law [was] to control liquor prices in other States,"[58] it violated the constitutional ban on "extraterritorial" state regulation.[59]

In *Healy v. The Beer Institute, Inc.*,[60] the Court took a step beyond *Brown-Forman* by striking down a rule that required large-scale beer distributors to ensure that prices charged to Connecticut wholesal-ers were not, at the very moment of sale, higher than the lowest prices it then was charging in any adjoining state. The Court emphasized that validat-ing the Connecticut law could produce a cascade of

57. *Id.* at 582. Justice Stevens, joined by Justices White and Rehnquist, dissented on the ground that speculation alone sup-ported the majority's fears that the certification rule actually determined pricing in other states. The dissenters noted that the challenged statute permitted mid-month reductions in certified sales prices by way of discretionary administrative action as long as the newly lowered price was charged not only elsewhere but in New York as well. This line of reasoning, however, did not assuage the majority's concerns. Just as surely as "New York could not require an out-of-state company to receive a license from New York to do business in other states," it could not "force appellant to seek regulatory approval from New York before it can reduce its prices in another State." *Id.* at 582 n.5.

58. *Id.* at 583.

59. *Id.* at 581.

60. 491 U.S. 324 (1989).

similar, retaliatory enactments, thus triggering a nationwide "price gridlock" wholly at odds with the sort of free-flowing commerce the Framers had envisioned.[61] According to the Court, extraterritoriality analysis based on "practical effects" must necessarily take fair account of the laws of other states.[62] Here, the Court reasoned, "because volume discounts are permitted in Massachusetts, New York and Rhode Island, but not in Connecticut, the effect of Connecticut's affirmation scheme is to deter volume discounts in each of these other States...."[63] After all, unless sellers declined to provide volume discounts in other jurisdictions, "the lowest of the volume-discounted prices would have to be offered as the regular price for an entire month in Connecticut."[64]

The *Brown-Forman* and *Beer Institute* cases demonstrate the Court's concern about state laws that

61. *Id.* at 340.

62. *Id.* at 336.

63. *Id.* at 339.

64. *Id.* The month-long nature of this effect of the Connecticut rule, and other problems as well, arose because other states required the posting of a fixed price for a month-long period. For example, even though Massachusetts did not tie permissible instate prices to charges imposed in other states, it did require posting the single price that would be charged throughout any particular month before that month began. One consequence was that when distributors decided on January 1 what price they would charge in Massachusetts throughout the month of February, they had to fix that price in light of their lowest planned February price in Connecticut because that state's rule precluded the Connecticut price from exceeding the Massachusetts price at any time. "In other words," the Court concluded, "the Connecticut statute has the extraterritorial effect, condemned in *Brown-Forman*, of preventing brewers from undertaking competitive pricing in Massachusetts based on prevailing market conditions." *Id.* at 338.

have significant extraterritorial effects. Nonetheless, the essential principle of those decisions may go no further than to jeopardize state laws that specifically tie requirements concerning in-state behavior to how one acts in other jurisdictions.[65] At the least, it is important to recognize that state rules do not offend the dormancy doctrine simply because they influence extraterritorial behavior. In *Dean Milk*, for example, the Court indicated that the city of Madison could prohibit local sales of milk not pasteurized in conformance with its generally applicable minimum health standards and then conduct out-of-state inspections to ensure that those standards were being honored.[66] Such a rule, particularly if replicated in neighboring localities, would push many non-Wisconsin bottlers into complying with sanitation requirements devised in Wisconsin. It seems clear, however, that this sort of "extraterritorial" effect could not support judicial invalidation of the very law that the Court in *Dean Milk* described as a "reasonable and adequate" regulatory alternative.[67]

65. *See* Pharmaceutical Research & Mfrs. of Am. v. Walsh, 123 S.Ct. 1855, 1871 (2003) (rejecting extraterritoriality challenge to state law that disadvantaged out-of-state drug suppliers that failed to provide price rebates to local pharmacies as part of a state effort to hold down drug prices; reasoning that, unlike in earlier cases, the law did not "regulate the price of any out-of-state transaction, by its express terms or its inevitable effect").

66. Dean Milk Co. v. City of Madison, 340 U.S. 349, 354 (1951).

67. *Id*. at 354. *See also* Regan, *supra* note 3, at 1271 (asserting that New Jersey "could deny access to [in-state] landfills to

Sometimes the Court weaves an evaluation of extraterritorial effects into the application of dormant Commerce Clause balancing analysis. In *Southern Pacific,* for example, the Court emphasized that the Arizona train-length law greatly altered railroad operations in other states as part of its calculation of the burdens that law imposed on interstate commerce.[68] On the other hand, the Court's decision *Edgar v. MITE Corp.*[69] reveals how the Court may consider extraterritoriality concerns in assessing the weight of the state's justification for the challenged law. In *Edgar,* the Court confronted an Illinois statute that restricted all corporate takeovers, including those involving only foreign corporations, as long as (1) Illinois residents owned at least 10% of the target company's stock or (2) the corporate target had its principal office in Illinois and specified amounts of its financial assets were located in the state, whether or not any of its shareholders actually resided there. In the process of invalidating this law through application of the *Pike* balancing test, the Court emphasized that the state had "no legitimate interest" in regulating transactions between non-resident firms and non-resident shareholders—which was just what the

entities, local or foreign, that did not comply with ... measures [that discouraged] the generation of waste" notwithstanding "the complaint that as applied to foreigners such legislation would be impermissibly extraterritorial").

68. *See supra* note 14 and accompanying text.

69. 457 U.S. 624 (1982).

statute did in many of its applications.[70] In *CTS Corp. v. Dynamics Corp. of America*,[71] the Court distinguished *Edgar* by emphasizing that Indiana's take-over statute (unlike Illinois's) applied only to *domestic* corporations, over which the state had regulatory authority that flowed from both conventional understandings of the effects of incorporation and the entity's voluntarily assumed relationship with the state.[72] Together, *Edgar* and *CTS* may be seen as standing for something like the flipside of the principle established by *Brown-Forman* and *Beer Institute*. Thus, just as surely as a state may not structure the terms of private trade in other jurisdictions, it lacks authority to justify the imposition of burdens on interstate transactions by relying on supposed regulatory benefits that accrue primarily to persons with whom the state lacks any meaningful connection.[73]

70. *Id.* at 644. Four Justices joined a portion of the opinion (section V.A) that relied solely on extraterritoriality principles in invalidating the law. A majority joined the separate portion of the opinion discussed in the text (section V.B) that relied on *Pike* balancing analysis.

71. 481 U.S. 69 (1987).

72. *Id.* at 93.

73. *See Edgar*, 457 U.S. at 644 (noting that "[w]hile protecting local investors is plainly a legitimate state objective, the state has no legitimate interest in protecting nonresident shareholders" and "there is nothing to be weighed in the balance to sustain the law" in this regard); *id.* at 645–46 (adding that "Illinois has no interest in regulating the internal affairs of foreign corporations").

D. Recurring Themes in the Court's Dormant Commerce Clause Analysis

What "big picture" lessons can one draw from the Court's non-discrimination, balancing and extraterritoriality rulings? First, all these cases—including those involving outright discrimination against interstate commerce—entail a weighing of state and federal interests. The Maine baitfish case, for example, reveals the Court's willingness to assess justifications offered by the state in support of even the most starkly discriminatory law.[74] This is not to say that the level of scrutiny lacks importance in dormant Commerce Clause litigation. In applying *Pike*'s balancing analysis to the *Clover Leaf Creamery* case, for example, the Court quickly dismissed recycling subsidies as too ineffectual to qualify as a reasonable alternative to the state's wholesale ban on nonreturnable plastic milk jugs. In applying the "virtually *per se*" rule in *Carbone*, however, the Court invalidated a forced-use rule for a local waste transfer station precisely because subsidization by the town did qualify as a "less restrictive means" for ensuring the facility's effective operation.[75]

Second, the Court has indicated that both the nature and the manifestation of the state's interests have significant roles to play in the balancing process. Thus, directly saving lives should logically

74. *See* Maine v. Taylor, 477 U.S. 131 (1986) (discussed *supra* Chapter X).

75. *See* C & A Carbone, Inc. v. Town of Clarkstown, 511 U.S. 383 (1994) (discussed *supra* Chapter X).

count for more than reducing illness, which should logically count for more than merely averting confusion among product purchasers. (Compare, for example, the Court's deference to the state's safety interests in *Bradley* with the Court's dismissal of a confused-buyer rationale in the *Washington State Apple Advertising* case.[76]) Likewise, the fit between the state's interest and the state law is of extreme importance. A state rule may fail because it advances the state's interest too tenuously, because its effectiveness is too speculative or because it is affirmatively counterproductive. (Recall, for example, the Court's concern in *Washington State Apple Advertising* that the state's "buyer protection" law perversely deprived product purchasers of useful information.) In addition, problems of overinclusiveness may place a state law in constitutional jeopar-

76. The Court overtly suggested the sliding-scale importance of different state interests in the *Washington Apple Advertising* case when it noted that such an interest, at least presumptively, "is *particularly strong* when the State acts to protect its citizenry in matters pertaining to the sale of foodstuffs." Hunt v. Washington State Apple Adver. Comm'n, 432 U.S. 333, 350 (1977) (emphasis added). *See also Pike*, 397 U.S. at 143 (noting that "[w]e are not ... dealing here with 'state legislation in the field of safety ... ' or with an Act designed to protect consumers ... from contaminated or unfit goods" but instead with a law enacted "simply to protect and enhance the reputation of growers within the state"); *id.* at 145–46 (describing this state interest as "tenuous," "minimal" and "certainly less substantial than a state's interest in securing employment for its people"). At the same time, there is much to be said against unrestrained judicial assessments of the relative importance of different state objectives, *see supra* Chapter VI (discussing rationale of *Garcia* case), and the Court's decisions in this field do not often (at least openly) get into the business of ranking the importance of state purposes in enacting legislation. *See also supra* note 3 (noting criticisms of unduly open-ended judicial balancing analysis).

dy.[77] The wholesale ban on baitfish importation upheld in *Maine v. Taylor*,[78] for example, might well become unconstitutional if, in the future, scientists devise ways to identify and exclude only those particular fish that carry destructive parasites.[79] It is equally true that underinclusiveness may lead a court to invalidate a commerce-burdening statute. Excluding only non-locally-generated hazardous waste from state disposal facilities, for example, is unjustifiable if locally generated hazardous waste poses exactly the same environmental threat.[80] These examples highlight the pervasive importance of so-called less-restrictive-alternative analysis in

77. A rule is over-inclusive if it reaches more persons than those involved in the mischief it has the purpose of addressing. Assume, for example, that a state wishes to deal with the growing problem of used newspapers being left in public places. A law that prohibited the possession of newspapers outside one's own yard would be over-inclusive because many persons who take newspapers outside their yards nonetheless properly dispose of them. A law that prohibited all purchases of newspapers would be even more over-inclusive, and a law that prohibited all littering would be over-inclusive as well, so long as the law's purpose was to stop only newspaper littering. Given such a purpose, a law that simply outlawed newspaper littering would not be over-inclusive (or at least not substantially so), but such a law might also not be very effective in rooting out the problem of visual blight caused by newspaper littering. *See generally* LOUIS MICHAEL SEIDMAN, CONSTITUTIONAL LAW, EQUAL PROTECTION OF THE LAWS 66–73 (2003).

78. 477 U.S. 131 (1986).

79. *See id.* at 147 (noting that "if and when such procedures are developed, Maine may no longer be able to justify its import ban").

80. *See* Oregon Waste Sys., Inc. v. Department of Envtl. Quality, 511 U.S. 93 (1994).

dormant Commerce Clause cases. In *City of Phila-delphia*, for example, New Jersey's selective ban on importation of out-of-state waste did not square with its stated goal of keeping its countryside from turning into one large landfill. If the state genuinely wished to limit the acreage gobbled up by solid waste, it should have put limits on the total volume of solid waste put in the ground, without regard to the waste generator's in-state or out-of-state loca-tion.[81] On the other side of the coin, the nature of some state interests may virtually foreclose successful dormancy doctrine challenges, at least in balancing cases. In *Exxon Corp. v. Governor of Maryland*, 437 U.S. 117 (1978), for example, the Court upheld a Maryland law that barred all petroleum producers and refiners from operating local gas stations. At least at first glance, the burden imposed by the law on interstate commerce seemed great because the law's practical effect fell solely on out-of-state businesses in that no gas was produced or refined in Maryland and almost all gas sold by non-local service stations operators came through producer-or-refiner operated facilities. The majority, however, found no undue burden on interstate commerce and in so doing made much of the fact that the law did not preclude ownership by all out-of-state businesses because some non-pro-ducer/non-refiner firms (such as Sears & Roebuck and Pantry Pride) could continue to operate gas stations in Maryland. *Id.* at 126 & n.15. As Justice Blackmun observed in dissent, however, the state legislature's failure to engage in "universal discrimina-tion" against out-of-state entities was not controlling. *Id.* at 146–47. In *Washington Apple Advertising Commission*, for exam-ple, the Court had found a dormant Commerce Clause violation because Washington apple producers were disadvantaged by a North Carolina packaging law even though that law had no ill-effects on many other out-of-state apple producers because they had not devised a distinctive grading and package-marking sys-tem. *See id.* at 146 n.14. Indeed, the Maryland law at issue in *Exxon* seemed more onerous for out-of-state competitors than the apple-packaging restrictions imposed by North Carolina be-

Third, just as surely as courts will carefully consider the precise state interests cited in support of challenged legislation, they also will look closely at the precise burden the challenged law places on interstate commerce. In *Southern Pacific*, for example, the Court emphasized the many ways in which Arizona's train-length law raised costs and delayed deliveries.[82] Likewise, in *Clover Leaf Creamery*, the Court refused to oversimplify the case by focusing myopically on the harms suffered by out-of-state resin producers. Instead, the Court also considered the law's impact on out-of-state milk bottlers, pulp producers and dairy farmers, many of whom received an advantage from the challenged prohibi-

cause the Maryland law *flatly excluded* many out-of-state business owners from the local market; it did not (as in the *Washington Apple* case) simply complicate out-of-staters' efforts to compete with local producers. Perhaps the key to understanding *Exxon* lies in focusing closely on Maryland's claimed state interest in countering vertical integration in the gasoline-distribution industry to solve such problems as unfair discrimination against non-vertically-integrated gas stations in allocating products in times of shortage. The point is that if one recognizes that prevention of vertical integration is itself a significant state interest, then further balancing in a case such as *Exxon* is (or at least is all but) unnecessary. Even though the Maryland law disproportionately burdened non-local gas station owners, there was simply no way to avoid that result (given the pre-existing location of refiners and producers) if the practice of vertical integration was to be discontinued. For this reason, although the Court's analysis in *Exxon* is open to criticism, the majority may not have overreached in concluding that Maryland's statute did not "impermissibly" burden interstate commerce. *Id*. at 127. *See also* Regan, *supra* note 3, at 1239 (asserting that "[c]ertainly there is a much more plausible legitimate purpose to credit ... in *Exxon* than ... in ... *Hunt*").

82. *See supra* notes 11–14 and accompanying text.

tion on the use of non-returnable plastic jugs.[83] The key point is that these cases have less to do with the incantation of legal platitudes than with close, and highly contextual, factual analysis. Lawyers called on to handle dormant Commerce Clause cases must roll up their sleeves, closely probe the particular law's underlying purposes and practical effects, seek to identify less restrictive alternatives, build a supportive evidentiary record with respect to both the law's burdens and the law's benefits and do all this against a checkerboard of past Supreme Court decisions that provide rich opportunities for argument by analogy and by distinction. In short, "Commerce Clause adjudication must depend in large part 'upon the thoroughness with which the lawyers perform their task in the conduct of constitutional litigation.' "[84]

Fourth, in assessing the constitutionality of any state law, the surrounding *legal* environment may well play a key role. In *Southern Pacific, Kassel* and *Beer Institute*, for example, the Court relied heavily on the commerce-burdening effects that flowed from the challenged measure's interaction with the laws of nearby states.[85] The interaction of the state rule and federal law will sometimes matter too. In

83. *See supra* notes 51–54 and accompanying text.

84. Raymond Motor Transp., Inc. v. Rice, 434 U.S. 429, 448 n.25 (1978).

85. *See also* Bibb v. Navajo Freight Lines, Inc., 359 U.S. 520, 529–30 (1959) (emphasizing that "a design out of line with requirements of almost all the other states may sometimes place a great burden of delay and inconvenience on those interstate motor carriers entering or crossing its territory"). This consideration played a significant role in pre-*Brown v. Board of Edu-*

Edgar, for example, the Court downplayed the state's interest in according shareholders of take-over-target corporations "withdrawal, proration, and equal consideration rights" because the federal Williams Act already protected these same interests. Although the Illinois statute went farther than the Williams Act in requiring corporate disclosures, the Court reasoned that—in light of the federal law's significant, freestanding disclosure requirements—the benefits supplied by the Illinois statute were too "speculative" to say that they outweighed the substantial burdens the statute placed on interstate transactions.[86]

Fifth, the Court sometimes uses rhetoric in deciding discrete dormant Commerce Clause questions that litigants must grapple with in handling later cases. In *Exxon Corp. v. Governor of Maryland*,[87] for

cation efforts to attack generally applicable racial-segregation requirements to the extent they applied to interstate transportation. *See* Morgan v. Virginia, 328 U.S. 373, 377, 381 (1946) (striking down segregation requirement as applied to interstate bus passengers in light of "related statutes of other states"; finding that law "unduly burdens [interstate] commerce in matters where uniformity is necessary" in part because, especially for sleeping or resting passengers, "reseating would be disturbing"). *Cf.* Colorado Anti–Discrimination Comm'n v. Continental Air Lines, Inc., 372 U.S. 714, 718–22 (1963) (rejecting airline's challenge of application to it of state ban on race-discrimination in hiring; noting that hiring is more "localized" than transporting passengers and that, unlike in *Morgan*, "threat of diverse and conflicting regulation" was "virtually nonexistent" because modern interpretations of Fourteenth Amendment would ban other states from excluding pilots on the basis of race).

86. *Edgar*, 457 U.S. at 644–45.

87. 437 U.S. 117 (1978).

example, the Court upheld a law that barred oil producers and refiners from owning local gas stations, even though all disadvantaged producers and refiners conducted these operations outside the state. In finding that the law did not place an impermissible burden on interstate commerce, the Court proclaimed that nothing in "the Commerce Clause protects the particular structure or methods of operation in a retail market."[88] But what does this statement mean? Surely it does not signify that a state may freely control all "methods of operation" in any market without worrying about the dormancy doctrine. The Court invalidated the law in *Washington State Apple Advertising Commission*, for example, even though it involved a "method of operation" with respect to product packaging.[89] This statement also cannot mean that the Court will never invalidate state laws that control business ownership structures. Just two years after *Exxon*, for example, the Court invalidated a Florida law that outlawed ownership of local investment advisory firms by out-of-state bank holding companies.[90] Probably the best reading of *Exxon*'s "particular structures or methods" language is that existing businesses, including out-of-state businesses, have no vested right to keep in place any pre-existing laws, including pre-existing laws about the permissibility of vertical integration. Just as surely as "variations in the experiences or habits of differ-

88. *Id.* at 127.

89. *See supra* notes 43–48 and accompanying text.

90. Lewis v. BT Inv. Managers, Inc., 447 U.S. 27 (1980).

ent communities may well call for different legislative regulations as to methods and manners of doing business,"[91] so too may shifts in conditions and values that take place over time.

Finally, it is important to see that dormant Commerce Clause cases do not always fit into a single, tidy pattern. Facially neutral laws, for example, may be evaluated under the *Pike* balancing test, under the specialized *Pike* rule apparently applicable in road-safety cases, under a categorization approach that asks whether the law is "discriminatory in effect," or under a "discriminatory purpose" or "extraterritoriality" analysis. All roads lead to Rome, however, and at least one of these analytical pathways is likely to produce a finding of invalidity if the challenged state law in fact substantially impedes the free flow of interstate commerce for no good reason. The key point is that lawyers and students can effectively use the Court's dormant Commerce Clause precedents to develop a "sense of smell" for problematic state laws. If such a law significantly trenches on the common-market values that have driven the dormancy principle for 150 years, it is likely that the Court will find in its precedents some rhetorical vehicle to support a determination of invalidity.

91.   Breard v. Alexandria, 341 U.S. 622, 641 (1951).

Chapter XII

Exceptions to the Dormant Commerce Clause Principle

From the earliest days of the dormancy doctrine, the Court has recognized important limitations on its operation. Three limitations continue to occupy prominent places in the pantheon of dormant Commerce Clause doctrine: the congressional-consent exception, the subsidy exception and the market-participant exception. We turn first, however, to the so-called quarantine exception and other limitations that have not fared well in the modern era.

A. The Modern Movement Away From Categorical Dormant Commerce Clause Exceptions

Notwithstanding the dormancy doctrine's far-reaching anti-discrimination principle, the Court indicated in a string of early decisions that states could adopt "quarantine" laws that flatly ban the importation of "noxious" items, such as "rags ... infected with the germs of yellow fever" or "animals having contagious or infectious diseases."[1] The Court retained, but narrowed, this quarantine principle when it struck down the prohibition on solid waste importation at issue in *City of Philadelphia v. New Jersey.*[2] The dissenters in that case argued that the "fact of life that New Jersey must somehow dispose of its own noxious items does not mean that it must serve as a depository for those of every other State."[3] Writing for the majority, however, Justice Stewart suggested that import-restricting quarantine laws are permissible only when the "very movement" of the excluded goods "risked

1. Bowman v. Chicago & Northwestern Ry. Co., 125 U.S. 465, 489, 491–92 (1888); *see, e.g.,* Mintz v. Baldwin, 289 U.S. 346, 350 (1933) (upholding prohibition on importation of cattle unless certified as coming from herds free of highly infectious Bang's Disease; concluding without difficulty that order did not "so unnecessarily burden[] interstate transportation as to contravene the commerce clause"). The earliest articulations of this principle also supported a state authority to "exclude from its limits convicts, paupers, idiots and lunatics," all of whom the Court seemed willing to liken to "persons afflicted by contagious or infectious diseases." *Bowman,* 125 U.S. at 492. The Court, however, abandoned this stance in *Edwards v. California,* 314 U.S. 160 (1941). In invalidating a California law that criminalized bringing any "indigent" nonresident into the state, the Court reasoned that the "the transportation of persons is commerce," *id.* at 172; that providing assistance to the needy and "the social phenomenon of large-scale interstate migration" were matters "of national concern," *id.* at 175; and that, whatever one may have thought a century earlier, "we do not think that it will now be seriously contended that because a person is without employment and without funds he constitutes a 'moral pestilence,' " *id.* at 177.

2. 437 U.S. 617 (1978).

3. *Id.* at 632 (Rehnquist, J., joined by Burger, C.J., dissenting).

contagion and other evils."[4] Because problems associated with solid waste—including leachate, vermin
and green space loss—arise only after the waste's
disposal, the Court refused to view the law at issue
in *City of Philadelphia* as the sort of quarantine
measure exempt from dormant Commerce Clause
attack.

In *Chemical Waste Management, Inc. v. Hunt*,[5]
the Court further eroded the quarantine exception
when it struck down an Alabama measure that
imposed a special charge on the importation of
hazardous waste produced in other states. Without
considering dangers posed by such waste while in
transit, the Court concluded that the challenged
rule was far removed from a genuine quarantine
measure because "Alabama permits both the generation and landfilling of hazardous waste ... and the
importation of still more hazardous waste subject to
payment of the additional fee."[6] After *City of Philadelphia* and *Chemical Waste Management*, the
would-be quarantine exception may be moving toward something like the following principle: A state
may foreclose the importation of items only if (1)
they are marked by a noxious condition that threatens infection or similar dangers, and (2) the state
has, within its own borders, sought to stamp out
the noxious condition, including by aggressively
minimizing exposure to it by people or property
that might be put at risk by the threat it poses. On
this view, the Court in *Chemical Waste Management* properly invalidated the challenged law not

4. *Id.* at 629.

5. 504 U.S. 334 (1992).

6. *Id.* at 346–47.

only because it tolerated the generation of hazardous waste as a foreseeable by-product of local business operations but also because the grant of authority to transport waste for a fee was inconsistent with an intention to invalidate any and all exposure to it.

Other once-recognized exceptions to the dormancy doctrine have met an even harsher fate. In a 19th-century case, *Geer v. Connecticut*,[7] the Court exempted wild-game laws—including a flatly discriminatory prohibition on killing ducks and geese for shipment outside the state—from Commerce Clause challenge. In *Hughes v. Oklahoma*,[8] however, the Court overruled *Geer,* describing its "state ownership" rationale as a "legal fiction" that ignored "practical realities."[9] Drawing on *Hughes*, the Court next abandoned its earlier endorsement of a wholesale exemption from Commerce Clause scrutiny for state water-export restrictions.[10] The Court concluded that "[a]lthough [the state's] greater ownership interest may not be irrelevant to Commerce Clause analysis, it does not absolutely remove [regulation of local] ground water from such scrutiny."[11]

7. 161 U.S. 519 (1896).

8. 441 U.S. 322 (1979).

9. *Id.* at 335–36.

10. Sporhase v. Nebraska, 458 U.S. 941 (1982) (refusing to follow Hudson County Water Co. v. McCarter, 209 U.S. 349, 357 (1908), which in turn had relied on *Geer*).

11. *Id.* at 951. At the same time, the Court in *Sporhase* endorsed a distinctly deferential approach to water regulations,

Other modern cases carry forward the tendency, reflected in both *Hughes* and *Sporhase*, of looking askance at broad categorical exceptions to the dormant Commerce Clause principle. In *Bacchus Imports, Ltd. v. Dias*, the Court declined to embrace an exception for liquor regulation, notwithstanding the Twenty–First Amendment's express grant to states of authority over the "transportation or importation" of alcoholic beverages.[12] In a less-noticed move, the Court in the same case appeared to reject any exception for discriminatory state laws (here, in the form of a discriminatory tax law) designed to bolster start-up or struggling local industries. Although arguments occasionally surface for state favoritism in this context,[13] the Court declared that "the propriety of economic protectionism may not be allowed to hinge upon the State's—or this Court's—characterization of the industry as either 'thriving' or 'struggling.' "[14]

including ostensibly discriminatory state efforts "to conserve and preserve *for its own citizens* this vital resource in times of severe shortage." *Id.* at 956 (emphasis added). In adopting this specialized approach, the Court relied in substantial part on the idea that water "has some indicia of a good publicly produced and owned" by the state as a result of conservation efforts. *Id.* at 957. This logic bears a close kinship to the logic that underlies the market-participant exception to the dormancy doctrine, which is discussed *infra* Chapter XII.

   12.   468 U.S. 263 (1984).

   13.   *See* Donald H. Regan, *The Supreme Court and State Protectionism: Making Sense of the Dormant Commerce Clause*, 84 MICH. L. REV. 1091, 1138 (1986) (noting argument for infant-industry protectionism).

   14.   *Id.* at 273.

Most recently, the Court rejected a dormant Commerce Clause exception proposed in a case that involved a tax break given by Maine only to those "benevolent and charitable institutions" that primarily served residents of the state.[15] Challenged by a religious summer camp that dealt with many nonresidents, the law fell victim to the anti-discrimination principle despite a stinging dissent written by Justice Scalia on behalf of four Justices. According to the dissenters, the Court should have used the case to endorse a "domestic charity exception" for resident-serving nonprofit institutions on the theory that they deliver "social services" that the state could limit to its own residents if the state provided those services itself.[16] The majority, however, was unmoved. In Justice Stevens's view, there was no justification for distinguishing for-profit from not-for-profit enterprises because "[e]ntities in both categories are major participants in interstate markets" and "[i]f there is need for a special exception for nonprofits, Congress ... has the power to create it."[17] We turn now to the congressional-consent exception that helped drive, in this prominent way, the majority's approach to the Maine summer camp case.

B. The Congressional–Consent Exception

The "congressional consent" exception is simple in its basic operation: If Congress so provides, state

15. Camps Newfound/Owatonna, Inc. v. Town of Harrison, 520 U.S. 564, 568 (1997).

16. *Id.* at 605 (Scalia, J., dissenting); *see id.* at 602–08.

17. *Id.* at 586–88.

laws that otherwise offend the dormant Commerce Clause are immune from challenge under it. Because this doctrine permits Congress to overturn ostensibly constitutional rulings without resort to the constitutional amendment process, it has sparked controversy from time to time. In the seminal *Cooley* decision, for example, the Court asserted that "[i]f the Constitution excluded the States from making any law regulating commerce, certainly Congress cannot re-grant, or in any manner re-convey to the States that power."[18] This dictum, however, has been submerged by a flood of later pronouncements. Most notably, in *Prudential Insurance Co. v. Benjamin*,[19] the Court declared that Congress could exercise its power to regulate interstate commerce, including by subjecting it to limitations and disadvantages, "in conjunction with coordinated action by the states."[20] Invoking this principle, the Court in *Prudential Insurance* went on to conclude that the federal McCarran–Ferguson Act exempted from dormant-Commerce–Clause scrutiny even outright state discrimination in the taxation of insurance companies chartered in other

18. Cooley v. Bd. of Wardens of Port of Philadelphia, 53 U.S. (12 How.) 299, 318 (1851).

19. 328 U.S. 408 (1946).

20. *Id*. at 434. One might say, to put the same point another way, that the dormant Commerce Clause is no longer dormant once Congress has spoken, including by declaring that particular state laws do not unduly burden interstate trade.

jurisdictions.[21]

Notwithstanding the modern Court's unwavering endorsement of the congressional-consent exception, it has applied that exception with restraint. As explained in *Maine v. Taylor*,[22] "because of the important role the Commerce Clause plays in protecting the free flow of interstate trade, this Court has exempted state statutes from the implied limitations of the Clause only when the congressional direction to do so has been unmistakably clear."[23] Citing this principle, the Court declined to rely on the congressional-consent principle to uphold the discriminatory ban on baitfish imports at issue in that case. In particular, the Court rejected the state's half-a-loaf argument that the federal government's extensive regulation of commerce in wildlife—while not amounting to outright consent—warranted a watered-down form of dormant Commerce Clause review. Instead, citing the "risk that unrepresented interests will be adversely affected by restraints on commerce," the Court found the "clear expression" rule fully applicable "regardless of whether the purported authorization takes the form of a flat exemption from Commerce Clause scrutiny or the less direct form of a reduction in the

21. *Id.* For a leading scholarly defense of the congressional-consent rule, see William Cohen, *Congressional Power to Validate Unconstitutional State Laws: A Forgotten Solution to an Old Enigma*, 35 STAN. L. REV. 387 (1983).

22. 477 U.S. 131 (1986).

23. *Id.* at 139. *Accord, e.g.*, Hillside Dairy, Inc. v. Lyons, 123 S.Ct. 2142, 2146–47 (2003).

level of scrutiny."[24]

The Court also limited the practical impact of the congressional-consent exception with its interpretation of the Equal Protection Clause in *Metropolitan Life Insurance Co. v. Ward*.[25] There, a foreign corporation challenged a state tax law that discriminated on its face in favor of domestic insurers. Writing for a five-Justice majority, Justice Powell conceded that the law was immune from dormant Commerce Clause challenge under the McCarran–Ferguson Act and the congressional-consent exception as applied in the *Prudential Insurance* case. He went on, however, to find the law unconstitutional under the Fourteenth Amendment's Equal Protection Clause, which is not subject to any congressional-consent exception. The problem with the challenged law was that "penalizing foreign insurers" to effectuate "parochial discrimination" was not the sort of "legitimate state purpose" that even minimal equal protection review requires of state legislation.[26]

As other analysts have noted, "[t]he implications of *Metropolitan Life* remain uncertain."[27] The decision drew a rebuke from an unusual coalition of four dissenting Justices (namely, Justices Brennan, Marshall, Rehnquist and O'Connor), who described

24. *Id.* at 139.

25. 470 U.S. 869 (1985).

26. *Id.* at 877–78.

27. KATHLEEN M. SULLIVAN & GERALD GUNTHER, CONSTITUTIONAL LAW 327 (14th ed. 2001); *see also* William Cohen, *Federalism In Equality Clothing: A Comment on* Metropolitan Life Insurance Company v. Ward, 38 STAN. L. REV. 1 (1985).

as "astonishing" the majority's unwillingness to view as legitimate a state purpose "to encourage capital investment within its borders."[28] In addition, later in the same term, the Court cabined the principle of *Metropolitan Life* when it upheld a congressionally authorized program established by Massachusetts and Connecticut that entirely barred the local operation of banks headquartered in any of the other 48 states.[29] Perhaps most significantly, the Court's reasoning in *Metropolitan Life* itself may signal that states can sidestep equal protection difficulties by simply coming up with *some* explanation for tax discrimination other than outright protectionism. States, for example, might seek to justify heightened taxation of non-resident firms on a theory that it roughly equalizes tax burdens placed on resident corporations by way of local property and other taxes. Such a justification—which almost always fails for dormant Commerce Clause purposes[30]—may nonetheless work for equal protection purposes to avert a fatal characterization of the law as "purely and completely discriminatory."[31]

28. *Metro. Life Ins. Co.*, 470 U.S. at 883 (O'Connor, J., dissenting).

29. *See* Northeast Bancorp, Inc. v. Board of Govs. of Fed. Reserve Sys., 472 U.S. 159 (1985). Seeming to grasp at analytical straws, the Court reasoned that, unlike in *Metropolitan Life*, neither Massachusetts nor Connecticut had excluded all interstate commerce (because each state permitted competition coming from the other) and that banking was (for some reason) a matter of distinctly "profound local concern." *Id.* at 177.

30. *See infra* Chapter XIII.

31. *Metro. Life Ins. Co.*, 470 U.S. at 878. There is case law support for the idea that equal protection law puts fewer re-

C. The Subsidy Exception

Prior discussion has shown that discriminatory tax laws, unless authorized by Congress, routinely violate the dormant Commerce Clause because they provide favored in-state firms with a competitive edge.[32] Basic "tax expenditure theory" teaches, however, that tax exemptions, credits and deductions are, as an economic matter, functionally indistinguishable from outright monetary grants.[33] Does it follow that cash subsidies for in-state businesses are unconstitutional because—just like discriminatory tax laws—they provide local firms with advantages *vis-à-vis* out-of-state competitors?

Although the Supreme Court has left itself wiggle room to reconsider the matter,[34] its precedents signal that the answer to this question is "no."[35]

straints than the dormancy doctrine on states' ability to adopt these sorts of "compensatory" taxes. *See* Associated Indus. v. Lohman, 511 U.S. 641, 651–52 (1994).

32. *See supra* Chapter X. *See also infra* Chapter XIII.

33. *See, e.g.,* Stanley S. Surrey, *Tax Incentives as a Device for Implementing Government Policy: A Comparison with Direct Government Expenditures,* 83 HARV. L. REV. 705, 717 (1970) ("A dollar is a dollar—both for the person who receives it and the government that pays it, whether the dollar comes with a tax credit label or a direct expenditure label.").

34. *See* Camps Newfound/Owatonna, Inc. v. Town of Harrison, 520 U.S. 564, 589 (1997) (noting that "[w]e have 'never squarely confronted the constitutionality of subsidies' ... and we need not address these questions today").

35. *See, e.g.,* Dan T. Coenen, *Business Subsidies and the Dormant Commerce Clause,* 107 YALE L.J. 965, 977–78 (1998).

Given the recurring theme that "practical realities" should guide dormant Commerce Clause decision making,[36] how can the Court justify this failure to equate discriminatory tax breaks with outright monetary subsidies? One explanation lies in the constitutional text. On this view, the Commerce Clause by its terms deals with the power to "regulate" interstate commerce, which forecloses taxation that "burdens" such commerce but not affirmative subsidization that operates only to "benefit" intrastate actors.[37] Another explanation lies in constitutional history. After all, it was not fear of unfair subsidization, but concern about "taxation without representation," that dominated American worries at the time of both the Revolution and the Constitutional Convention.[38]

The best explanation, however, seems to lie in concerns about "pragmatism"[39] and "practical consequences"[40] that the Court has consistently trumpeted as critical in applying the dormant Commerce Clause doctrine. Tax breaks and subsidies may not be *economically* different, but they are *politically* different. In particular, monetary subsidies are likely to encounter distinctive political checks because they involve straightforward and visible government spending; they are subject to reconsideration

36. Hughes v. Oklahoma, 441 U.S. 322, 335 (1979).

37. For a criticism of this view, see Coenen, *supra* note 35, at 1013–14.

38. *See id.* at 980–81.

39. Quill Corp. v. North Dakota, 504 U.S. 298, 310 (1992).

40. Nippert v. City of Richmond, 327 U.S. 416, 431 (1946).

in each year's budgeting process; and they lack the built-in appeal, for many, of government tax reduction.[41] As a result, the tax-break/subsidy distinction dovetails with the Court's recognition that judicial review under the dormancy principle may properly moderate when a "State's own political processes will act as a check on local regulations that unduly burden interstate commerce."[42]

When does a government program or rule fall within the subsidy exception? One governing principle is that the exception does not reach any form of discriminatory *tax* relief afforded by state law, regardless of whether that relief takes the form of a favorable exemption, deduction, credit, rebate or refund.[43] A more difficult question, which was squarely presented in *West Lynn Creamery, Inc. v. Healy*,[44] is whether there are instances in which a benefit characterized by the state as a "subsidy" or "payment" may be recharacterized by the courts as an unconstitutionally discriminatory tax break.[45] *West Lynn Creamery* involved a two-part Massachusetts program designed to aid the state's struggling dairy farming industry. The first part of the pro-

41. *See* Coenen, *supra* note 35, at 984–97.

42. Raymond Motor Transp., Inc. v. Rice, 434 U.S. 429, 447 (1978).

43. *See* Dan T. Coenen & Walter Hellerstein, *Suspect Linkage: The Interplay of State Taxing and Spending Measures in the Application of Constitutional Antidiscrimination Rules*, 95 MICH. L. REV. 2167, 2203–14 (1997) (elaborating this principle and noting possible qualifications of it).

44. 512 U.S. 186 (1994).

45. *Id.* at 194.

gram entailed the imposition of a tax on dealers for all milk they sold to retailers, whether or not that milk had come from inside or outside the state. The second part of the program required that all proceeds of this tax be used to make monetary payments to Massachusetts dairy farmers.

According to the dissenting opinion of Chief Justice Rehnquist, who was joined by Justice Blackmun, the state's program was constitutional because it embodied a permissible nondiscriminatory tax and state pay-outs that were unobjectionable under the subsidy exception to the dormant Commerce Clause.[46] The Court's majority, however, rejected this analysis. Reasoning that the two features of the challenged program could not be viewed in isolation, the majority opinion written by Justice Stevens recharacterized the state's payments to its dairy farmers as discriminatory tax "refunds" or "rebates."[47] It was inconsequential to the majority that the supposed tax relief went to beneficiaries (that is, dairy farmers) who were not the target of the tax (that is, milk dealers). The overarching problem, according to Justice Stevens, was that the Massachusetts program "in its practical effect" violated "the cardinal principle that a State may not 'benefit in-state economic interests by burdening out-of-state competitors.' "[48]

46. *Id*. at 212 (Rehnquist, C.J., dissenting).

47. *Id*. at 197.

48. *Id*. at 199 (quoting New Energy Co. v. Limbach, 486 U.S. 269, 273–74 (1988)).

The *de facto* refund principle of *West Lynn Creamery* raises troublesome problems of legal labeling. To begin with, the Court in that case focused on the subsidy program's unusually close linkage with a specialized state tax. But how should courts decide whether any particular tax-subsidy linkage is close enough to raise a constitutional red flag? Must the payment and tax programs appear in the same law? Must they be enacted simultaneously or at least close in time? Does an adequate linkage exist only when, as Justice Scalia claimed in his concurrence, the tax proceeds never find their way into the general treasury but instead go directly into a segregated fund from which all payments are made?[49] These and other questions about the requisite connection between subsidies and taxes loom on the horizon of dormant Commerce Clause law.[50]

49. *Id.* at 211 (Scalia, J., concurring).

50. For detailed treatments of these questions, as well as related questions raised in the tax-immunity context, see Coenen & Hellerstein, *supra* note 43, at 2215–27; and Coenen, *supra* note 35, at 1037–53. For a recent and narrowing gloss on *West Lynn Creamery*, see *Pharmaceutical Research & Manufacturers of America v. Walsh*, 123 S.Ct. 1855, 1871 (2003) (refusing to apply *West Lynn Creamery* rule where payments effectively required by Maine from out-of-state drug manufacturers resulted in financial benefit to local pharmacies and consumers; finding *de facto* tariff principle inapplicable because "payments to the local pharmacists provide no special benefit to competitors of [out-of-state] manufacturers," which would receive no benefit from the program even "by opening production facilities in Maine").

D. The Market–Participant Exception

Closely related to the Court's treatment of subsidies is its recognition of the "market participant" exception to the dormancy doctrine. Indeed, the Court first applied the market-participant exception in *Hughes v. Alexandria Scrap*[51] to validate a novel cash-subsidy program. In *Alexandria Scrap,* the Court faced a challenge to a Maryland law under which payments by the state went to scrap processors as part of an effort to rid local roadsides of unsightly junk cars. The fly in the ointment was that Maryland imposed more onerous and costly documentation requirements for obtaining state pay-outs on out-of-state than on in-state scrap processing firms. The Court, however, rejected an out-of-state processor's challenge to this patently discriminatory feature of the Maryland program. According to Justice Powell, who wrote for six Justices, the non-discrimination rule had no role to play in the case because the state had not sought to regulate private market behavior. Instead, because Maryland had "entered the market, in effect, as a purchaser," it was free to choose its own trading partners.[52] The dissenters worried that the Court had taken a wrong turn by "treating what is essentially a problem of striking a balance between com-

51. 426 U.S. 794 (1976).

52. *Id.* at 808.

peting interests as an exercise in absolutes."[53] For the majority, however, the governing principle was straightforward: "Nothing in the purposes animating the Commerce Clause prohibits a State, in the absence of congressional action, from participating in the market and exercising the right to favor its own citizens over others."[54]

The Court consolidated the market-participant exception in *Reeves, Inc. v. Stake*[55] by holding that, in a time of shortage, South Dakota could restrict sales from a state-owned cement plant to South Dakota residents. Then, in *White v. Massachusetts Council of Construction Employers, Inc.*,[56] the Court invoked the exception to uphold a Boston law that required building contractors engaged by the city to give a specified minimum percentage of resulting jobs to city residents. In effect, the Court's decision in *White* embodied two separate holdings. First, the Court effectively shielded from dormant Commerce Clause scrutiny the common practice of favoring state or municipal residents in hiring state or municipal employees. Second, the Court extended this principle to permit a city to force a private contractor that was working on a city construction project to favor local residents in its own hiring for that project. The Court justified this second holding by reasoning that persons employed to work on such a project, although paid and supervised by a private

53. *Id.* at 819 (Brennan, J., dissenting) (quoting H. P. Hood & Sons, Inc. v. Du Mond, 336 U.S. 525, 564 (1949) (Frankfurter, J., dissenting)).

54. *Id.* at 810.

55. 447 U.S. 429 (1980).

56. 460 U.S. 204 (1983).

firm, were "in a substantial, if informal, sense, 'working for the city.' "[57]

The market-participant exception to the dormant Commerce Clause, like the congressional-consent and subsidy exceptions, has proven controversial. Each of the Court's rulings—in *Alexandria Scrap*, *Reeves* and *White*—came from divided Courts, and Justice Brennan suggested that the Court's disagreements "point up the inherent weakness of the doctrine."[58] Commentators have challenged the exception on the ground that, among other things, it threatens efficiency and creates incentives for states to engage in business operations best handled by private firms.[59] Even so, the market-participant rule seems well entrenched. No majority opinion has

57. *Id.* at 211 n.7.

58. South–Central Timber Dev., Inc. v. Wunnicke, 467 U.S. 82, 101 (1984) (Brennan, J., concurring). The Court's ruling in *Reeves* came in a five-four decision, and Justice Powell, who had written for the majority in *Alexandria Scrap*, wrote the dissenting opinion. The Court's ruling in *White* came in a seven-to-two decision, and Justice Blackmun, who had written for the majority in *Reeves*, wrote the dissenting opinion. The Court's later ruling in *South-Central Timber*, to which Justice Brennan specifically alluded, in effect resulted from a four-to-two vote on the dormant Commerce Clause issue, due to the filing of a separate concurrence by Justice Powell, joined by Chief Justice Burger, and Justice Marshall's non-participation in the case. Justice Rehnquist, who had written for the Court's majority in *White*, penned the dissent in *South-Central Timber*.

59. *See, e.g.*, Christine H. Kellett, *The Market Participant Doctrine: No Longer "Good Sense" or "Sound Law,"* 9 TEMP. ENVTL. L. & TECH. J. 169 (1990). Professor Tribe has written that "[t]he Court's reasoning in these cases is in some respects problematic." LAURENCE H. TRIBE, AMERICAN CONSTITUTIONAL LAW, § 6–11, at 1090 (3d ed., vol. one, 2000). *See also id.* at 1090 n.20 (collecting authorities that have questioned the doctrine).

ever questioned the doctrine. Nine different Justices contributed to the majorities that handed down the decisions in *Alexandria Scrap, Reeves* and *White*.[60] And no Justice who later joined the Court has spoken ill of the doctrine.

So just what considerations justify recognition of the market-participant exception? In *Reeves* the Court pointed to history, conventional understanding, fairness and federalism in claiming that the exception reflects "good sense and sound law."[61] As to history, the Court reasoned that the Commerce Clause grew out of concerns about the imposition of obstructive taxes and regulations on private parties engaged in private transactions, and not state favoritism toward residents when the state itself engages in buying and selling.[62] As to convention, the Court cited the "long recognized right of trader or manufacturer, engaged in an entirely private business, freely to exercise his own independent discretion as to parties with whom he will deal."[63] As to fairness, the Court reasoned that state citizens should be able to reap where they have sown, including by insisting that the state may "limit[] benefits gener-

60. The Justices joining various majorities in *Alexandria Scrap, Reeves* and *White* were Chief Justice Burger and Justices Blackmun, Brennan, Marshall, O'Connor, Powell, Rehnquist, Stevens, and Stewart.

61. Reeves, Inc. v. Stake, 447 U.S. 429, 436 (1980). *See generally* Dan T. Coenen, *Untangling the Market–Participant Exemption to the Dormant Commerce Clause*, 88 MICH. L. REV. 395 (1989).

62. *Reeves*, 447 U.S. at 437.

63. *Id*. at 438–39.

ated by a state program to those who fund the State treasury."[64] Finally, as to federalism, the Court reasoned that the market-participant rule comported with the value of state experimentation. Justice Blackmun noted that the South Dakota cement plant had benefited both the state and the region since the early 1900s. He wondered, however, whether South Dakota would have ever built the plant at all if it had known that it would have to hold back supplies from its own residents to fill orders from out-of-state buyers in times of greatest need.[65] The Court's actual experience in applying the market-participant exception may also aid the case for retaining it. The key point is that the Court has wielded the exception with restraint by surrounding it with an array of important limits. In so doing, the Court has neutralized "worst fears" arguments about the market-participant doctrine's susceptibility to abuse.

E. Limits on the Market–Participant Exception

Just as surely as the Court has applied the market-participant exception in several cases, it has

64. *Id.* at 442. The Court also noted that state proprietary activities commonly are subject to the same restrictions applicable to private business; thus "[e]venhandedness suggests that, when acting as proprietors, States should similarly share existing freedoms from federal constraints, including the inherent limits of the Commerce Clause." *Id.* at 439.

65. *Id.* at 441.

declined to apply the exception in others. In *New England Power Co. v. New Hampshire*,[66] for example, the state relied on its "ownership" of the Connecticut River in passing a law that restricted the ability of privately owned plants located on the river to export hydroelectric power. The Court, however, invalidated the law, reasoning that the federal government had primary control over navigable waters and that the challenged law, in any event, targeted electric power and not the waters of the river itself.[67] In *Camps Newfound/Owattona*,[68] the state again tried to shoehorn an overtly discriminatory measure—here in the form of tax relief provided only to those non-profit corporations that favored residents—into the market-participant mold. A five-Justice majority, however, could not see how affording tax breaks to private entities even remotely qualified as "market participation" by the state. The majority also observed that the tax exemption differed from the "discrete" program in *Alexandria Scrap* and the "narrow" program in *Reeves* because "it sweeps to cover broad swathes of the nonprofit sector."[69]

66. 455 U.S. 331 (1982).

67. *Id*. at 338 n.6.

68. *See supra* notes 15–17 and accompanying text.

69. *Id*. at 594. The Court's "broad swathes" rationale may well surface again as the Court grapples with market-participant issues in other contexts. It could, for example, influence the Court's evaluation of an issue that has divided the circuit courts—namely, whether states may require all local governments to put in place buy-local and similar proprietary programs. *Compare* W.C.M. Window Co. v. Bernardi, 730 F.2d 486 (7th Cir. 1984) (holding that such state laws are not sustainable on a

Most important, the plurality opinion in *South-Central Timber Co. v. Wunnicke*[70] pointed to three possible "exceptions to the exception" in the market-participant field. At issue in the case was an Alaska rule that required purchasers of the state's standing timber to process that timber within the state prior to exportation. In rejecting the law, the Court emphasized that it (1) involved a natural resource; (2) impeded international, as well as interstate, commerce; and (3) not only imposed restrictions on the state's own timber sales but also "impose[d] conditions downstream in the timber-processing market."[71] Finally, Supreme Court authorities apart from *South-Central Timber* signal that a fourth "exception to the exception" applies when the state seeks to restrict access to channels of commerce that the state itself owns. We now turn to each of these four possible "exceptions to the exception" embedded in the Court's market-participant rulings.

1. *Natural resources*. In *Reeves*, the Court distinguished cement—the product of an elaborate manufacturing process that works on raw materi-

market-participant theory), *with* National Solid Waste Mgmt. Ass'n v. Williams, 146 F.3d 595, 599 (8th Cir. 1998) (declining to follow *W. C. M. Window*); Trojan Tech., Inc. v. Pennsylvania, 916 F.2d 903 (3d Cir. 1990) (same). *See generally* Coenen, *supra* note 61, at 481–84.

70. 467 U.S. 82 (1984).

71. *Id.* at 95. Arguably, the Court looked at these factors in the aggregate. But *South-Central Timber,* and other cases as well, lend support to the view that each of these "factors" may independently limit the operation of the market-participant exception.

als—from natural resources located "by happenstance" within the state.[72] The Court thus implied that two mutually reinforcing justifications might support recognition of a natural-resources exception to the market-participant doctrine. First, the lucky chance of possessing such resources gives a state less of a claim to hoard them, particularly in light of the exception's fairness-based sow-and-reap rationale. Second, the restriction of access to natural resources threatens interstate commerce in unique ways because those resources constitute the essential building blocks of production. As usual, these justifications have spawned critiques. The extraction of many natural resources, for example, involves substantial outlays by their owner, and buyers denied access to state-owned natural resources can always look elsewhere for market substitutes. In *South-Central Timber*, however, the Court plurality reiterated *Reeves*'s emphasis that special considerations might well be present if "a natural resource 'like coal, timber, wild game, or minerals' [is] involved."[73]

Assuming a natural-resource exception exists, borderline questions will arise about whether particular state transactions fall within it. Take the case of state-owned landfills. Does land constitute a natural resource so that a state may deny nonresidents access to any landfill that the state itself owns and operates? The better answer is "no." Whatever label one attaches to land, all states have it. It follows that the key justifications for the natural

72. *Reeves*, 447 U.S. at 444.

73. *South-Central Timber*, 467 U.S. at 96.

resources exception, based on happenstance and scarcity, do not apply with much force in this context—as lower courts in effect have concluded.[74]

2. *Foreign Commerce.* In *South-Central Timber*, the Court emphasized that much Alaska timber was exported to Japan and that, for this reason, the state's processing restriction significantly impeded international, as well as interstate, commerce. The Court reasoned that this fact helped support invalidation of the law because it brought into play the additional policy concern that "the Federal Government [should speak] with one voice when regulating commercial relations with foreign governments."[75] These few words leave it far from clear whether a full-fledged foreign-commerce "exception" to the market participant doctrine stands on the brink of judicial recognition. The Court, however, has paid attention to this factor in other contexts[76] and is likely to follow the lead of *South-Central Timber* by according it at least some weight in the market-participant calculus.[77]

74. *E.g.*, Swin Resource Sys., Inc. v. Lycoming County, 883 F.2d 245 (3d Cir. 1989) (applying dormant Commerce Clause to invalidate discrimination by publicly owned waste facility); County Comm'rs v. Stevens, 473 A.2d 12 (Md. 1984) (same).

75. *South-Central Timber*, 467 U.S. at 100.

76. *See* Japan Line, Ltd. v. Los Angeles County, 441 U.S. 434 (1979) (invalidating state *ad valorem* property tax, as applied to Japanese shipping companies' cargo containers which were used exclusively in foreign commerce, because the tax was inconsistent with Congress's power to regulate commerce with foreign nations).

77. *See* Brannon P. Denning & Jack H. McCall, Jr., *The Constitutionality of State and Local "Sanctions" Against Foreign*

3. *Downstream Restraints.* Writing for the Court's four-Justice plurality in *South-Central Timber*, Justice White placed primary emphasis on the special threats to a free-flowing commerce posed by the "State's attachment of restrictions on dispositions subsequent to the goods coming to rest in private hands."[78] According to Justice White, such "downstream restrictions" properly negate application of the "market *participant*" label because they have the "*regulatory* effect" of controlling the behavior of purely private trading partners—in *South-Central Timber*, private log owners and private timber processors.[79] Seeking to develop this notion, Justice White continued: "The limit of the market-participant doctrine must be that it allows a State to impose burdens on commerce within a market in which it is a participant, but allows it to go no further." In addition, he urged that the market that the state has entered must be "relatively narrowly defined" lest the market-participant exception "swallow[] up" the dormant Commerce Clause rule.[80]

The plurality opinion then proceeded to apply these principles by contrasting the facts of *White* with those of *South-Central Timber*. In the *White* case, Justice White explained, Boston had entered

Countries: Affairs of State, States' Affairs, or a Sorry State of Affairs, 26 HASTINGS CONST. L.Q. 307, 351–68 (1999) (arguing that market-participant exception should not extend to foreign commerce).

78. *South-Central Timber,* 467 U.S. at 98.

79. *Id.*

80. *Id.* at 97–99.

the market for employment because construction workers employed by private contractors "substantially ... worked for the City" in "the course of an ongoing commercial relationship in which the city retained a continuing proprietary interest." In *South-Central Timber*, by contrast, Alaska was not "participating in the processed timber market" because it merely "restricts the post-purchase activity of the purchaser" and "participates in no way in the actual processing."[81]

As the Court's efforts to distinguish these two cases reveal, application of the "downstream restraint" principle is complicated by the rich variety of forms such restraints may take.[82] If a state gives high school graduates scholarships for strong performance, but only if they attend in-state colleges, has it imposed a discriminatory restriction "on a market in which it is not a participant"? Does the answer to the question depend on whether the program benefits private-college, as well as public-college, students? (The argument seems strong, after all, that states are participants in the market for public education, but less strong that they are participants in the private-education market as well.) Are downstream restraint problems negated if the state issues checks directly to in-state private

81. *Id.* at 98–99.

82. *See, e.g.*, New England Power Co. v. New Hampshire, 455 U.S. 331, 338 n.6 (1982) (invalidating state ban on private company's exportation of hydroelectric power generated by river state claims to own because law restricts "the sale of electric energy, a product entirely distinct from the river waters used to produce it").

schools, rather than to students, because this form of payment injects the state into the private-education market in its capacity as a payor? (Note, in this regard, the Court's unwillingness in *South-Central Timber* "to say that the State could evade the reasoning of this opinion by merely including a provision ... that title [to the timber] does not pass until the processing is complete" because "the substance of the transaction ... governs."[83]) Does the state remain a participant in both the public-education and private-education markets, so that there is no downstream-restraint problem, if it monitors student performance following the award grant with a view to assessing continuing eligibility for scholarship grants? Is talk about "markets" entirely irrelevant in the cash-grant scholarship context because it involves a subsidy, rather than a market-participant, problem? And for that matter, is talk about state participation in particular markets ever appropriate, given that the ruling in *South-Central Timber* came from a mere plurality of four Justices, only one of whom (Justice Stevens) still sits on the Court?[84]

4. *Channels of Commerce.* A final exception to the market-participant doctrine applies when the state grants access to the channels of commerce in which it maintains a proprietary interest. Consider the Court's road cases, such as *Bibb*, *Raymond* and

83. *Id.* at 99 n.11.

84. *See generally* Note, *Dormant Danger?: A Potential Constitutional Challenge to Georgia's Hope Scholarship*, 34 GA. L. REV. 1381 (2000).

Kassel.[85] Basic doctrine condemns state laws that discriminate against or unduly burden interstate users of roadways. Yet states pay for, build and own state roads, so that—at least as a matter of theory—the market participant exception might be invoked in this context. One senses that a refusal to apply the market-participant exception in these cases reflects the special importance of the infrastructure of commerce to interstate movement and trade. But how far does this "exception to the exception" extend? Without saying as much, one circuit court applied the channels-of-commerce exception to validate a state's discrimination against nonresident vendors who sought to rent space in a state-owned farmers' market.[86] Another application of this exception has come in cases that involve highway and airport "user fees."[87] To understand those cases, however, we must first consider how the dormant Commerce Clause relates to state tax laws, a subject to which we now turn.

85. *See supra* Chapter XI.

86. Smith v. Department of Agric., 630 F.2d 1081 (5th Cir. 1980). *See* Coenen, *supra* note 61, at 451–53 (analyzing case along these lines).

87. *See infra* Chapter XIII.

CHAPTER XIII

THE DORMANCY DOCTRINE AND STATE TAX LAWS

The Supreme Court has wrestled with state taxes under the Commerce Clause in much the same way that it has wrestled with state regulatory measures.[1] Applying a variety of verbal formulae, the Court has struck down hundreds of state tax laws while upholding hundreds of others, sometimes drawing highly formalistic distinctions between one program and another.[2] In *Complete Auto Transit, Inc. v. Brady*,[3] the Court sought to fashion a modern, functional synthesis of its taxation jurisprudence based upon "economic realities."[4] Pulling together prior strands of dormant Commerce Clause doctrine, the Court declared that state tax laws

1. From the earliest years of the dormancy doctrine, the Court has recognized that state taxation may qualify as "in effect, a regulation" subject to displacement by the grant to Congress of authority to "regulate" interstate and international commerce. *See* Walling v. Michigan, 116 U.S. 446, 455 (1886).

2. *Compare* Railway Express Agency v. Virginia, 347 U.S. 359 (1954) (holding that a tax for "the privilege of doing business in this state" is unconstitutional), *with* Railway Express Agency, Inc. v. Virginia, 358 U.S. 434 (1959) (allowing similar tax when renamed a "franchise tax").

3. 430 U.S. 274 (1977).

4. *Id.* at 279.

offend constitutional requirements unless they are (1) nondiscriminatory with respect to interstate commerce; (2) applicable to activity with a substantial nexus to the state; (3) fairly apportioned; and (4) fairly related to services provided by the taxing jurisdiction. The Court crafted the *Complete Auto Transit* test with the nation-preserving purposes of the dormant Commerce Clause firmly in mind, and the modern cases reflect an attentiveness to tax-law policies that comport with the same common-market principle the Court has sought to vindicate in the regulatory context.[5] Those policies include ensuring that the taxing state has a meaningful relationship to the taxed activity, avoiding the imposition of discriminatory or duplicative burdens on cross-border business operations, and seeing to it that interstate commerce bears no more than its "fair share" of state taxation.[6]

The *Complete Auto Transit* test applies to all forms of state exactions—income taxes, sales taxes, license taxes, real estate taxes, and whatever other sort of tax might come down the pike.[7] It takes into account all features of the state's taxing scheme, focusing attention not only on the definition of tax bases and apportionment formulas but also on deductions, exemptions, credits, and other forms of

5. *See generally supra* Chapter II.

6. Goldberg v. Sweet, 488 U.S. 252, 261 (1989).

7. *See, e.g.,* Camps Newfound/Owatonna, Inc. v. Town of Harrison, 520 U.S. 564, 574–75 (1997) (concluding that a "tax on real estate, like any other tax, may impermissibly burden interstate commerce").

tax relief.[8] In short, the Court's *Complete Auto Transit* jurisprudence—particularly as refined in recent decisions applying the so-called "internal consistency" and "external consistency" tests—provides a roadmap for exploring the consistency of any state taxing system with the dormant Commerce Clause principle. We turn now to a more detailed examination of each of the *Complete Auto Transit* requirements.[9]

A. Tax Discrimination

In scores of cases the Court has invalidated state taxes on the ground that they unlawfully discriminate against interstate commerce. These decisions have flowed in part from the Court's vigilant application of the core anti-discrimination feature of the dormancy doctrine and its general unwillingness to dilute that principle in the state-taxation context with complex and expansive exceptions and limitations. The Court, for example, has consistently refused to authorize tax discrimination defended on

8. *See, e.g.,* Maryland v. Louisiana, 451 U.S. 725, 756 (1981) (invalidating state's "first use" tax on natural gas because it "unquestionably discriminates against interstate commerce in favor of local interests as the necessary result of various tax credits and exclusions").

9. This treatment offers nothing more than an introduction to a highly complex subject. The leading scholarly treatment appears in Volume I, Part III of Jerome R. Hellerstein & Walter Hellerstein, State Taxation ¶¶ 4.01 to 4.24 (3d ed. 1998 with supp.). The leading casebook in this field is Jerome R. Hellerstein & Walter Hellerstein, State and Local Taxation, Cases and Materials (7th ed. 2001).

the basis that interstate business operators have suffered no injury because they "passed on" added tax increments to in-state purchasers with whom they have dealt. Rather, the Court has eschewed "economic incidence analysis" because it involves a "morass" and raises "a certain potential for error."[10] In similar fashion, the Court has rejected claims for relief from the rule of strict equality based on assertions that (1) the challenged tax involves only "*de minimis* discrimination";[11] (2) the discriminatory feature of the law affects only a small number of taxpayers;[12] and (3) the challenged tax relief involves subsidy-like business development incentives for start-up or struggling local enterprises.[13] In essence, the Court has recognized

10. Fulton Corp. v. Faulkner, 516 U.S. 325, 342 (1996); *accord, e.g.,* Bacchus Imports, Ltd. v. Dias, 468 U.S. 263, 272 (1984).

11. *Fulton Corp.*, 516 U.S. at 333 n.3.

12. New Energy Co. v. Limbach, 486 U.S. 269, 276–77 (1988) (stating, in a case in which the challenged law affected only one local firm and one non-local firm, that "the size or number of the in-state businesses favored or the out-of-state businesses disfavored [is not] relevant to our determination"; reasoning that "[v]arying the strength of the bar against economic protectionism according to the size and number of in-state and out-of-state firms" would produce undesirable complexity).

13. For elaborate discussions of this subject, see Peter D. Enrich, *Saving the States from Themselves: Commerce Clause Constraints on State Tax Incentives for Business*, 110 HARV. L. REV. 377 (1996); Walter Hellerstein & Dan T. Coenen, *Commerce Clause Restraints on State Business Development Incentives*, 81 CORNELL L. REV. 789 (1996); and Philip M. Tatarowitz & Rebecca F. Mims–Velarde, *An Analytical Approach to State Tax Discrimination Under the Dormant Commerce Clause*, 39 VAND. L. REV. 879 (1986).

only one exception to the sweeping prohibition on tax discrimination. Under the so-called compensatory tax doctrine, the state may lay a specialized tax on interstate transactions to equalize tax burdens otherwise placed solely on comparable intrastate activity. Thus, in *Henneford v. Silas Mason Co.*,[14] the Court upheld a use tax imposed on persons who bought goods outside the state for in-state consumption. This tax was proper, in the Court's view, because it was part of a broader taxing scheme under which all goods—whether purchased inside or outside the state—were subject to nondiscriminatory taxation in that the tax on in-state purchases was simply labeled a "sales," rather than a "use," tax.[15] Later cases have put the compensatory tax exception on such a short leash that it almost never operates outside the sales and use tax setting.[16] In

14.   300 U.S. 577 (1937).

15.   *See supra* Chapter X (discussing *Silas Mason* case in greater detail).

16.   In particular, the Court in *Fulton Corp.* (*see supra* note 10) drew on its prior decision in *Oregon Waste* (*see infra* note 18) to declare that the exception applies only if three conditions are met: "First, a State must, as a threshold matter, identify the intrastate tax burden for which the State is attempting to compensate. Second, the tax on interstate commerce must be shown roughly to approximate—but not to exceed—the amount of the tax on intrastate commerce. Finally, the events on which the interstate and intrastate taxes are imposed must be substantially equivalent; that is, they must be sufficiently similar in substance to serve as mutually exclusive proxies for each other." 516 U.S. at 332–33 (internal quotation marks and citations omitted). For a pre-*Silas Mason* case in which the Court upheld a compensatory tax, see *Hinson v. Lott*, 75 U.S. (8 Wall.) 148 (1869) (upholding tax on imported liquor because it compensated for a tax imposed on all liquor distilled in the state). In *Fulton*

this way the Court has advanced its more general agenda of avoiding "the creation of new uncertainties in an already complex field."[17]

Often unlawful tax discrimination is stark.[18] In *New Energy Co. v. Limbach*,[19] for example, the state sought to defend an Ohio sales tax credit for gasoline that contained the grain-based fuel, ethanol. The Court, however, struck down the exemption because the state granted it only for ethanol made in Ohio or in a state that afforded Ohio ethanol similarly favorable tax treatment. The reciprocity provision did not save the exemption because Ohio could not pass a law, even with the aim of generally stimulating interstate ethanol sales, that in effect

Corp., the Court identified *Hinson* as the "only exception" to its pattern of applying the compensatory tax doctrine exclusively to "traditional sales/use taxes." 516 U.S. at 342 n.8. *See generally* Walter Hellerstein, *Complementary Taxes as a Defense to Unconstitutional State Tax Discrimination*, 39 TAX LAW. 405 (1986).

17.   New Energy Co. v. Limbach, 486 U.S. 269, 277 (1988).

18.   *See, e.g.*, Oregon Waste Sys., Inc. v. Department of Envtl. Quality, 511 U.S. 93 (1994) (invalidating law that imposed surcharge on out-of-state waste that was 2–1/2 times more than the charge imposed for identical in-state waste); Chemical Waste Mgmt., Inc. v. Hunt, 504 U.S. 334 (1992) (invalidating waste disposal fee that applied only to out-of-state waste); Tyler Pipe Indus., Inc. v. Washington State Dept. of Revenue, 483 U.S. 232 (1987) (invalidating manufacturing tax imposed, in practical effect, on goods sold outside the state but not on goods sold in the state); Westinghouse Elec. Corp. v. Tully, 466 U.S. 388 (1984) (holding unconstitutional tax credits for in-state businesses that discriminated against export shipping from other states); Boston Stock Exch. v. State Tax Comm'n, 429 U.S. 318 (1977) (invalidating stock transfer tax that was higher for out-of-state sales than for in-state sales).

19.   486 U.S. 269 (1988).

punished states for not treating an Ohio product as favorably as Ohio would have liked.[20] Nor did it matter that Ohio had acted with the purposes of reducing pollution and promoting a modern, environment-friendly industry. States are free to pursue such aims, the Court proclaimed, but they may not do so with programs that overtly discriminate against interstate commerce.[21]

Some cases have brought before the Court legislative schemes in which unlawful discrimination is not obvious on the face of the challenged tax law. In *South Central Bell Telephone Co. v. Alabama*,[22] for example, the Court struck down a franchise tax calculated for Alabama corporations based on their par value and calculated for non-Alabama corporations based on their actual value. A unanimous Court found that this scheme violated the non-discrimination rule because in-state firms could set par value at any level they wished under Alabama corporation law, thus reducing their tax liability to minimal amounts by way of a unilateral choice.[23] A trickier tax-discrimination issue came before the Court in *Associated Industries v. Lohman*.[24] At issue

20. *Id*. at 274–76. *See also supra* Chapter X (discussing reciprocity requirements in the non-tax context, including the one invalidated in Great Atl. & Pac. Tea Co. v. Cottrell, 424 U.S. 366 (1976)).

21. *New Energy*, 486 U.S. at 278–79.

22. 526 U.S. 160 (1999).

23. The Court in effect looked at the state's tax law and its corporation law together in finding that "[t]he tax ... facially discriminates." *Id*. at 169.

24. 511 U.S. 641 (1994).

in that case was the constitutionality of a Missouri taxing scheme marked by two key components. First, the state imposed a sales tax, triggered by the in-state purchase of goods, that varied from 4.225% to 7.725% of the purchase price depending on whether the local government exercised an option under state law to raise the minimum rate. Second, the state imposed a uniform 5.725% use tax, triggered by local use of goods purchased outside the state, which was designed to compensate for the sales tax pursuant to the principle of the *Silas Mason* case.[25] The upshot of this statutory pattern was that "over 93% of the dollar volume of sales in the State occurred in jurisdictions where the local sales tax exceeded the use tax."[26] Focusing on this fact, the Missouri courts upheld the taxing scheme in its totality because on average it greatly favored interstate over intrastate trade. The Supreme Court, however, rejected this overall-impact approach. Instead, citing *Dean Milk* and its progeny,[27] the Court required a comparison of tax burdens on a locality-by-locality basis and invalidated the taxing scheme in each place where the local government had not imposed a sales tax equal to or greater than the 5.725% use-tax rate. Again sounding a theme of simplicity and straightforwardness, the Court reasoned that "patent discrimination in one part of the operation of a tax scheme [cannot] be rendered inconsequential for Commerce Clause

25. *See supra* notes 14–15 and accompanying text.

26. *Associated Indus.*, 511 U.S. at 645.

27. *See supra* Chapter XI.

purposes by advantages given to interstate commerce in other facets of a tax plan or in other regions of a State."[28]

The Court probably has pushed the anti-discrimination rule to its furthest point in striking down facially non-discriminatory charges placed on door-to-door sellers, sometimes called "drummers," who solicit orders for delivery at a later time. In *Robbins v. Shelby County Taxing District*,[29] the Court reasoned that, as a practical matter, "the tax on drummers operates greatly to [out-of-state firms'] disadvantage in comparison with the merchants and manufacturers of Memphis" because those local operators typically sell their wares from "regular, licensed houses of business."[30] Placing an important limit on this principle, the Court in later cases distinguished taxes that target "drummers" from taxes placed on "peddlers" who carry goods with them and complete sales on the spot. The Court appears to have justified its differing approach to these cases by relying on the less-than-airtight theory that drummers almost always work for out-of-state suppliers, while peddlers may well represent local businesses so that state taxation of them does not discriminate in favor of in-state stores.[31]

28. *Id.* at 649.

29. 120 U.S. 489 (1887).

30. *Id.* at 498; *accord, e.g.,* Nippert v. City of Richmond, 327 U.S. 416 (1946); Best & Co. v. Maxwell, 311 U.S. 454 (1940).

31. *See, e.g.,* Caskey Baking Co. v. Virginia, 313 U.S. 117 (1941) (allowing state to collect peddler tax imposed on out-of-state baker); Wagner v. City of Covington, 251 U.S. 95, 102–04 (1919) (collecting authorities and noting that goods sold by

Even while recognizing few limits on the nondiscrimination rule, the Court has been careful to restrict its application to cases that involve "a comparison of substantially similar entities."[32] In *Alaska v. Arctic Maid*,[33] for example, the Court considered state laws concerning the taxation of salmon under which (1) fishing operators had to pay a 4% tax for salmon frozen on board ships for transport and later canning outside the state and (2) fishing operators had to pay a 1% tax for salmon frozen on

peddler "might just as well have been manufactured within the State"); *see also* Dunbar–Stanley Studios, Inc. v. Alabama, 393 U.S. 537 (1969) (holding that state tax imposed at a higher rate on transient photographers than on fixed-location photographers did not unlawfully discriminate against interstate commerce). A related case is *Breard v. Alexandria*, 341 U.S. 622 (1951), in which the Court upheld a general prohibition on door-to-door solicitation, as applied to a drummer, against a dormant Commerce Clause challenge. How does one reconcile the case with *Robbins*? At least three possibilities come to mind. First, the ordinance in *Breard* did not involve a tax at all and was supported by a weighty state interest in safeguarding residential privacy. Second, *Breard* (unlike *Robbins*) did not present potential problems of placing cumulative unapportioned tax obligations on commercial operators (including small operators) who happened to operate in a variety of jurisdictions; rather, the law's constraint "affected interstate drummers and local drummers in exactly the same way—both were put out of business." Donald H. Regan, *The Supreme Court and State Protectionism: Making Sense of the Dormant Commerce Clause*, 84 MICH L. REV. 1091, 1199 (1986). Finally, the law at issue in *Breard* appeared to reach both drummers and peddlers. Thus, although *Breard* itself involved a challenge by drummers, the Court might have found the constitutional challenge to the ordinance controlled by its peddling-fee cases, rather than its drumming-fee cases, in part because the law's application to peddlers might have tended to ensure a greater measure of local opposition to its enactment.

32.   General Motors Corp. v. Tracy, 519 U.S. 278, 298 (1997).

33.   366 U.S. 199 (1961).

shore for later local sale as fresh-frozen fish. Despite allegations of discrimination offered up by freezer ship operators, the Court found that the case involved a faulty attempt to equate economically dissimilar business operations. After all, the Court explained, freezer ship operators sold fish to canners and thus did not compete at all in the retail fresh-frozen fish market to which the 1% tax applied. The dormant Commerce Clause, the Court continued, simply does not impose an " 'iron rule of equality' between taxes laid by a State on different types of business."[34]

As *Lohman*, *Robbins* and *Arctic Maid* reveal, the Court's conscientious efforts to simplify the nondiscrimination rule has not sheltered this field from all difficulties of characterization and line drawing. Taxing schemes come in so many shapes and sizes that hard questions about the presence or absence of discrimination will inevitably arise. The existence of some subtleties, however, should not obscure the overarching message of the Court's decisions: "[I]n the process of competition no state may discriminatorily tax the products manufactured or the business operations performed in any other state."[35]

34. *Id.* at 205. A recent application of this principle came in *General Motors Corp. v. Tracy*, 519 U.S. 278 (1997). There the Court upheld a state's imposition of different tax rates on sales of natural gas by local utilities and sales by independent operators, whose primary operations took place outside the state. Relying on *Arctic Maid*, the Court reasoned that regulated utilities and nonregulated independent sellers operate in separate markets.

35. Boston Stock Exch. v. State Tax Comm'n, 429 U.S. 318, 337 (1977).

B. The Substantial Nexus and Fair Apportionment Requirements

Just as surely as settled constitutional principles require "minimum contacts" for a state to assert personal jurisdiction over a nonresident,[36] no state may assert taxing jurisdiction over any person or firm with whom it lacks a meaningful connection. The Due Process Clause of the Fourteenth Amendment imposes an irreducible "nexus" requirement on state governments in this regard. In *Quill Corp. v. North Dakota*,[37] however, the Court made it clear that the dormant Commerce Clause goes beyond what the minimum nexus mandate of due process demands. The issue in *Quill* was whether a state could require a mail-order business to collect and remit a use tax on items sold for delivery into the state. Reaffirming *National Bellas Hess, Inc. v. Department of Revenue*,[38] the Court rejected this assertion of state authority because the seller lacked a local "physical presence" in the form of facilities or sales personnel.[39] In so ruling, however, the Court

36. International Shoe Co. v. Washington, 326 U.S. 310, 316 (1945).

37. 504 U.S. 298 (1992).

38. 386 U.S. 753 (1967).

39. In a number of cases, the Court has found a sufficient physical presence to support execution of state tax-related authority over out-of-state firms. *See* National Geographic Soc'y v. California Bd. of Equalization, 430 U.S. 551 (1977) (allowing collection of use tax from out-of-state company because of existence of in-state retail sales outlets); Scripto, Inc. v. Carson, 362

took care to rely only on the dormant Commerce Clause and not on due process principles. This move carried with it significant consequences in light of the "congressional consent" exception to the dormancy doctrine.[40] Thus, as the Court emphasized in *Quill*, "Congress is now free to decide whether, when, and to what extent the States may burden interstate mail-order concerns with a duty to collect use taxes."[41]

U.S. 207 (1960) (allowing state to collect use tax from out-of-state seller because seller employed in-state independent contractors to solicit sales); General Trading Co. v. State Tax Comm'n, 322 U.S. 335 (1944) (upholding duty to collect use tax for items ordered as the result of solicitations by traveling salespeople sent into the state by an out-of-state company); Nelson v. Sears, Roebuck & Co., 312 U.S. 359 (1941) (allowing state to impose duty to collect use tax based on out-of-state corporation's mail order sales because it had retail stores in the state, even though those stores did not account for the mail-order catalogue sales that triggered the use tax).

40. *See supra* Chapter XII.

41. *Quill*, 504 U.S. at 318. Related to these decisions are cases that involve dormancy doctrine restraints on state power to force foreign corporations to register to do business, thus subjecting themselves to the general personal jurisdiction and taxing authority of the state. These cases require application of the "manipulable and at times anachronistically metaphysical" principle, LAURENCE H. TRIBE, AMERICAN CONSTITUTIONAL LAW, § 6–14, at 1104 (3d ed., vol. one 2000), that a state may not demand registration of a firm that engages solely in "interstate commerce" but may demand registration if the firm "is engaged in intrastate as well as interstate aspects of the ... business." Eli Lilly & Co. v. Sav-On-Drugs, 366 U.S. 276, 279 (1961) (upholding qualification requirement for foreign corporation that, in addition to selling drugs to New Jersey wholesalers—which would not itself support registration—also maintained an office and had 18 employees promoting its product to hospitals and pharmacies in the state). The Court's most recent decision in this line,

Tied at the hip to the notion of "substantial nexus" is the separate *Complete Auto Transit* standard that mandates "fair apportionment" of state taxes. To take a simple example, assume that a multistate firm, Mega–Metal Fabricating Corporation, does 10% of its business in the state of Taxomania and has a substantial nexus with that state because a local sales force, showroom and warehouse establish its "physical presence" there. Common sense (if not common decency) suggests that Taxomania should not be able to tax 100% of the net profits generated by Mega–Metal's nationwide activities even though the *Quill* nexus requirement is met. After all, if Taxomania could tax 100% of Mega–Metal's income, many other states could do so as well. The consequence would be that Mega–Metal would pay much more in state taxes than a firm that generated exactly the same revenues and profits but operated within only one jurisdiction.

To counter the "risk of multiple taxation" pre-

Allenberg Cotton Co. v. Pittman, 419 U.S. 20 (1974), concerned a corporate cotton merchant, headquartered in Tennessee, that (1) contracted, through a Mississippi broker, to buy Mississippi farmers' cotton; (2) took title under those contracts in Mississippi, where the cotton was stored in warehouses; and (3) shipped the cotton to buyers located outside Mississippi. The Court ruled that—whether or not Mississippi could tax the firm for local storage of the cotton or for other in-state components of these transactions, *see id.* at 33–34—it could not require registration. In reaching this conclusion, the Court emphasized that the corporate cotton merchant had no local office; did not own or operate the local warehouses; had no employees working in Mississippi "on a regular basis"; and essentially operated through an independent broker who lacked authority to contract on the corporation's behalf. *Id.* at 23.

sented by scenarios of this kind,[42] the Court has insisted that states may tax only "that aspect of the interstate commerce to which the State bears a special relation."[43] Since the late 19th century, states have limited their imposition of property taxes on instrumentalities of interstate commerce— such as railroads, express companies, and telephone lines—through use of apportionment formulas, and since the early 20th century, they have adopted apportionment-based techniques in imposing income-based taxes on firms with unitary multistate operations. Historically, the most common income-tax apportionment formula gave equal weight to three separate factors: sales, property and payroll. For example, if Taxomania used this three-factor formula, it could tax 10% of Mega Metal's total income if 15% of the firm's total sales, 10% of its total property and 5% of its total payroll were attributable to Taxomania.[44]

Not all states, however, take this three-factor apportionment approach.[45] In *Moorman Manufacturing Co. v. Bair*,[46] for example, an interstate firm challenged Iowa's single-factor formula, which considered only the percentage of nationwide *sales* at-

42. *Id*. at 309.

43. Central Greyhound Lines v. Mealey, 334 U.S. 653, 661 (1948).

44. *See* Butler Bros. v. McColgan, 315 U.S. 501 (1942) (upholding standard three-factor apportionment formula).

45. Indeed, most states today give greater weight to the sales factor than to other factors, and several states have adopted the single-factor sales formula described immediately below.

46. 437 U.S. 267 (1978).

tributable to the taxing state. The firm argued that this sales-only approach offended the dormant Commerce Clause goal of fostering "tax neutral decisions"[47] by rewarding firms that located their physical facilities and work force within, rather than outside, the taxing state. (After all, unlike in three-factor states, locating employees and property in Iowa did not raise the firm's tax bill by even one cent.) The Court, however, rejected this argument, emphasizing the difficulties of judicial micro-management of facially non-discriminatory apportionment methodologies.[48]

Moorman Manufacturing comports with the historic disinclination of the Court to scuttle apportionment techniques unless they raise very obvious problems of fairness.[49] In more recent years, however, the Court has devised a new approach for assessing both apportionment problems and related difficulties: the so-called internal-consistency test.[50] A state law satisfies this test if, but only if, "the imposition of a tax identical to the one in question by every other State would add no burden to interstate commerce that intrastate commerce would

47. Boston Stock Exch. v. State Tax Comm'n, 429 U.S. 318, 331 (1977).

48. *Moorman Mfg.*, 437 U.S. at 278.

49. *E.g.*, Norfolk & W. Ry. Co. v. Missouri State Tax Comm'n, 390 U.S. 317, 326 (1968) (invalidating tax where state's methodology led to a "grossly distorted" tax levy).

50. *See generally* Walter Hellerstein, *"Is Internal Consistency Foolish?": Reflections on an Emerging Commerce Clause Restraint on State Taxation*, 87 MICH. L. REV. 1381 (1988).

not also bear.''[51] For example, the tax challenged on fair-apportionment grounds in *Oklahoma Tax Commission v. Jefferson Lines, Inc.*[52] passed the internal-consistency test with flying colors. There, Oklahoma had imposed a 4% sales tax on ticket purchases for every bus trip that originated in the state regardless of the trip's destination. The tax raised a knotty fair-apportionment problem because it fully taxed the purchase of bus trips that began in Oklahoma whether 1% or 100% of the trip occurred within the state. The tax, however, posed no problem at all under the internal-consistency test because any particular bus trip, whether interstate or intrastate, can originate in only one jurisdiction. Thus, even assuming that all states imposed this same taxing scheme, each bus trip would be subject to one, and only one, tax payment so that interstate bus operators would fare no worse than similarly situated intrastate competitors.[53]

In contrast, the Court in *American Trucking Associations, Inc. v. Scheiner,*[54] found that a flat, unapportioned "axle tax," which applied to any large truck that operated in Pennsylvania without

51. Oklahoma Tax Comm'n v. Jefferson Lines, Inc., 514 U.S. 175, 185 (1995).

52. *Id.*

53. The taxing scheme challenged in *Moorman Mfg.* also posed no internal-consistency problem. If every state applied a single-factor sales-based apportionment formula, every multi-state firm would be taxed on 100%, but no more than 100%, of its total income just as surely as a firm that made all its sales intrastate would pay tax on 100% of its income.

54. 483 U.S. 266 (1987).

regard to mileage traveled, ran afoul of the internal-consistency mandate. The problem was apparent: If all states exacted the same fixed fee, a truck that traveled throughout the continental United States during the tax year would pay 48 times the tax paid by a truck that traveled exactly the same distance solely within Pennsylvania. The Court in *Scheiner* noted that "the Commerce Clause does not require the States to avoid flat taxes when ... the use of a more finely graduated user-fee schedule would pose genuine administrative burdens."[55] In *Scheiner* itself, however, the state could easily have tied its charge for highway use to miles actually traveled, in keeping with the practice of many other states and of Pennsylvania itself for other truck-tax purposes.

State laws sometimes raise internal-consistency problems because they are phrased in the disjunctive. In *Goldberg v. Sweet*,[56] for example, the Court confronted an Illinois tax that applied to phone calls *either* sent to *or* sent from the state. Had the law stopped there, it would have violated the internal consistency test because, if adopted by all states, it would have produced double taxation of interstate, but not intrastate, calls. In fact, however, the law did not stop there because it specified that the tax applied only to those calls that were billed to an Illinois service address. This feature of the law removed internal-consistency problems because, as the Court explained, "if every State taxed only those interstate phone calls which are charged to an

55. *Id.* at 296.
56. 488 U.S. 252 (1989).

in-state service address, only one State would tax each interstate telephone call."[57] Another technique that states may use to avoid internal-consistency problems is to provide a credit for taxes paid in other jurisdictions.[58] Indeed in *Goldberg* itself, although the Court did not focus on the point, the challenged law included a credit provision that reduced the Illinois telecommunications tax to the extent that the taxpayer paid similar charges to other states. This credit provision, no less than the law's billing address limitation, negated internal-consistency problems because if every state taxed every phone call, but gave a credit for taxes on the same call paid anywhere else, the taxpayer involved in either an interstate or intrastate call would of necessity pay one, but only one, tax.[59]

The Court's modern cases carry forward the traditional requirement of fair apportionment by requiring not only internal consistency but so-called external consistency as well.[60] Under this aspect of the Court's jurisprudence, even the most internally consistent tax will run afoul of the Commerce Clause if it lacks "all appropriate proportions to the

57. *Id.* at 261.

58. *See* D.H. Holmes Co. v. McNamara, 486 U.S. 24, 31 (1988) (concluding that the "Louisiana taxing scheme is fairly apportioned, for it provides a credit against its use tax for sales taxes that have been paid in other states").

59. *Cf. Goldberg*, 488 U.S. at 264 (noting, although in portion of opinion not focusing specifically on internal-consistency concerns, that "the credit provision contained in the Tax Act operates to avoid actual multiple taxation").

60. *Jefferson Lines*, 514 U.S. at 185.

business transacted ... in that State, or has led to a grossly distorted result."[61] In practice the Court has seldom condemned state taxes on this ground. In an important line of cases, for example, the Court has deemed any requirement of fair apportionment essentially inapplicable to the "conventional sales tax" imposed on a local transfer of goods notwithstanding arguments that the transferred product has close connections with other states.[62] Even so, internally consistent taxes occasionally run afoul of the external-consistency requirement.

Consider a flat $500 tax placed on any train trip, but only if the trip's longest intrastate segment occurs within the taxing state. Such a tax would be internally consistent because every train trip—whether interstate or intrastate in nature—can have only one longest intrastate segment. The practical effect of such a tax, however, would be to give an artificial taxing advantage to geographically large states by permitting them to tax *in toto* many train trips that occur largely, or even primarily, in

61. *Id.* at 195 (quoting Container Corp. v. Franchise Tax Bd., 463 U.S. 159, 170 (1983)).

62. *Id.* at 188. *See, e.g.*, State Tax Comm'n v. Pacific State Cast Iron Pipe Co., 372 U.S. 605, 606 (1963) (upholding full application of generally applicable sales tax even though particular sold items were to be immediately shipped outside the state); Browning v. Waycross, 233 U.S. 16, 23 (1914) (state may fully tax local installer of lightning rods even though manufactured outside the state). *See generally* Walter Hellerstein, Michael J. McIntyre & Richard D. Pomp, *Commerce Clause Restraints on State Taxation After* Jefferson Lines, 51 TAX L. REV. 47, 86 (1995) (noting both this phenomenon and the inherent differences between sales-based and income-based taxes).

other states. In times gone by, the Court might have dealt with this problem by blocking state taxation of cross-border train trips altogether, perhaps on the theory that states lack the ability to tax interstate commerce "directly."[63] In the modern era, however, the Court would likely hold that such a tax violates the principle of "external consistency" by unfairly permitting large states to cash in on out-of-state attributes of only quasi-intrastate train traffic.

A leading "external consistency" case is *Norfolk & Western Railway Co. v. Missouri State Tax Commission.*[64] There the Court confronted a property tax applicable to the rolling stock of railroad companies. Because train engines and cars constantly moved in and out of Missouri, the state adopted a convenient apportionment formula based on track length. In particular, the state multiplied the total value of all the company's rolling stock as of the tax day times a ratio determined by comparing all track "owned, leased, or controlled by the N & W ... in Missouri" to all track owned, leased or controlled by the company anywhere in the United States.[65] The problem was that, due to substantial real-world traffic-density variations, this formula subjected 8.2824% of the firm's rolling stock to state taxation even though in actuality only about 3.16% of its total fleet (in terms of its taxable value) was located in Missouri on an average day. Even while acknowl-

63. Freeman v. Hewit, 329 U.S. 249, 258 (1946).

64. 390 U.S. 317 (1968).

65. *Id.* at 321.

edging that states were entitled to "broad toler-
ance" in fashioning apportionment formulas, the
Court found the Missouri statute unconstitutional
as applied because it had generated "a grossly distorted result."[66] The governing principle, in the
Court's view, was that the Constitution would not
"tolerate any result, however distorted, just because
it is the product of a convenient mathematical formula which, in most situations, may produce a
tolerable product."[67]

Did the law involved in *Goldberg* offend the "external consistency" standard because it taxed a
party billed for a phone call based on 100% of its
cost even though that call involved the sending of
signals across state lines to a distant location? Distinguishing physical-movement cases such as
Scheiner, the Court said "no" because an "apportionment formula based on mileage or some other
geographic division of individual telephone calls
would produce insurmountable administrative and
technological barriers."[68] What about the law involved in *Jefferson Lines*, which imposed a flat 4%
sales tax on the price of all bus trips that originated
in the state, whatever the distance traveled inside
or outside Oklahoma? In *Central Greyhound Lines,
Inc. v. Mealey*,[69] the Court had mandated mileage-
based apportionment of a New York "gross receipts
tax" laid on all revenues obtained "by reason of any

66. *Id.* at 326–27.

67. *Id.* at 327.

68. *Goldberg*, 488 U.S. at 264–65.

69. 334 U.S. 653 (1948).

sale ... made" in the state by a bus line operator.[70] Because aggregate in-state ticket "sales" under the Oklahoma statute equaled aggregate "gross receipts" under the New York formula, the dissenters in *Jefferson Lines* could see no reason not to extend the external-consistency-based ruling in *Central Greyhound* to the *Jefferson Lines* case.[71] Even while acknowledging the "striking" similarities of the cases, however, the majority found no external-consistency problem because *Jefferson Lines* involved a sales tax formally imposed on ticket buyers, whereas *Central Greyhound* involved a gross receipts tax formally imposed on ticket sellers. According to Justice Souter, because a "sale of goods is most readily viewed as a discrete event facilitated by the laws and amenities of the place of sale"[72] and because a "sale of services can ordinarily be treated as a local state event just as readily as a sale of tangible goods,"[73] a state that places a sales tax on the transfer of a bus ticket is permitted to ignore the interstate elements of the service that the ticket represents. To the dissenters the difference between the sales tax and the gross receipts tax was purely "formal" because both exactions "as a practical matter" required sellers to remit unapportioned tax payments calculated by focusing on exactly the same tax base.[74] The majority, however, was pre-

70. *Id.* at 664.

71. *Jefferson Lines*, 514 U.S. at 201, 203–07 (Breyer, J., joined by O'Connor, J., dissenting).

72. *Id.* at 186.

73. *Id.* at 188. *See supra* note 32.

74. *Jefferson Lines*, 514 U.S. at 204.

pared to declare that "economic equivalence alone has ... not been (and should not be) the touchstone of Commerce Clause jurisprudence."[75] This division of the Court reflected differing visions of what was required by a dormant Commerce Clause jurisprudence focused on "practical effects."[76] The result in the case, however, left no doubt about the Court's continuing hesitation to carry over to the sales tax context a jurisprudence of fair apportionment developed to deal with taxes based on income and property values.

C.   The Fair–Relation Requirement

In theory, the *Complete Auto Transit* test requires states to ensure that taxes are "fairly related to the services provided by the state."[77] In practice, however, the Court has never insisted that taxes paid and services received match one another in any meaningful sense. In *Commonwealth Edison Co. v. Montana*,[78] for example, the Court considered Montana's imposition of a severance tax for coal, 90% of which was shipped outside the state. The challengers asserted that the tax violated the fair relation requirement because it allegedly brought into the state's coffers about 100 times the amount the state

75.   *Id*. at 196 n.7.

76.   *Id*.

77.   *Complete Auto Transit*, 430 U.S. at 279.

78.   453 U.S. 609 (1981).

had to spend for roads, police and other services attributable to intrastate coal mining.[79] The Court, however, found that the challengers, in making this argument, "completely misunderstood the nature of the inquiry under the fourth prong," which Montana had satisfied simply by tying its tax to the amount of coal extracted from the earth.[80] It is not surprising, in light of this holding, that a leading authority has written that "[t]he 'fairly related test' appears to have little independent significance."[81]

In *Commonwealth Edison*, however, the Court signaled that the fair-relation requirement might well continue to play a meaningful role in judicial assessments of state user fees. Distinguishing earlier decisions involving such exactions, the Court emphasized that *Commonwealth Edison* itself did not involve " 'user' charges," but instead concerned a "true" tax in the "technical sense."[82] The Court also suggested that the dormant Commerce Clause might well require a tighter linkage between the value of services provided and the level of user fees exacted because such fees partake "of a rent charged by the State based upon its proprietary interest in its public property."[83] This seemingly simple statement, however, raised a subject of significant complexity, to which we now turn.

79. *Id.* at 620 n.10.

80. *Id.* at 621.

81. TRIBE, *supra* note 41, § 6–18, at 1126 n.9.

82. *Commonwealth Edison*, 453 U.S. at 622 n.12.

83. *Id.*

D. The Dormancy Doctrine and State User Fees

As *Commonwealth Edison* illustrates, the Court has indicated on several occasions that the *Complete Auto Transit* test extends to state exactions characterized as user fees. Indeed, *Commonwealth Edison* went one step further, suggesting that user fees are subject to an even more probing form of the *Complete Auto Transit* test than applies to ordinary taxes, at least with regard to the fair-relation requirement.

There is reason to conclude that this suggestion makes no sense. After all, the imposition of state user fees—whether for landfill services, college educations, park access or recreational activities—would seem to fit squarely within the rubric of "market participation," which (as we have seen before) is *wholly exempt* from *any* type of dormant Commerce Clause review.[84] Put another way, the Court's distinctively activist Commerce Clause user fee jurisprudence seems set on a "collision course" with its hands-off approach to state market participation.[85] What on earth is going on here?

The difficulty is that the Court has not shown care in its use of the user fee label. It has broadly proclaimed, for example, that the term embraces any "specific charge imposed by the State for the

84. *See supra* Chapter XII.

85. Dan T. Coenen, *State User Fees and the Dormant Commerce Clause*, 50 VAND. L. REV. 795, 802 (1997).

use of state-owned or state-provided transportation *or other facilities and services.*"[86] In actuality, however, the Court has never invoked, and could not logically invoke, the dormant Commerce Clause to invalidate resident-favoring price discrimination in the sale of items such as educational services or state-made products.[87] In *Reeves, Inc. v. Stake*,[88] for example, the Court held that South Dakota could totally exclude non-residents from purchasing the state's cement. Because the greater power of total exclusion must include the lesser power of partial exclusion, it seems clear as crystal that the state could let out-of-state buyers enter this market even while charging them a higher price than it might impose on its own residents.

What then is one to make of cases like *Commonwealth Edison*, which suggest that the *Complete Auto Transit* test operates full bore in the user-fee context? Close inspection reveals that the Court has actually applied its *Complete Auto Transit* dormant Commerce Clause jurisprudence *only* to user fees charged in making available to interstate operators the *channels of interstate commerce*.[89] Just as surely as the state may not invoke the market-participant label to dodge the dormant Commerce Clause in roadway cases such as *Kassel v. Consolidated Freightways Corp.*,[90] the state cannot invoke the

86. *Or. Waste Sys.*, 511 U.S. at 103 n.6.

87. *See* Coenen, *supra* note 85, at 807 n.60.

88. 447 U.S. 429 (1980).

89. *See* Coenen, *supra* note 85, at 816–23.

90. 450 U.S. 662 (1981). *See generally supra* Chapter XII.

market-participant exception in charging discriminatory user fees for access to state-owned highways,
wharves or airports. Indeed, the national interest in
keeping these channels of commerce wide open is so
strong that, as *Commonwealth Edison* indicates, the
Court has intensified the "fair relationship" inquiry
in this context.

The bottom line is that the market-participant
rule will shelter from dormant Commerce Clause
attack many, perhaps most, state decisions about
setting prices for goods and services the state choos-
es to sell. When, however, the state charges "user
fees" for access to roads and other components of
the nation's transportation infrastructure, not only
does the market-participant exception fall away but
an invigorated version of the *Complete Auto Transit*
test apparently will take hold.

CHAPTER XIV

THE PRIVILEGES AND IMMUNITIES CLAUSE AND OTHER EXPRESS PROTECTIONS OF NATIONHOOD

The dormant Commerce Clause does not stand alone as a bulwark against state interferences with the goal of fostering union. Express prohibitions set forth in the Constitution serve the same end, albeit in more focused ways. The Privileges or Immunities Clause of the Fourteenth Amendment, for example, safeguards an ill-defined, yet long-recognized, corpus of rights that "owe their existence to the Federal government" and "its National character."[1] Commerce-related rights of this kind include "free access to the [the Nation's] seaports, through which all operations of foreign commerce are conducted," the ability "to come to the seat of government to assert any claim" upon it, and the "right to use the navigable waters of the United States, however they may penetrate the territory of the several States."[2] Protecting national cohesiveness in a different way, the Tonnage Clause of Article I, § 10, substantially disables states from imposing taxes for the use of harbors and shorelines, thus facilitating free-flow-

1. Slaughter–House Cases, 83 U.S. (16 Wall.) 36, 79 (1873).

2. *Id.*

ing maritime shipping through all ports of the nation.[3]

Drawing on concerns akin to those that underlie the dormant Commerce Clause principle, the Import–Export Clause specifies that "[n]o State shall, without the Consent of the Congress, lay any Imposts or Duties on Imports or Exports, except what may be absolutely necessary for executing its inspection Laws."[4] In *Woodruff v. Parham*,[5] the Court limited the reach of this Clause by reading it to inhibit state interferences with only international, and not interstate, trade.[6] In other cases, the Court first embraced and then rebuffed the "original package" doctrine, which woodenly prohibited all state taxation of imported goods not yet removed from the containers in which they had arrived.[7]

3. U.S. CONST. art. I, § 10, cl. 3. This principle, however, does not prohibit state charges for the use of towing services, wharves and other state-provided improvements, even when calculated according to the ship's holding capacity or weight. *See* Dan T. Coenen, *State User Fees and the Dormant Commerce Clause*, 50 VAND. L. REV. 795, 816–17 (1997) (collecting cases). The compatibility of such state user fees with the dormant Commerce Clause principle is addressed *supra* Chapter XIII.

4. U.S. CONST. art. I, § 10, cl. 2.

5. 75 U.S. (8 Wall.) 123 (1868).

6. Justice Thomas has criticized this holding. *See* Camps Newfound/Owatonna, Inc. v. Town of Harrison, 520 U.S. 564, 609 (1997) (Thomas, J., dissenting). So has Professor Denning. Brannon P. Denning, *Justice Thomas, the Import–Export Clause, and* Camps Newfound/Owatonna v. Harrison, 70 U. COLO. L. REV. 155 (1999).

7. *See Camps Newfound/Owatonna*, 520 U.S. at 633–34 (Thomas, J., dissenting) (discussing the Court's acceptance of the "original package" doctrine in Woodruff v. Parham, 75 U.S. (8

Nowadays, in applying the Import–Export Clause, the Court focuses more closely on its underlying policies, including the goals of ensuring federal control over foreign affairs, protecting federal revenues from state encroachment, and keeping coastal states located along trade routes from bilking "States not situated as favorably geographically."[8] In the seminal modern decision, *Michelin Tire Corp. v. Wages*,[9] the Court found no affront to these policies in Georgia's application of a nondiscriminatory *ad valorem* tax to imported tires, whether or not still in their "original packages," because that property enjoyed the benefits of state police patrols, fire protection and other public benefits no less than other good stored in and taxed by the state.[10]

Perhaps the most important express constitutional protection of nation-building values lies in the Privileges and Immunities Clause of Article IV, § 2.[11] That clause provides that "Citizens of each State shall be entitled to all the Privileges and Immunities of Citizens of the several states" and

Wall.) 123 (1868), and Low v. Austin, 80 U.S. (13 Wall.) 29 (1871), while noting its demise in Michelin Tire Corp. v. Wages, 423 U.S. 276 (1976)).

8. Michelin Tire Corp. v. Wages, 423 U.S. 276, 285–86 (1976).

9. *Id.*

10. *Id.* at 288. For an extensive discussion of the Import–Export Clause, see JEROME R. HELLERSTEIN & WALTER HELLERSTEIN, STATE TAXATION ¶¶ 5.01 to 5.09 (3d ed. 1998).

11. Also of great consequence is the Full Faith and Credit Clause, which requires state courts to honor the judgments issued by tribunals in other states. U.S. CONST. art. IV, § 1. The impact of that clause is beyond the scope of this book.

thus affords "to a citizen of State A who ventures into State B the same privileges which the citizens of State B enjoy."[12] This clause, for example, bars any state from denying basic police protection to non-residents simply because they are non-residents temporarily visiting within the state's borders.[13]

The protections provided by the Article IV guaranty are both narrower and broader than those provided by the dormancy doctrine.[14] They are narrower for three reasons. First, the Privileges and Immunities Clause, in contrast to the dormant Commerce Clause principle, affords no protection to corporations or other non-individual plaintiffs.[15] Thus, for example, Reeves, Inc. (a Wyoming corporation) could not have successfully challenged South Dakota's discriminatory cement-sales program by relying on the privileges-and-immunities prohibition.[16] Second, the Court has never supplemented Article IV's express ban on outright discrimination

---

12. Toomer v. Witsell, 334 U.S. 385, 395 (1948).

13. *See* Laurence H. Tribe, American Constitutional Law, § 6–37, at 1264 (3d ed., vol. one, 2000); Jonathan D. Varat, *State Citizenship and Interstate Equality*, 48 U. Chi. L. Rev. 487, 539 (1981) (discussing Privileges and Immunities Clause and related constitutional limits in detail).

14. *See generally* Brannon P. Denning, *Can the Privileges and Immunities Clause of Article IV Replace the Dormant Commerce Clause Doctrine?*, 88 Minn. L. Rev. ___ (2003) (detailing differences between the clauses).

15. *See* Paul v. Virginia, 75 U.S. (8 Wall.) 168 (1868).

16. *See* Reeves, Inc. v. Stake, 447 U.S. 429 (1980) (discussed *supra* Chapter XII). Of course, this principle forecloses use of the Privileges and Immunities Clause by the large numbers of other corporate plaintiffs that typically (and often successfully) bring

with a supplementary prohibition on facially neutral laws that impose an undue burden on interstate commerce or on anything else. For this reason, even individual truck operators could not have succeeded by invoking the Privileges and Immunities Clause in *Kassel v. Consolidated Freightways Corp.*,[17] at least unless the challenged vehicle-length rule somehow generated discrimination in "practical effect" between Iowa and non-Iowa residents that those drivers had standing to assert.[18]

dormant Commerce Clause challenges. *See, e.g.,* Dean Milk Co. v. City of Madison, 340 U.S. 349 (1951).

17. 450 U.S. 662 (1981) (discussed *supra* Chapter XI).

18. Chalker v. Birmingham & Northwestern Ry. Co., 249 U.S. 522, 527 (1919) (applying clause to invalidate state tax imposed at higher level on individuals whose principal office was outside the state because "the chief office of an individual is commonly in the State of which he is a citizen"). In *Hillside Dairy, Inc. v. Lyons*, 123 S.Ct. 2142 (2003), the Court reaffirmed that successful pursuit of a Privileges and Immunities Clause claim does not require "an express statement in [state] laws and regulations identifying out-of-state citizenship as a basis for disparate treatment." *Id.* at 2147. The Court added that: "Whether *Chalker* should be interpreted as merely applying the Clause to classifications that are but proxies for differential treatment against out-of-state residents, or as prohibiting any classification with the practical effect of discriminating against such residents, is a matter we need not decide...." *Id.* There is, by the way, another problem in finding a Privileges and Immunities Clause problem in *Kassel* and cases like it. The problem is that the clause protects nonresidents "*in* the several states." Yet the non-resident taxpayers and road users primarily disadvantaged by the Iowa truck-length law were not so disadvantaged while or because they were present in Iowa. In fact, they were disadvantaged precisely because Iowa had *exported* safety, road wear, and related financial costs to neighboring jurisdictions. *See* Donald H. Regan, *The Supreme Court and State Protectionism:*

Third, even the clause's ban on outright discrimination extends only to state infringement of interests "which are in their nature fundamental"[19] or (to put the same point another way) "basic to the maintenance or well-being of the Union."[20] What is the sort of "fundamental" or "basic" interest that Article IV safeguards against discriminatory denial or interference? From the start, courts have protected the right to ply a private trade, "to institute and maintain actions of any kind in the courts of the state," and to be free of "higher taxes or impositions than are paid by the other citizens of the state."[21] In *Toomer v. Witsell*,[22] for example, the Court deemed pursuit of the shrimping business a sufficiently fundamental interest to block state taxation of non-resident shrimpers at 100 times the rate applied to resident competitors. In *Supreme Court of New Hampshire v. Piper*,[23] the Court drew on the same principle to hold that the "opportunity to practice law" qualified as "fundamental."[24] And in *Doe v. Bolton*,[25] the Court struck down Georgia's

Making Sense of the Dormant Commerce Clause, 84 MICH. L. REV. 1091, 1203–05 & n.236 (1986).

19. Saenz v. Roe, 526 U.S. 489, 525 (1999) (quoting Corfield v. Coryell, 6 F.Cas. 546, 551 (C.C.E.D.Pa.1823)).

20. Baldwin v. Fish and Game Comm'n, 436 U.S. 371, 388 (1978).

21. Corfield v. Coryell, 6 F.Cas. 546, 552 (C.C.E.D.Pa.1823) (Washington, J., sitting on circuit). *See., e.g.,* Austin v. New Hampshire, 420 U.S. 656, 661 (1975) (describing *Corfield* as "the first, and long the leading, explication of the Clause").

22. 334 U.S. 385 (1948).

23. 470 U.S. 274 (1985).

24. *Id.* at 281.

25. 410 U.S. 179 (1973).

residency requirement for obtaining abortions from privately operated hospitals and clinics, reasoning that if the Privileges and Immunities Clause "protects persons who enter other states to ply their trade, so must it protect persons who enter Georgia seeking the medical services that are available there."[26]

Cases such as *Toomer, Piper* and *Doe* reveal that the Court's notion of "fundamental rights" is expansive and multifaceted. In *Baldwin v. Montana Fish and Game Commission*,[27] however, the Court made it clear that this concept has limits. *Baldwin* concerned the common state practice of charging non-residents more than residents for hunting licenses. Deeming this stark form of discrimination immune from Privileges and Immunities Clause attack, the Court emphasized that bagging elk is "not a means to the nonresident's livelihood."[28] "Whatever rights or activities may be 'fundamental under the Privileges and Immunities Clause,' " the Court declared, "elk-hunting by nonresidents in Montana is not one of them."[29]

The majority's conclusion was hardly self-evident in light of the nation-building purposes of the Privileges and Immunities Clause.[30] Ordinary citizens,

26. *Id.* at 200.

27. 436 U.S. 371 (1978).

28. *Id.* at 388.

29. *Id.*

30. *See, e.g., id.* at 394 (Brennan, J., dissenting) (worrying about Montana's "invidiously discriminating against nonresi-

for example, might well miss the chance to develop valuable ties with America's rich natural and cultural diversity if blocked by individual states from the pleasures of roaming hunting grounds, bird habitats or fishing streams.[31] Nonetheless, the result in *Baldwin* was understandable. Given longstanding precedent that the "fundamental right" principle puts some limits on Article IV protections, the Court found itself unable to apply that rubric to an activity that was only "a recreation and a sport."[32]

The specialized "fundamental right" limitation on the scope of the Privileges and Immunities Clause reveals how, in some ways, it affords a narrower protection than the dormant Commerce Clause doctrine, which embodies no similarly restrictive principle. On the other hand, the Privileges and Immunities Clause may reach beyond the dormancy doctrine in some cases for the simple reason that that doctrine by definition concerns only *commerce*. In *Lopez v. United States*,[33] for example, the Court excluded the regulation of gun possession near schools from Congress's affirmative commerce power. It probably follows that the Court lacks authority to disrupt state legislation in this same field by invoking the Commerce Clause in its dor-

dents seeking to enjoy natural treasures it alone among the 50 States possesses").

31. *See, e.g.*, Varat, *supra* note 13, at 515–16.

32. *Id*. at 388.

33. 514 U.S. 549 (1995) (discussed *supra* Chapter IV).

mant state.[34] Thus, if a state passed a law barring only non-residents from possessing guns near schools, that law would seem immune to challenge under the dormancy doctrine despite its patent disadvantaging of non-residents. The same law, however, would raise a serious Privileges and Immunities Clause problem because the Court has always described as fundamental the right "to take, *hold* and dispose of property."[35] Moreover, this hypothetical gun law on its face denies to nonresidents "the same privileges" that residents possess with regard to the potentially life-saving entitlement to carry a firearm.[36] The key point is that the Privileges and Immunities Clause may permit the Court to disrupt some forms of state regulation that lay beyond the grasp of the dormant Commerce Clause principle because of their inherently non-economic character.

The Privileges and Immunities Clause also differs from the dormancy doctrine because the latter, but not the former, is subject to the "market participant" exception.[37] The Court highlighted this dis-

34. *But cf.* TRIBE, *supra* note 13, § 6–5, at 1050 n.1 (suggesting that ban on possessing nonlocally, but not locally, produced guns might well violate the dormancy doctrine).

35. *Baldwin*, 436 U.S. at 384 (quoting Corfield v. Coryell, 6 F.Cas. 546, 552 (C.C.E.D.Pa.1823)) (emphasis added).

36. Toomer v. Witsell, 334 U.S. 385, 395 (1948).

37. It also seems settled that the two protections differ because the Privilege and Immunities Clause is not subject to a congressional-consent exception. *See, e.g.*, Hillside Dairy, Inc. v. Lyons, 123 S.Ct. 2142 (2003) (assuming this point). Moreover, if the Privileges and Immunities Clause is subject to a local-subsidy "exception," that would seem to be the case not because such a freestanding exception exists (as in the dormant Commerce

tinction with its decisions in *White v. Massachusetts Council of Construction Employers, Inc.*,[38] and *United Building & Construction Trades Council v. Mayor & Council of Camden.*[39] In *White*, the Court had invoked the market-participant exception to thwart a dormant Commerce Clause challenge to a Boston law that forced contractors dealing with the city to hire a minimum percentage of local residents for work on city building projects. In the *United Building* case, however, the Court refused to apply the market-participant exception to block a Privileges and Immunities Clause challenge aimed at a functionally identical ordinance enacted by Camden, New Jersey.[40] In essence, the Court reasoned that the Commerce Clause by implication limits the pow-

Clause context), but because such subsidies do not concern the sort of "fundamental" interests that give rise to "Privileges and Immunities" protected by the Clause in the first place. *See infra* note 43 and accompanying text.

38.   460 U.S. 204 (1983).

39.   465 U.S. 208 (1984).

40.   The Court, on the other hand, did hold that the Privileges and Immunities Clause blocks local as well as state-wide discrimination in the same fashion that such discrimination is controlled by the dormant Commerce Clause. *See supra* Chapter X. Writing only for himself, Justice Blackmun dissented from this portion of the Court's opinion, reasoning that discrimination on the basis of municipal residence should not be covered by the Clause because "disadvantaged state residents who turn to the state legislature to displace ordinances like Camden's [will] further the interests of non-residents as well as their own." *Id.* at 231. The majority, in response, reasoned that out-of-staters necessarily "will not enjoy the same privileges as the New Jersey citizen residing in Camden" and that nonresidents, unlike similarly disadvantaged residents, "lack the chance to remedy at the polls any discrimination against them." *Id.* at 217.

er of states to "regulate" interstate commerce, but not their power to "participate" in commerce in whatever ways they might see fit. No similar line of reasoning, the Court continued, justified recognizing a market-participant exception to the Privileges and Immunities Clause, which focuses on state disruption of "interstate harmony" rather than state "regulation affecting interstate commerce." Because working for a construction firm was a "common calling" that qualified as a "fundamental," the plaintiffs in the *United Building* case could invoke the protections of the Article IV clause notwithstanding the Court's earlier ruling in *White*.[41]

What the Court in *United Building* gave with one hand, however, it largely took away with the other. First, in defining what rights merit protection under the Privileges and Immunities Clause, the Court sharply distinguished Camden's restriction on private firms' hiring of private workers from a preference imposed in hiring local residents for employment by the city itself. By thus indicating that genuinely *public* employment does not qualify as a "fundamental right,"[42] the Court in effect forged an exception to the Privileges and Immunities Clause that mirrored the market-participant exception in its applications to the most orthodox resident-preference hiring programs. Second, *United Building* left no doubt that the universe of non-fundamental government-bestowed interests, unprotected by the Privileges and Immunities Clause, stretches beyond

41. *Id*. at 219–20.

42. *Id*.

state employment. In particular, the Court signaled that the clause would not bar price differentials for (or even total exclusions of non-residents from) public educational services and other benefits provided directly by the state itself.[43] In charting this path, the Court suggested that its work with the Privileges and Immunities Clause would take broad account of the same resident-favoring "reap and sow" logic that underpins the market-participant exception to the dormancy doctrine.[44]

Finally, even in *United Building* itself, the Court—while declining to dismiss the case on market-participant grounds—did not go so far as to invalidate the challenged private-employee hiring preference. Instead, the Court remanded the case for a determination of whether the state's discrimination against outsiders bore a "close relation" to a "substantial" state interest. No less important, in fashioning this remand, the Court again alluded to the same values that underpin the market-participant doctrine by noting that "caution is particularly appropriate" in judicial application of the "close

43. *See* TRIBE, *supra* note 13, § 6–37, at 1262–63 (suggesting that this principle, which flows from a state's constitutional nature as a "separate political community," extends to state discrimination in affording access to "public libraries, public schools, state universities, state-supported hospitals, and other public welfare programs").

44. *See supra* Chapter XIII (discussing the "sow and reap" concept). In particular, the Court noted that the case did not involve a state's direct use of its own resources, but instead involved "efforts to bias private employment decisions." *United Building,* 465 U.S. at 221.

relation" test when access to the state's own funds is at issue.[45]

The Court's remand in *United Building* illustrates a foundational aspect of Privileges and Immunities Clause doctrine. "Like many other constitutional provisions, the Privileges and Immunities Clause is not an absolute."[46] Rather, even in cases that involve fundamental rights, the clause bans discrimination against non-residents only if "there is no substantial reason for the discrimination beyond the mere fact that they are citizens of other states" or if (to put the same point a bit differently) non-residents constitute a "peculiar source" of an "evil" a state may properly attack.[47] In *Hicklin v. Orbeck*,[48] for example, the Court drew on these formulations to strike down an Alaska program that forced private firms to prefer residents in any employment "resulting from" oil-and-gas and pipeline projects that involved the state.[49] The Court reasoned that non-resident workers were not a "peculiar source" of the widespread unemployment this program sought to rectify.[50] Rather, local joblessness stemmed primarily from a lack of training and a dearth of specialized work skills among Alaska's home-grown labor force. In addition, and once again in keeping with the underlying logic of the market-

45. *United Building*, 465 U.S. at 222—23.

46. Toomer v. Witsell, 334 U.S. 385, 396 (1948).

47. *Id.* at 396, 398.

48. 437 U.S. 518, 524 (1978).

49. *Id.* at 524.

50. *Id.* at 526.

participant rule, the Court refused to approve the "Alaska-hire" program on the ground that the state was merely steering its own oil and gas assets into the hands of its own residents. While acknowledging the "often ... crucial" importance of "a State's ownership of the property with which the statute is concerned," the Court found that Alaska had chosen a means to advance its supposed "reap and sow" purpose that swept too broadly.[51] The problem was that:

> [The] Alaska Hire [law] extends to employers who have no connection whatsoever with the State's oil and gas, perform no work on state land, have no contractual relationship with the State, and receive no payment from the State. The Act goes so far as to reach suppliers who provide goods or services to subcontractors who, in turn, perform work for contractors despite the fact that none of these employers may themselves have direct dealings with the State's oil and gas or ever set foot on state land.... In sum, the Act is an attempt to force virtually all businesses that benefit in some way from the economic ripple effect of Alaska's decision to develop its oil and gas resources to bias their employment practices in favor of the State's residents. We believe that Alaska's ownership of the oil and gas that is the subject matter of Alaska Hire simply constitutes insufficient justification for the pervasive discrimination against nonresidents that the Act mandates.[52]

51. *Id*. at 529.

52. *Id*. at 530–31.

The Court's recurring resort to means-ends analysis under the Privileges and Immunities Clause likens its operation to that of the dormant Commerce Clause principle.[53] In each setting, the Court looks to see whether there is some good reason for the state to lay a special burden on outsiders who lack fair representation in local lawmaking assemblies. In the absence of such a reason—in *Toomer* and *Hicklin* no less than in *City of Philadelphia*[54] and *Dean Milk*[55]—the Court will impose by judicial decree the sort of even-handed treatment the state's political process has failed to provide.

53. *See supra* Chapter XI (discussing significance of judicial assessment of less restrictive alternatives and means-end fit).

54. City of Philadelphia v. New Jersey, 437 U.S. 617 (1978).

55. Dean Milk Co. v. City of Madison, 340 U.S. 349 (1951).

CHAPTER XV

THE SUPREMACY CLAUSE AND PREEMPTION

The Supremacy Clause of Article VI renders federal statutes "the supreme Law of the Land ... anything in the Constitution or Laws of any State to the Contrary notwithstanding."[1] The Supreme Court has given life to this provision with many rulings that federal enactments preempt state common-law or statutory rules. Each of these decisions turns on the distinctive features of the particular federal and state laws involved in the case, thus frustrating efforts to encapsulate this body of doctrine in a few short pages.[2] At the same time, "[m]ost problems pertaining to preemption have arisen in close connection with the Commerce Clause" because these problems typically arise in cases "involving federal legislation enacted pursuant to that clause."[3] Because the pervasiveness of preemption litigation lends it great practical importance, an overview of this field is in order.

1. U.S. CONST. art. VI, cl. 3.

2. A more detailed and comprehensive discussion than the one offered here appears in LAURENCE H. TRIBE, AMERICAN CONSTITUTIONAL LAW, §§ 6–28 to 6–32 (3d ed., vol. one, 2000).

3. *Id.* § 6–28, at 1173.

To begin with, preemption decisions—unlike, for example, dormant Commerce Clause or Privilege and Immunities Clause rulings—hinge on questions of *statutory* interpretation. In each preemption case, the Court must determine whether an "act of Congress fairly interpreted is in actual conflict with the law of the State."[4] As in most cases involving the application of federal statutes, tough issues arise because Congress has not focused with precision on the particular interpretive conundrum that has found its way under the judicial microscope. Consequently, courts must employ the tools of the judicial craft to identify the most reasonable interpretation of federal statutory law with respect to the precise preemption question presented.

The most straightforward cases involve claims of so-called express preemption. In these cases, the parties battle over the scope of federal legislation that explicitly provides for the displacement of some category of state law. The Federal Cigarette Labeling and Advertising Act, for example, mandates printing the now familiar "Surgeon General's Warning" on every pack of cigarettes sold in the United States. Less well known is the fact that this statute includes an additional provision that preempts any "requirement or prohibition based on smoking and health ... imposed under State law with respect to the advertising or promotion of any cigarettes the packages of which are ... labeled" in conformance with federal rules.[5] In *Cipollone v.*

4. Savage v. Jones, 225 U.S. 501, 533 (1912).
5. 15 U.S.C. § 1334(b).

Liggett Group, Inc.[6] the Court held that this express preemption provision displaces state tort-law regimes (whether founded on statutes, common law or both) to the extent they authorize recoveries based on the marketer's failure to warn of product dangers in communications designed to induce cigarette sales. The Court also held, however, that the federal statute did not negate state law causes of action for breach of express warranty because the "requirement" that gives rise to such a claim is not "imposed under State law, but instead imposed *by the warrantor.*"[7] In addition, the Court found no preemption of claims based on the making of fraudulent statements, including in cigarette advertising. Those claims, the Court reasoned, do not involve "a duty 'based on smoking or health' " but instead "a more general obligation—the duty not to deceive."[8] Finally, the Court held that the statutory preemption provision did not bar claims based on failures to warn of product dangers in communications made to governing bodies such as an "administrative agency."[9] Again focusing on the express preemption provision's precise terms, the Court explained that, even if these suits involve a "requirement based on smoking and health,"[10] they remain available because they focus on failures "to disclose . . . facts through channels of communication *other*

6. 505 U.S. 504 (1992).

7. *Id.* at 525 (emphasis in original).

8. *Id.* at 528.

9. *Id.* at 528.

10. *Id.* at 526.

than advertising or promotion."[11] The results and reasoning in *Cipollone* are less important than the basic message they convey: In express preemption cases, the Court engages in highly contextual, text-driven analysis to determine whether particular state rules fall within or without the federal statutory mandate of displacement.[12]

More controversial, and often more difficult, than cases like *Cipollone* are cases based on claims that federal law blocks a state law from operating even in the absence of an express preemption provision. In addressing these "implied preemption" cases, the Court has spoken of both "conflict preemption" (which applies when state law contravenes federal purposes or requires action that violates federal law) and "field preemption" (which applies when federal regulation of a field is so "pervasive" or federal interests are "so dominant" that "state laws on the same subject" should not operate).[13] The Court has also noted, however, that these categories are not "rigidly distinct," and judicial inquiries inevitably focus on whether state law "stands as an obstacle to the accomplishment and execution of 'the full purposes and objectives of Congress.' "[14]

11. *Id*. at 528 (emphasis added).

12. *See* TRIBE, *supra* note 2, § 6–31, at 1210 n.27 (asserting that "one must remember that preemption analysis is ... thoroughly a function of the federal statute's specific text and history").

13. English v. General Elec. Co., 496 U.S. 72, 79 & n.5 (1990).

14. *Id*. (quoting Hines v. Davidowitz, 312 U.S. 52, 67 (1941), and adding that "field pre-emption may be understood as a

In *Burbank v. Lockheed Air Terminal, Inc.*,[15] for example, the Court found implied preemption of a city ordinance that barred jet takeoffs from a local airport between 11:00 p.m. and 7:00 a.m. Enforcement of this ordinance, the Court concluded, would conflict with the Federal Aviation Act, even though that Act included no express preemption provision, because the city's "timing of takeoffs and landings would severely limit the flexibility of FAA in controlling air traffic flow."[16] In addition, the "pervasive nature of the scheme of federal regulation of aircraft noise" supported a determination that the local rule could not stand.[17]

On the other hand, the Court in *Pacific Gas & Electric Co. v. State Energy Resources Conservation & Development Commission (PG & E)*[18] declined to find that the Atomic Energy Act preempted a California moratorium on the building of new nuclear power plants that resulted from worries about mounting volumes of radioactive waste for which no effective disposal system had yet been developed. The Court first rejected the would-be plant operator's contention that the moratorium conflicted with federal efforts to occupy "the entire field of species of conflict pre-emption" in that a "state law that falls within a pre-empted field conflicts with Congress' intent ... to exclude state regulation" from that field).

15. 411 U.S. 624 (1973).

16. *Id*. at 639. *See also id*. at 633 (noting that "[t]here is, to be sure, no express provision of pre-emption in the 1972 Act").

17. *Id*. at 633.

18. 461 U.S. 190 (1983).

nuclear safety concerns."[19] The Court conceded both that Congress intended to assume exclusive control of nuclear safety matters and that spent fuel rods posed safety problems as they built up in cooling ponds on plant sites. The Court concluded, however, that California had not adopted the moratorium for safety reasons but instead had acted with the permissible *economic* purpose of avoiding the power disruptions that would result if continuing waste build-ups required future nuclear plant shutdowns. The Court also found unpersuasive the utility's alternative argument that the moratorium was unlawful because "a primary purpose of the Atomic Energy Act was, and continues to be, the promotion of nuclear power."[20] According to the Court, this argument suffered from a failure to see that Congress had not sought to promote nuclear power "at all costs."[21] Rather, by specifically permitting states to regulate the economic elements of nuclear power, Congress had signaled its willingness to tolerate just the sort of non-safety-based regulatory measure adopted by the state.[22]

In the preemption context, as elsewhere, the level of generality at which courts characterize legisla-

19. *Id.* at 212.

20. *Id.* at 221.

21. *Id.* at 222.

22. In finding a congressional intent *not* to preempt state economic regulation related to nuclear plants, the Court relied on a federal statutory mandate that "[n]othing in this section shall be construed to affect the authority of any state or local agency to regulate activities for purposes other than protection against radiation hazards." *Id.* at 210 (quoting 42 U.S.C. § 202(k)). These sorts of non-preemption or "savings" statutes appear with frequency in federal enactments and often play a

tive purposes often proves all-important. In *PG & E*, for example, the Court declared in broad terms that Congress had occupied the field of nuclear power safety. Nonetheless, in *Silkwood v. Kerr–McGee Corp.*,[23] the Court refused to preempt an award of punitive damages against a nuclear plant operator for recklessly exposing an employee to radiation injuries. The majority reasoned that Congress's purpose to occupy the safety field did not extend to interfering with traditional "state tort remedies."[24] The dissenters reasoned that Congress at least meant to preempt state punitive damages remedies (as opposed to compensatory damages remedies) because of their essentially "regulatory" purpose of punishing and deterring safety-related lapses.[25] The nuclear power industry might well have advocated yet a third position—namely, that the "comprehensive" federal authority recognized in *PG & E* mandated preemption of even compensatory remedies for a nuclear-plant safety breach.[26] Each of these three positions, in keeping with *PG & E*, acknowledges that Congress has roped off an "impliedly preempted field" with regard to nuclear power safety.[27] Each position, however, also reflects

key role in decisions concerning whether state law must give way in the face congressional exercises of its powers.

23. 464 U.S. 238 (1984).

24. *Id.* at 253.

25. *Id.* at 274 (Powell, J., dissenting)

26. *Id.* at 281.

27. Pacific Gas & Elec. Co. v. State Energy Res. Conservation & Dev. Comm'n, 461 U.S. 190, 205 (1983).

a different view about how far Congress meant for that field to extend. Fortunately for the plaintiff in the *Silkwood* case, the Court majority embraced the view most hospitable to the retention of state authority.

In rejecting claims of preemption in both *PG & E* and *Silkwood*, the Court sounded the theme of restraint that surfaces on a regular basis in modern preemption decisions. From the time of its ruling in *Rice v. Santa Fe Elevator Corp.*,[28] the Court often has proclaimed that when "Congress legislate[s] . . . in a field which the States have traditionally occupied, . . . we start with the assumption that the historic police powers of the State were not to be superseded by the Federal Act *unless that was the clear and manifest purpose of Congress.*"[29] Sometimes the Court sidesteps application of this canon by finding that the challenged measure lies outside a field "traditionally occupied" by the states.[30] On other occasions, the court finds Congress's preemptive purpose sufficiently clear that the *Rice* presumption is overcome.[31] There can be no doubt,

28. 331 U.S. 218 (1947) (holding that federal warehousing act preempted state warehousing laws because preemptive purpose was shown).

29. *Id.* at 230 (emphasis added). *Accord, e.g.,* United States v. Locke, 529 U.S. 89, 108 (2000) (citing the " 'assumption' of non-preemption" established by *Rice*).

30. *See, e.g., Locke,* 529 U.S. at 108 (declining to apply *Rice* preemption presumption to field of oil tanker regulation because "Congress has legislated in the field [of maritime transport] from the earliest days of the Republic").

31. *See, e.g.,* Crosby v. National Foreign Trade Council, 530 U.S. 363, 374 n.8 (2000) (invalidating state law that restricted trade with firms that dealt with Myanmar in light of federal

however, that the *Rice* rule often has contributed to decisions that federal law lacks preemptive effect. In *Cipollone*, for example, Justice Stevens insisted that "we must fairly but—in light of the strong presumption against preemption—narrowly construe the precise language" set forth in the express preemption provision of the federal cigarette-labeling law.[32]

Modern commentators have raised important questions about the nature and scope of federal preemption doctrine. For example, some analysts have questioned whether arguments based on implied preemption should ever succeed in light of the *Rice*'s ostensible "plain statement rule."[33] Even the federalism-minded Rehnquist Court, however, has stuck with the longstanding view that a congressional "purpose" to preempt may be "clear and manifest" even in the absence of an express preemption provision.[34] Other analysts have sought to statutory treatment of the same subject matter even while "[a]ssuming, *arguendo*, that some presumption against preemption is appropriate" in this context).

32. *Cipollone*, 505 U.S. at 523.

33. Stephen Gardbaum, *Rethinking Constitutional Federalism*, 74 TEX. L. REV. 795, 828–29 (1996) (further arguing for congressional duty to engage in focused deliberation for any would-be preemptive action to qualify as "proper" under the Necessary and Proper Clause in light of federalism concerns that preemption of state law implicates); *cf. Cipollone*, 505 U.S. at 546–47 (Scalia, J., concurring and dissenting) (finding operation of "'plain statement' rule" in implied-preemption context "more than somewhat odd").

34. *E.g.*, Geier v. American Honda Motor Co., 529 U.S. 861 (2000) (concluding that a Federal Motor Vehicle Safety Standard

draw on the political process rationale of *Garcia v. San Antonio Metropolitan Transit Authority*[35] and *South Carolina v. Baker*[36] in an effort to cabin federal preemption based on agency action.[37] In particular, they assert that administrative rule-making is not marked by the same sort of state-protective structural features that operate when Congress itself passes laws. They thus contend that the Court should seldom, if ever, give preemptive effect to the pronouncements of federal agencies.[38]

impliedly preempted state tort rules authorizing a no-airbag negligence action, even though no express statutory preemption provision covered such common-law claims); Gade v. National Solid Wastes Mgmt. Ass'n, 505 U.S. 88 (1992) (finding state licensing requirements for hazardous waste workers preempted by federal Occupational Safety and Health Act). *See also supra* note 31 (discussing *Crosby* case). Indeed, some commentators have observed that the current Justices most closely identified with a "states' rights" perspective seem, ironically, most inclined to find that federal statutes have preempted state laws. *See* Richard H. Fallon, Jr., *The "Conservative" Paths of the Rehnquist Court's Federalism Decisions*, 69 U. CHI. L. REV. 429, 432, 462–63 (2002); *see also* TRIBE, *supra* note 2, § 6–30, at 1203 n.66. One explanation for this perhaps surprising result may be that these Justices (or at least some of them) tend to value private autonomy from regulatory controls no less than they value local regulatory autonomy. On this view, these Justices are drawn to preemption because its typical effect—as cases such as *Cipollone*, *PG & E* and *Silkwood* reveal—is to exempt business interests from state-imposed constraints that reach beyond, if not far beyond, parallel controls imposed by federal authorities.

35. 469 U.S. 528 (1985).

36. 485 U.S. 505 (1988).

37. *See generally supra* Chapter VI (discussing these cases).

38. *See, e.g.,* Calvin R. Massey, *Etiquette Tips: Some Implications of "Process Federalism,"* 18 HARV. J. L. & PUB. POL'Y 175, 193, 213 (1994).

Again, however, the Court, has not embraced this state-protective argument, at least in its strongest forms. Indeed, the Court has gone so far as to give implied preemptive effect to agency action not embodied in formally and finally promulgated regulations.[39]

39. *See* Geier v. American Honda Motor Co., 529 U.S. 861 (2000); *id.* at 887, 907–10 (Stevens, J., dissenting) (complaining that preemption of state airbag suits was "the product of the Court's interpretation of the final commentary accompanying an interim administrative regulation and the history of airbag regulation generally"; also suggesting the need, in light of political-process considerations, for agency rule "to address preemption explicitly"). In cases decided prior to *Geier*, the Court had signaled some degree of heightened intolerance for agency preemption, both to protect the "federal-state balance" and "because agencies normally address problems in a detailed manner [so that] we can expect that they will make their intentions clear if they intend for their regulations to be exclusive." Hillsborough County v. Automated Med. Labs., Inc., 471 U.S. 707, 717–18 (1985) (refusing to find county ordinances preempted by FDA regulations); *see also* California Coastal Comm'n v. Granite Rock Co., 480 U.S. 572, 583 (1987) (citing *Hillsborough County* in observing that "it is appropriate to expect an administrative regulation to declare any intention to preempt state law with some specificity"). The majority in *Geier*, however, distinguished these cases on the ground that they did not involve a circumscribed claim of frustration-of-purpose-based conflict preemption, but instead involved an assertion of field preemption of "*all* state law in a particular area" due to "the mere 'volume and complexity' of agency regulations." *Geier*, 529 U.S. at 884 (emphasis in original). Whatever form of preemption the case involves, the Court may well be less willing to set aside a state law based on rules promulgated by a private industry group (as opposed to a full-fledged federal agency) pursuant to a delegation of congressional authority. In *Florida Lime & Avocado Growers v. Paul*, 373 U.S. 132 (1963), for example, the Court declined to give a federal regulation preemptive effect in part because it had not been drafted "by impartial experts in Washington . . ., but rather

How does the Court's preemption jurisprudence relate to the dormant Commerce Clause principle? There is no market-participant exception to the preemption doctrine.[40] There clearly is, on the other hand, a congressional-consent exception to that doctrine in the sense that Congress may (and often does) declare that federal statutes do *not* displace specified forms of state regulation otherwise subject to preemption-based attack.[41]

Federal preemption law, whatever its size and shape, carries with it great practical significance in fixing the balance of federal and state power. The Supreme Court, for example, routinely issues more decisions that concern preemption than rulings that

by the South Florida Avocado Administrative Committee." *Id.* at 150–51.

40. *See* Wisconsin Dep't of Indus., Labor & Human Relations v. Gould Inc., 475 U.S. 282, 289–90 (1986) (applying exclusive-federal-remedy principle of National Labor Relations Act to preempt state rule barring governmental purchases from three-time NLRA violators). Put another way, as Professor Regan has written, "the state-as-market-participant doctrine is *not* aptly regarded" as the sort of "doctrine about 'state sovereignty' " that Congress lacks authority to overrule. Donald H. Regan, *The Supreme Court and State Protectionism: Making Sense of the Dormant Commerce Clause*, 84 MICH. L. REV. 1091, 1198 n.210 (1986) (emphasis in original). *See generally supra* Chapter VI (considering "external constraints" on congressional powers).

41. Congressional consent, so to speak, often comes in the form of "savings statutes." *See, e.g., supra* note 22 (discussing operation of such a statute in the *PG & E* case). *See also* New England Power Co. v. New Hampshire, 455 U.S. 331, 343 (1982) (discussing effect of statutory " 'nonpreemption' clause" and distinguishing its effect from that of a statute that affirmatively consents to state laws that otherwise would violate the dormant Commerce Clause principle).

construe the Commerce Clause in either its power-granting or dormant dimensions. This observation, however, should not obscure the fact that the Court's expansive preemption-law caseload has an intimate connection to the Court's Commerce Clause jurisprudence. The modern proliferation of preemption disputes is, after all, the direct result of the sweeping scope the Court has ascribed to the commerce power in the post–1937 period.

TABLE OF CASES

References are to Pages.

INDEX

References are to pages

381

†